# Queering the Subversive Stitch

# Queering the Subversive Stitch

Men and the Culture of Needlework

Joseph McBrinn

BLOOMSBURY VISUAL ARTS
LONDON • NEW YORK • OXFORD • NEW DELHI • SYDNEY

BLOOMSBURY VISUAL ARTS
Bloomsbury Publishing Plc
50 Bedford Square, London, WC1B 3DP, UK
1385 Broadway, New York, NY 10018, USA
29 Earlsfort Terrace, Dublin 2, Ireland

BLOOMSBURY, BLOOMSBURY VISUAL ARTS and the Diana logo
are trademarks of Bloomsbury Publishing Plc

First published in Great Britain 2021

Copyright © Joseph McBrinn, 2021

Joseph McBrinn has asserted his right under the Copyright, Designs
and Patents Act, 1988, to be identified as Author of this work.

For legal purposes the Acknowledgements on p. xix constitute an
extension of this copyright page.

Cover design: Sam Clark, bytheskydesign.com
Cover image Sailor in the British Navy embroidering, from *The British Workman*,
1867 (© Hulton Archive/Getty Images)

All rights reserved. No part of this publication may be reproduced or transmitted
in any form or by any means, electronic or mechanical, including photocopying,
recording, or any information storage or retrieval system, without prior
permission in writing from the publishers.

Bloomsbury Publishing Plc does not have any control over, or responsibility for, any
third-party websites referred to or in this book. All internet addresses given
in this book were correct at the time of going to press. The author and publisher
regret any inconvenience caused if addresses have changed or sites have
ceased to exist, but can accept no responsibility for any such changes.

A catalogue record for this book is available from the British Library.

Library of Congress Cataloging-in-Publication Data
Names: McBrinn, Joseph, author.
Title: Queering the subversive stitch : men and the culture of needlework / Joseph McBrinn.
Description: London ; New York : Bloomsbury Visual Arts, 2021. | Includes
bibliographical references and index.
Identifiers: LCCN 2020035591 (print) | LCCN 2020035592 (ebook) | ISBN
9781472578044 (paperback) | ISBN 9781472578051 (hardback) | ISBN
9781472578068 (epub) | ISBN 9781472578075 (pdf)
Subjects: LCSH: Needlework–Social aspects. | Masculinity. | Queer theory. |
Male domination (Social structure)
Classification: LCC TT705 .M333 2021  (print) | LCC TT705  (ebook) | DDC 746.4–dc23
LC record available at https://lccn.loc.gov/2020035591
LC ebook record available at https://lccn.loc.gov/2020035592

| ISBN: | HB: | 978-1-4725-7805-1 |
|---|---|---|
|  | PB: | 978-1-4725-7804-4 |
|  | ePDF: | 978-1-4725-7807-5 |
|  | eBook: | 978-1-4725-7806-8 |

Typeset by Integra Software Services Pvt. Ltd.
Printed and bound in India

To find out more about our authors and books visit www.bloomsbury.com
and sign up for our newsletters.

... to all actresses who have played actresses, to all women who act, to all men who act and become women, to all the people who want to be mothers. To my mother ...
(Pedro Almodóvar, 1999)

*For my mother ...*

# Contents

| | | |
|---|---|---|
| Illustrations | | viii |
| Preface | | xvii |
| Acknowledgements | | xix |
| 1 | 'Only sissies and women sew': An introduction | 1 |
| 2 | Needlework and the creation of masculinities: 'The prick' of patriarchy | 11 |
| 3 | 'Killing the angel in the house': Victorian manliness, domestic handicrafts and homosexual panic | 49 |
| 4 | 'The mesh canvas': Amateur needlecrafts, masculinity and modernism | 87 |
| 5 | Masculinity and 'the politics of cloth': From the 'bad boys' of postmodern art to the 'boys that sew club' of the new millennium | 119 |
| 6 | Conclusion: 'Men who Embroider' | 157 |
| Notes | | 163 |
| Select Bibliography | | 214 |
| Index | | 225 |

# Illustrations

## Plates

1 Elaine Reichek, *Sampler (Hercules)*, 1997, hand embroidery on linen, 22 x 17¼ in. (55.9 x 45.1 cm), Collection Melva Bucksbaum, Photo. Adam Reich, © Elaine Reichek

2 Stephen Beal, *Periodic Table of the Artist's Colors*, 2004, hand-embroidered cotton floss, cotton canvas, 30 x 36 in. (76.2 x 91.4 cm), © Museum of Arts and Design, New York, Collection of Mr and Mrs Robert Lipp, 2007, Photo. Ed Watkins, 2008

3 William Morris, *If I Can*, 1857, wool and cotton thread on cloth, 66.3 x 73.5 in. (168.5 x 187 cm), Photo. Courtesy of Bridgeman Images. © Kelmscott Manor, Oxfordshire/Society of Antiquities of London

4 Fine Cell Work/Inmates of HMP Wandsworth in collaboration with the Victoria and Albert Museum, *HMP Wandsworth Quilt*, 2010, pierced, appliquéd and embroidered cotton on linen, 76.7 x 102 in. (195 x 260 cm), acquired with support of the Friends of the V&A, © Victoria and Albert Museum, London (T.27–2010)

5 Jim Hodges, *Here's Where We Will Stay*, 1995, printed nylon, painted chiffon and silk head scarves with thread, embroidery, sequins, 216 x 204 in. (548.6 x 518.2 cm) overall, Photo. Mark Bower, © Christie's Images/Bridgeman Images, © Jim Hodges, Courtesy of Gladstone Gallery, New York and Brussels

6 Ernest Thesiger embroidering at home, 6 Montpelier Terrace, Knightsbridge, London, undated press photo, c.1920s/30s, EFT/000161, Ernest Thesiger Archive, © The University of Bristol Theatre Collection/ArenaPAL

7 Russell Lynes embroidering at home, 427 East 84th Street, New York, published in 'The Pleasure of Making It.' *House & Garden*, 142(1)

(July 1972): 51, © The Estate of Russell Lynes, Photo. Courtesy of Dean Brown/House & Garden, © Condé Nast

8   Charles LeDray, *Army, Navy, Air Force, Marines*, 1993, fabric, wire, vinyl, silkscreen, zipper, 26¾ x 54 in. (67.9 x 137.2 cm) overall. Photo. Courtesy of the artist and Peter Freeman, Inc. Private Collection, Houston, TX. Photo. Tom Powel, © Charles LeDray

9   Grayson Perry, *Turner Prize Dress*, 2003, silk, lace, polyester and cotton, 38 ⅝ x 36 x 4 ⅜ in. (98 x 66 x 11 cm), Courtesy of the artist and Victoria Miro Gallery, London/Venice, © Grayson Perry

10  Nicolas Moufarrege, *Untitled* (detail), 1985, thread, pre-printed needlepoint canvas, fabric and needlepoint canvas 18 x 31 in. (45.7 x 78.7 cm), © The Artist's Estate, Courtesy Nabil Mufarrej and Gulnar 'Nouna' Mufarrij, Photo. Neil Johnson for Visual AIDS, New York

11  Nick Cave, *Soundsuit #5*, 2010, mixed media – knitted fabric with appliquéd found flowers, embroidery, sequins, metal armature, © Nick Cave. Courtesy of the artist and Jack Shainman Gallery, New York

12  Jochen Flinzer, *53 Wochen Glück (53 Weeks of Happiness)* (detail), 1994–5, embroidery thread on silk, 169 x 12.7 in. (430 x 32.5 cm), Photo. © MMK Museum für Moderne Kunst Frankfurt am Main, Photo. Axel Schneider, © Jochen Flinzer, Courtesy Thomas Rehbein Galerie, Köln

13  Francesco Vezzoli with an embroidery hoop in front of a display of his *Crying Divas from The Screenplays of an Embroiderer*, 1999, thirty black-and-white laser prints on canvas with metallic embroidery, each frame 13 x 17 in. (33 x 43.2 cm), overall 39 x 194 ⅞ in. (99.1 x 494.9 cm), Photo. Giorgio Lotti/Archivio Giorgio Lotti/Mondadori Portfolio/Getty Images

14  Chan-Hyo Bae, *Existing in Costume 1*, 2006, C-print, 31.1 x 25.1 in. (79 x 64 cm), Photo. © Chan-Hyo Bae

15  James Merry and Björk, *Moth* headpiece for *Vulnicura* tour, 2015, Photo. © Santiago Felipe

16  Nicholas Hlobo, *Macaleni iintozomlambo*, 2010, ribbon on tea paper, 30.3 x 41.3 in. (77 x 105 cm), © Tate London, 2018 © Nicholas Hlobo, Courtesy Stevenson Gallery, Cape Town, South Africa

# Figures

| | | |
|---|---|---|
| 1.1 | 'Jack's Christmas Present.' *The British Workman*, no. 156 (2 December 1867): 141, © The British Library Board (LOU.LON 23) | 5 |
| 1.2 | Capt. Garrison Burdett Arey, *Bird of Paradise*, c.1865–9, woollen yarn on canvas, 21.5 x 27.5 in. (54.6 x 69.8 cm), Courtesy of the collections of the Museum of Old Newbury | 6 |
| 2.1 | Edmund Harrison, *Circumcision of Christ*, c.1687, linen silk, gold thread, silver thread on linen, 43 x 28. 5 in. (110 x 73 cm), © National Museums Scotland (A.1987.317) | 15 |
| 2.2 | Ron Gerelli, *James Norbury Knitting*, c.1930s, © The Hulton Archive/Getty Images | 17 |
| 2.3 | Portrait of Kaffe Fassett sewing by David Cripps on the cover of *Glorious Inspiration: Kaffe Fassett's Needlepoint Source Book* (London: Ebury Press, 1991), Reproduced by permission of The Random House Group Ltd/Penguin Books Ltd. © 1991 and Courtesy of the artist | 18 |
| 2.4 | Mark Newport, *Freedom Bed Cover/Zachary*, 2006, hand-embroidered cotton thread and ribbon on comic book pages, 80 x 65 x 1 in. (2.03 m x 165.1 cm x 2.5 cm), Courtesy of Greg Kucera Gallery Inc. Seattle, © Mark Newport | 19 |
| 2.5 | Norman Willis, 'How I Got Stitched Up …' *Cross Stitcher* 72 (August 1998): 74, Courtesy of *Cross Stitcher*/Dennis Publishing Ltd | 20 |
| 2.6 | Ernest Gimson and Phyllis Lovibond, *Sampler*, c.1890s, cotton thread on linen, 18.5 x 13.4 in. (47 x 34 cm), © Crafts Study Centre/University for the Creative Arts (T.81.54) | 23 |
| 2.7 | Jamie Chalmers aka 'Mr. X-Stitch.' © Jamie Chalmers | 25 |
| 2.8 | Arthur Hopkins, 'Amusements on Board an Ocean Liner: A Sewing Match for Men.' *The Graphic* (10 November 1894): 549, Private Collection © Look and Learn/Illustrated Papers Collection/Bridgeman Images | 28 |
| 2.9 | John Lockwood Kipling, *Men at an Embroidery Frame for Jewelled and Spangled Cloth*, November 1870, pencil, pen and wash on paper, 10.4 x 14.4 in. (26.3 x 36.7 cm), © Victoria and Albert Museum (0929:31/(IS)) | 29 |

| | | |
|---|---|---|
| 2.10 | Charlie Chaplin, *Modern Times*, 1936, film still, © The Estate of Charlie Chaplin/Roy Export SAS, Paris, 2018 | 30 |
| 2.11 | 'Style-Art Needlepoint Inc, (M502)', unexecuted needlepoint scrim, 1978, 18 x 12¾ in. (46 x 32 cm), Private Collection | 36 |
| 2.12 | David Shenton, 'Make Yourself a Cuddly Clone' knitting pattern from *Stanley and the Mask of Mystery* (London: Gay Men's Press, 1983), © David Shenton | 37 |
| 2.13 | Tom of Finland, 'Shipwrecked.' Cross-stitch kit, © Tom of Finland/Artists Rights Society (ARS), New York/DACS, London, 2019 | 38 |
| 2.14 | David Medalla, *A Stitch in Time*, 1968–72, Arts Council Collection, © David Medalla | 38 |
| 2.15 | Richard Saja, *Diversity Quilt*, cotton, 2009, 93 x 97 in. (236.2 x 246.3 cm), Photo. Andy Duback, Collection of the Shelburne Museum, Gift of Richard Saja | 39 |
| 2.16 | 'Mr. M'Neil.' Postcard, June 1905, Private Collection | 41 |
| 2.17 | Martin Parr, *Liam Moore, RSA Academy, Tipton*, 2010, © Martin Parr/Magnum Photos | 46 |
| 3.1 | James Wilson, *Sampler*, 1828, cotton thread on linen, 13 x 16.7 in. (33.5 x 42.5 cm), Courtesy of Haslemere Educational Museum | 51 |
| 3.2 | John Glazbey Crumpler, *Sampler*, 1841, cotton thread on cloth, 7 x 8.46 in. (17.78 x 21.5 cm), Private Collection | 53 |
| 3.3 | 'Instruction of Pauper Children in the South Metropolitan District School, Sutton.' *The Illustrated London News* LX (4 May 1872): 425, © DEA/Biblioteca Ambrosiana/GETTY Images | 54 |
| 3.4 | Edmund Blampied, 'Everybody Can Help.' *The Sketch* (9 December 1914): IV, © The British Library Board (MFM.MLD52) | 61 |
| 3.5 | George Plank, 'Aunt Georgie.' From E.F. Benson's *The Freaks of Mayfair* (London: T.N. Foulis, 1916), facing p. 40, Private Collection | 61 |
| 3.6 | Mary Hogarth, 'Modern Embroidery.' *Vogue* (London) (late October 1923): 66–7, Courtesy of *Vogue* © The Condé Nast Publications Ltd., Photo. © The British Library Board (Zc.9.d.565) | 71 |
| 3.7 | Duncan Grant (designer), Vanessa Bell, Mary Hogarth, Miss Elwes and Mrs Antrobus (embroiderers), *Ecclesiastical Banner*, 1925, appliquéd fabrics, wool and silk threads, pearls and beads, 72 x 36 in. (182.8 x 91.5 cm), © Estate of Duncan Grant. All rights | |

|      |                                                                                                                                                                                                                                                                                                |     |
|------|----------------------------------------------------------------------------------------------------------------------------------------------------------------------------------------------------------------------------------------------------------------------------------------------|-----|
|      | reserved, DACS 2018, Photo. © Victoria and Albert Museum, London (T.52.1935)                                                                                                                                                                                                                 | 73  |
| 3.8  | '27. Embroidered Chair Seat. Duncan Grant. Worked by Mrs. Bartle Grant. The Property of Mrs. Maynard Keynes / 28. Embroidered Footstool Cover. Victorian.' From Margaret H. Bulley, *Have You Good Taste? A Guide to the Appreciation of the Lesser Arts* (London: Methuen & Co., 1933), Private Collection | 73  |
| 3.9  | *Weldon's Antique Tapestry. Part 2* (London: Weldons Ltd., Fashion, Pattern and Transfer Publishers, n.d. [*c.*1920]), pp. 10–11, Private Collection                                                                                                                                         | 75  |
| 3.10 | John Craske, *Beach Scene: The Foreshore*, 1931, wool and silk threads on canvas, 15.7 x 46.7 in. (40 x 118.5 cm), © Britten-Pears Foundation (5–9400060)                                                                                                                                     | 76  |
| 3.11 | D.H. Lawrence and Frieda Lawrence, *Etruscan Figure*, cotton threads on unbleached linen, *c.*1920s, 10.6 x 12.9 in. (27.5 x 33 cm), Courtesy of The University of Tulsa, McFarlin Library, Department of Special Collections & University Archives (1976.013.3.2.4)                         | 76  |
| 3.12 | 'Mr. Ernest Thesiger Teaching Petit Point to Two Disabled Men.' From 'Embroideries by Disabled Soldiers.' *The Queen* (27 May 1931): 19, © The British Library Board (MFM.MLD45)                                                                                                             | 79  |
| 3.13 | Ernest Thesiger, *Sampler*, signed and dated 1946, cotton thread on linen, 12.2 x 14.1 in. (31 x 36 cm), Private Collection, © John S. Thesiger, Photo. © Jake Shaw, Courtesy of Bearnes Hampton & Littlewood                                                                                 | 82  |
| 3.14 | Ernest Thesiger, 'Needlework as a Hobby.' *The Home Magazine* XXXIV(119) (March 1926): 27, Photo. © The Bodleian Libraries, The University of Oxford (Per. 2705 d.45)                                                                                                                        | 84  |
| 3.15 | From Lady Smith-Dorrien, 'Convalescing Soldiers.' In *Needlework in War-Time: Suggestions for Teaching Beginners and Convalescents* (London: The Royal School of Needlework, n.d. [*c.*1940]), p. 3, Private Collection                                                                      | 85  |
| 4.1  | Ben Nicholson and Mary Berwick, *Animal Squares*, 1925–9, rag rug, 42 x 67 in. (106 x 170 cm), Photo. Whitworth Art Gallery, University of Manchester, © Angela Verren Taunt, All Rights Reserved, DACS 2019                                                                                 | 88  |

| | | |
|---|---|---|
| 4.2 | First World War veteran H.B. McDermott's winning entry in a 'fancy needlework contest' at a St. Paul hospital, Minnesota, dated 27 April 1925, unidentified press photo, Private Collection | 90 |
| 4.3 | King Gustaf V of Sweden's final embroidery (left unfinished), silk threads on linen, *c.*1950, 19.3 x 15 in. (49 x 38.1 cm), © Livrustkammaren/The Royal Armoury, Stockholm, Photo. Erik Lernestål | 92 |
| 4.4 | George Platt Lynes, *Embroidered Christmas Card for Monroe Wheeler after a Design by Paul Klee*, wool on canvas, 1944, 6 x 6 in. (15 x 15 cm), Monroe Wheeler Papers, Photo. Yale University Collation of American Literature, Beinecke Rare Books & Manuscript Library, Yale University (YCAL MSS 136), © The Estate of George Platt Lynes | 99 |
| 4.5 | Allen Porter, *Untitled*, *c.*1955, wool on linen, 27 x 33 in. (68.5 x 84 cm), Courtesy of the Leslie-Lohman Museum of Gay and Lesbian Art, New York, Gift of Timothy Stuart-Warner | 100 |
| 4.6 | George Platt Lynes (and Russell Lynes), *Cushion Cover*, wool on canvas, *c.*1955, 6 x 6 in. (15 x 15 cm), Bernard Perlin Papers, Photo. Yale University Collation of American Literature, Beinecke Rare Books & Manuscript Library, Yale University (YCAL MSS 849), © The Estate of George Platt Lynes | 101 |
| 4.7 | Louis Gartner, *Facsimile of a Painting by Paul Cadmus*, signed and dated 1960, petit point needlepoint tapestry, 27 x 30.75 in. (68.58 x 78.11 cm), Photo. Courtesy of the Canvassed Gallery, Los Angeles | 102 |
| 4.8 | Frank Stella ('and Mrs. Leo Castelli'), *Cushion Covers*, wool on needlepoint canvas, 15 x 15 in. (38 x 38 cm), originally published in Russell Lynes, 'The Mesh Canvas.' *Art in America* 56(3) (May/June 1968): 43, © The Estate of Russell Lynes | 107 |
| 4.9 | Frontispiece from Robert E. Illes, *Men in Stitches* (New York: Van Nostrand Reinhold Co., 1975), Courtesy of John Wiley & Sons | 112 |
| 4.10 | *Rosey Grier's Needlepoint for Men* (New York: Walker and Co., 1973), Private Collection | 114 |
| 4.11 | 'Man That Needle.' *Life*, 70(20) (28 May 1971): 80–1, Images by Yale Joel and Michael Rougie, © Time Inc. All rights reserved. © 1971 Time Inc. All rights reserved. Reprinted/Translated from LIFE | |

and published with the permission of Time Inc. Reproduction in any manner in any language in whole or in part without written permission is prohibited    114

4.12 Ed Rossbach, *Mickey Mouse Lace*, cotton and rayon needlepoint lace, 1971, 3½ x 3 in. (8.9 x 7.6 cm) © The Estate of Ed Rossbach, Photo. © The Museum of Fine Arts, Boston, The Daphne Farago Collection (2004–2111)    117

4.13 Andy Warhol, *Male Nude*, 1987, four photographs, silver gelatin print on paper and thread, 28 x 22 in. (71.1 x 55.9 cm) © Tate, London 2018 © The Andy Warhol Foundation for the Visual Arts, Inc/Licensed by DACS, London and ARS, New York, 2018    118

5.1 Mike Kelley, *More Love Hours than Can Ever Be Repaid and the Wages of Sin*, 1987, stuffed fabric toys and afghans on canvas with dried corn; wax candles on wood and metal base, 120¾ × 151¾ × 31¾ in. (306.7 × 385.4 × 80.6 cm), Whitney Museum of American Art, New York; purchase with funds from the Painting and Sculpture Committee 89.13a-d. © Mike Kelley Foundation for the Arts. All Rights Reserved/VAGA at ARS, New York and DACS, London 2018    122

5.2 Robert Gober, *Wedding Gown*, 1989, silk satin, muslin, linen, tulle, welded steel, 54¼ x 57 x 38½ in. (137.2 x 144.8 x 96.5 cm), © Robert Gober, Courtesy Matthew Marks Gallery    124

5.3 'My Name Is Duane Kearns Puryear ... ' NAMES Project Memorial Quilt, 1992, Courtesy the NAMES Project, Photo. Fred W. McDarrah, © Premium Archive/Getty Images    127

5.4 José Leonilson, *O Penélope*, 1993, thread on voile, 90.1 x 31.4 in. (229 x 80 cm), © Tate, London 2018 © Projeto Leonsilson    130

5.5 Dutes Miller and Stan Shellabarger, *Untitled (Pink Tube)*, 2003–present, performance view, Museum of Contemporary Art, Chicago, 2013, Photo. Courtesy of Nathan Keay, © Dutes Miller and Stan Shellabarger and Museum of Contemporary Art, Chicago    132

5.6 Leo Chiachio and Daniel Giannone, *Marineritos*, 2005, hand embroidery with cotton thread, graphite and stone appliqué on fabric, 31.5 x 41 in. (80 x 105 cm), © Leo Chiachio and Danny Giannone    134

| | | |
|---|---|---|
| 5.7 | Kang Seung Lee, *Untitled (Me as Aunt Georgie)*, 2013, C-Print, 16 x 24 in. (40.6 x 60.9 cm), © Kang Seung Lee | 136 |
| 5.8 | Nigel Hurlstone, *What Pleasure*, 2013, cotton, organdie, cotton and burmilana thread, digital print, couching, 85.8 x 37 in. (218 x 94 cm), © Nigel Hurlstone | 136 |
| 5.9 | Aaron McIntosh, *The Couch* (detail), 2010, 'Colonial Revival'-style vintage couch, digital prints (from romance novels, gay pornography and gay erotica) on cotton canvas, batting, thread, 35 x 72 x 36 in. (89 x 183 x 91 cm), Photo. Terry Brown, © Aaron McIntosh | 136 |
| 5.10 | Grant Neufeld (second left) and the Revolutionary Knitting Circle (RKC) knitting protest at the G8 Summit, Calgary, Alberta Canada, 26 June 2002, Photo. Don MacKinnon © Getty Images | 139 |
| 5.11 | Julie Morstad, illustration for 'Lords of the Strings.' *BUST* (136) (December 2005/January 2006): 82 © Julie Morstad, Courtesy of *BUST* magazine | 140 |
| 5.12 | Michael Brennand-Wood, *Flower Head – Narcissistic Butterfly*, 2005, machine-embroidered blooms, mirror, wire, photographs, beads, fabric, thread and acrylic paint on a wood base, 23.6 x 23.6 x 15.7 in. (60 x 60 x 40 cm), collection of the artist, Photo. Peter Mennim, © Michael Brennand-Wood | 142 |
| 5.13 | Jochen Flinzer, *53 Wochen Glück (53 Weeks of Happiness)*, 1994–5, embroidery thread on silk, 169 x 12.7 in. (430 x 32.5 cm), installation view, Photo © MMK Museum für Moderne Kunst Frankfurt am Main, Photo. Axel Schneider, © Jochen Flinzer, Courtesy Thomas Rehbein Galerie, Köln | 144 |
| 5.14 | Yinka Shonibare MBE, *Big Boy*, 2002, Dutch wax-printed cotton fabric, fibreglass figure, 84 x 66 x 55 in. (215 x 170 x 12 cm), plinth 86 in. (220 cm) diameter, Gift of Susan and Lewis Manilow (2004.759), Chicago (IL), Art Institute of Chicago. © 2019, The Art Institute of Chicago/Art Resource, NY/Scala, Florence | 144 |
| 5.15 | Michael Raedecker, *material*, 2009, acrylic and thread on canvas, 40 ⅛ x 46 ½ in. (102 x 118 cm), Private Collection, Photo. Courtesy of the Artist and the Grimm Gallery, Amsterdam and New York, © Michael Raedecker | 145 |

5.16  Brett Alexander, *Playing with Dolls*, 2003–6, dimensions variable, © Brett Alexander   146

5.17  Gavin Fry, *Orlando*, nine panels, dimensions variable, hand embroidery on second-hand, mass-produced sewing kits and Berlin woolwork, 2010, © Gavin Fry   148

5.18  'Gentlemen of the Needle.' *Country Life* CXVI(6) (February 1997): 28–9, © Country Life Picture Library   150

5.19  Cover of *Needle Arts*, XXIX(2) (June 1998), Courtesy of *Needle Arts*, Courtesy of the Embroiderers' Guild of America   151

5.20  Francesco Vezzoli, *Who's Afraid of Virginia Woolf (Double Portrait after Man Ray)*, 2011, inkjet print on canvas with metallic embroidery, 11.8 x 11.8 in. (30 x 30 cm), Private Collection, Photo. © Christie's Images/Bridgeman Art Library, © Francesco Vezzoli   152

5.21  Josh Faught, *It Takes a Lifetime to Get Exactly Where You Are*, 2012, handwoven sequin trim, handwoven hemp, cedar blocks, cotton, polyester, wool, cochineal (made from ground-up bugs), straw hat with lace, toilet paper, paper towels, Jacquard woven reproduction of panel from the AIDS quilt, silk handkerchief, indigo, political pins, disaster blanket, gourd, gold leaf, plaster cat, cedar blocks and nail polish, 96 x 240 in./8 x 20 ft. (243 x 610 cm), Photo. Courtesy of the Artist and Lisa Cooley, New York, © Josh Faught   153

5.22  Matt Smith, *Piccadilly 1830*, 2012, turkey and ostrich feathers, ceramic, metal cage, wool, linen, mirror-backed beads, approx. 90.5 x 23.6 x 11.8 in. (230 x 60 x 30 cm), © Unravelled Arts, Photo. Sussie Ahlberg   153

5.23  Satoru Aoyama, *Embroiderers (Dedicated to Unknown Embroiderers) #10*, 2015, embroidery on inkjet print, 7 x 10 in. (18 x 26 cm), Photo. Kei Miyajima, © Satoru Aoyama, Courtesy of Mizuma Art Gallery, Tokyo   155

6.1  'Men who Embroider.' Unattributed magazine cutting (early mid-1950s), EFT/000066/13, Ernest Thesiger Archive, © The University of Bristol Theatre Collection/ArenaPAL   159

Whilst every effort has been made to contact copyright holders, the author and publisher would nevertheless welcome relevant information on any oversight which may have occurred.

# Preface

'The history of men's opposition to women's emancipation is more interesting perhaps than the story of that emancipation itself. An amusing book might be made of it,' so wrote Virginia Woolf in 1929.[1] Woolf is widely known to have struggled with the conventional markers of idealized femininity such as embroidery. She was conscious of never becoming fully proficient at sewing (unlike her mother and sister), yet it was often prescribed to her as a cure for her 'nerve troubles', purely on account of her sex. Woolf found her own personal and political liberation through writing but witnessed, during the course of her lifetime, needlework transformed from a means of enforcing a feminine stereotype to one of emancipation from it.

Needlework's uncanny ability to be both symbol of oppression and tool of liberation in women's lives found its most compelling and complete exposition in Rozsika Parker's groundbreaking *The Subversive Stitch: Embroidery and the Making of the Feminine* (1984). Between the publication of Woolf's and Parker's books, and ever since, men's opposition to women's emancipation has stimulated much less debate. Although many would agree that it is a far less interesting avenue of exploration, little remains known of the motivations of men. And not all men were opposed to gender equality. Perhaps more interesting (and certainly more amusing) than the men who were are those who took up needle and thread not only in support of liberating women from the strictures of gender stereotypes but themselves too. This book is about such men.

The historical processes that sanctioned the complete omission or the covert marginalization of men within the culture of needlework remain little known. In this book I map and explore men's presence in needlework's past and present not only to think through the continued relevance of feminist interventions such as Woolf's or Parker's but also to explore the social construction of masculinity – as something that only really exists in relation to femininity. If men who took up needlework have often been seen as *queer* by *queering* (disrupting the normative readings of) needlework it is possible to reveal just how such cultural practices have been implicated in the making of the masculine (through exclusion, effacement and elision) as much as the feminine (through emphasis, enforcement and inculcation). This is the first book ever published about men's needlework and I do hope readers will find it not only amusing but also interesting.

# Acknowledgements

I have spent many years working on this book and as such I have incurred innumerable debts. I will be forever grateful to Frances Arnold, my editor, for her remarkable patience and perseverance as I completed the research and grappled with the manuscript. I am also indebted to Yvonne Thouroude for all her guidance and kindness. Agnes Upshall, Pari Thomson, Hannah Crump, Ariadne Godwin and Geraldine Billingham supported the book through its early stages and many other staff at Bloomsbury enabled it to reach completion. Rebecca Hamilton expertly supported me through the final stages. Adriana Brioso designed the lovely cover, and Vincy Sagayaraj, Vaishnavi Purushothaman and Amy Jordan made the production process a pleasure. I am also grateful to the anonymous peer-reviewers whose comments and insights proved invaluable. Friends and colleagues supported me through the process. Elaine Reichek and Michael Brennand-Wood were my inspiration. Gavin Fry shared his own research and kept me right. Suzanna Chan, Juliette MacDonald, Eleanor Flegg, Janice Helland, John Potvin, Alla Myzelev and the late Sandra Alfoldy all discussed the book with me and read (or listened to) parts of the manuscript in draft form. Christopher Reed was generous with his time and knowledge. Tanya Harrod and Jorunn Veiteberg offered suggestions and much other sage advice. I am heartbroken that Nikki Gordon Bowe, my supporter-in-chief, my confidant and the most scrupulous and generous interlocutor, is not here to see the book finally realized.

Other aspects of my research on masculinity and needlework have been published elsewhere, and I am very grateful to friends, colleagues and editors for encouragement that proved crucial to the completion of this book: Glenn Adamson and Stephen Knott (*The Journal of Modern Craft*), Catherine Harper (*Textile: Cloth and Culture*), Polly Leonard and Beth Smith (*Selvedge*), Lynn Hulse (*TEXT: Journal for the Study of Textile Art, Design and History*) and especially Jo Hall (*Embroidery*). I am equally grateful to Elaine Cheasley Patterson and Susan Surette, Zoë Thomas and Miranda Garrett, and Johanna

Amos and Lisa Binkley for invitations to contribute to their volumes on contemporary craft, modern feminism and the history of needlework that helped shape and sharpen some of my ideas and arguments. I am also deeply indebted to all the artists who permitted their work to be included in this book: Brett Alexander, Satoru Aoyama, Nick Cave, Jamie Chalmers, Kaffe Fassett, Josh Faught, Jochen Flinzer, Leo Chiachio and Daniel Giannone, Robert Gober, Nicholas Hlobo, Jim Hodges, Nigel Hurlstone, Chan-Hyo Bae, Charles LeDray, Kang Seung Lee, David Medalla, James Merry, Aaron McIntosh, Mark Newport, Martin Parr, Grayson Perry, Michael Raedecker, David Shenton, Dutes Miller and Stan Shellabarger, Matt Smith and Francesco Vezzoli. Several other artists kindly talked to me about their work: Raymond Dugan, Nigel Cheney, Joe Cunningham, Stuart Easton, Oliver Herring, James Hunting, John Thomas Paradiso, Fernando Marques Penteado, Skårt and Ernie Smith. Decedents of other artists aided my search for archives and images. Miranda Seymour, Matthew Sturgis, Henry Porter, John S. Thesiger and Josh Lynes all helped in different ways. I am saddened that Henrietta Garnett is not here to see the book completed as she provided much crucial support and encouragement.

I spent a good deal of my time doing research for this book in libraries and I thank all the staff I have exhausted and exasperated especially at the Queen's University and Ulster University libraries, Belfast; the National Library of Ireland, Dublin; the National Art Library, Victoria and Albert Museum and the British Library, London; and the Beinecke Rare Book & Manuscript Library, Yale. I am especially indebted to David Crabtree, Patricia Doyle, Stephen Milligen, Michaela Hewitt, Sineaid Carson, Janice Bell, Marion Khorshidian and Lorna Reid at Belfast School of Art Library. I am also grateful to several colleagues – Natalie Dallat, Justin Magee, Paul Brown, Marie Mallon, Wendy Aitken and Louise Harbinson. I am also thankful for help to the staff at DACS, London; Scala, Florence; ARS, New York; *Country Life*; Time Inc; *Vogue*; and Condé Nast.

Several curators assisted me in locating archive material, rare publications, specific photographs and other information: Janis Jefferies, Goldsmiths University; Dean Daderko, Contemporary Arts Museum, Houston; Natalie King, University of Melbourne; Malin Grundberg, Livrustkammaren/The Royal Armory, Stockholm; Ludmila Egorova; and Sarah Quinton, Textile

Museum of Canada. For help in locating images and information I am also grateful to: Elissa Auther; Grace Beaumont, Arts Council Collection; Alissa Bennett, Gladstone Gallery; Lexi Campbell, Matthew Marks Gallery; Maurice Berger; Julia Blackburn; Cheryl Christian and Brad Cape, the Embroiderers' Guild of America; Luca Corbetta, Francesco Vezzoli Studio; Riann Coulter; Carolyn Cruthirds, Museum of Fine Arts, Boston; Durk Dehner and Jordan Green, Tom of Finland Foundation; Gabriela Dias, Projecto Leonilson; Allan Downend, The E.F. Benson Society; Edwina Erhman, Victoria and Albert Museum; Moira Fitzgerald, Beinecke Rare Book & Manuscript Library; Christopher Fletcher, Alan Brown and Helen Gilio, Bodleian Library, University of Oxford; Allison Foster, Tate Gallery Archive; Michelle Gearon, Monash University Museum of Art; Elyse Gonzales and Rebecca Harlow, Museum of Art, Design & Architecture, University of California; Sabrina Gschwandtner; Allison Harig, Shelburne Museum; Christopher Hilton, Britten-Pears Foundation; Ruth Hoffmann, Magnum Photos; Ellen J Holdorf, Museum of Arts and Design; Rosie Holman, Kaffe Fassett Studio; Susan Isken, Craft & Folk Art Museum, Los Angeles; Susan Kay-Williams, Royal School of Needlework; Charlotte King, Martin Parr Studio; Peter Hughes, Madresfield Court; Melissa Kunz, Special Collections, McFarlin Library, University of Tulsa; Emily Lawrence and Emily Schafer of the History Society of Old Newbury; David Leddick; Arnold Lozano and Kate Guyonvarch, Roy Export S.A.S., Paris; Paul Kennedy; Shan McAnena; Nicolette Makovicky, University of Oxford; Susanne Mayor and Clare Reed, Lamb House, Rye, Sussex, The National Trust; Rebecca Mecklenborg, Jack Shainman Gallery; Julia Morstad; Makiko Mikawa, Mizuma Art Gallery; Simon Mills; Micah Musheno, Whitney Museum of American Art; Robert Neller, Haslemere Educational Museum; Linda Newington, Winchester School of Art; Sisipho Ngodwana, Stevenson Cape Town; Claire Regnault and Sara Guthrie, National Museum of New Zealand Te Papa Tongarewa; Heather Romaine, The University of Bristol Theatre Collection; Susan Penny, *Cross Stitcher*; Christopher Phillips, Ernest Brown & Phillips; Siân Phillips, Bridgeman Art Library; Fr. Nicholas Schofield, Our Lady of Lourdes & St. Michael's Church, Uxbridge and Archdiocese of Westminster Archives; Albi Schottenstein; Thomas Schroeder, Museum für Moderne Kunst Frankfurt am Main; Jake Shaw; Julie Ann Stevens; Ruth Southorn, *The World of Cross Stitching*; Lynn

Szygenda; Sarah Toso and Lucinda Moore, Mary Evans Picture Library; Jorien de Vries, Grimm Gallery; Branden Wallace, Leslie-Lohman Museum of Gay and Lesbian Art; Simon Watson; Alexander Whitehead, Peter Freeman, Inc; Hannah van den Wijngaard, Victoria Miro; and Margaret Wilson, National Museums Scotland.

Like all writers I am dependent on the kindness and support of my loved ones – I thank my parents, sisters, nieces and nephews and especially my partner, Gareth.

# 1

# 'Only sissies and women sew': An introduction

Following the publication of her book, *The Subversive Stitch: Embroidery and the Making of the Feminine*, towards the end of 1984, Rozsika Parker appears to have given a single press interview. During the course of a short conversation, in response to Parker's contention that 'the art of embroidery has been the means of educating women into the feminine ideal, and of proving that they have attained it, but it has also provided a weapon of resistance to the constraints of femininity', the journalist Anne Caborn asked why there were no men in the book.[1] Parker had, in fact, opened the book with reference to men that she had found in a recent government statistics report on 'leisure activities' that revealed: 'Needlework is the favourite hobby of two per cent of British males, about equal to the number who go to church regularly. Nearly one in three fills in football coupons, in an average month, or has a bet.'[2] From this both women agreed, somewhat humorously, that 'real men gamble and fill in football coupons: only cissies and women sew and swell congregations.'[3] Writing up her interview Caborn remained struck by Parker's 'juxtaposition of needleworkers and churchgoers' which she thought 'neatly picks out the unspoken presumption' that for men needlework of any sort was emasculating and carried the stigma of not just effeminacy but further of homosexuality: 'Your average hot blooded male is no more likely to whip his embroidery out in a public place, than he is to turn up in the local wearing purple hot pants. Well, it's not really what you'd call macho. Tough. Is it?'

Caborn drew up a short list of male needleworkers from the well-known (the Duke of Windsor, formerly the Prince of Wales and briefly King Edward VIII) and the obscure (Sir Alec Douglas-Home, 14th Earl of Home and Conservative Prime Minister, 1963–4) to the surprising (Rock Hudson, one-time Hollywood matinée idol), actively and playfully disrupting Parker's stress on embroidery's critical role in 'the making of the feminine' alone. In reply, Parker pointed out that the issue of men's erasure from the history of embroidery had actually been, from an early stage, a factor in her thinking. In the 1970s, as part of the Women's Art History Collective, when Parker first began to reconsider embroidery, she was struck by the prominent position men often held in its history. Embroidery had not always been 'women's work'.[4] Unlike the similar research being done by contemporary feminist art critics, art historians and artists in America, such as Patricia Mainardi, Rachel Maines, Toni Flores Fratto, Lucy Lippard and Judy Chicago, whose work Parker read and reviewed, she remained perturbed by the fact that the history of needlework seemed to oppress women further by its omission of men.[5] Parker had been 'taught to embroider aged 6 or 7,' but, she recalled, it was considered too 'soppy and sissy' for her brothers who were given toy guns to play with.[6]

Towards the end of the interview with Caborn, Parker reflected, 'Why is it that a man impairs his masculinity if he embroiders?' She was not alone in her thinking. In 1984, as Parker's book appeared, the American historian Joan Jensen acknowledged that 'Men have been tailors and factory workers; sailors at sea have sewn their own clothing,' practices that were related, yet somehow removed, from the realities of women's experiences of needlework.[7] Studies of women's needlework proliferated in the nineteenth and twentieth centuries but to date there has not been a single book-length study about men and the culture of needlework. To understand better how needlework became so associated with the feminine ideal Parker analysed over a thousand years of its history in Britain. Over the past five hundred years, in particular, she located 'transitional' moments when embroidery became a social and economic, as much as a cultural, factor in the separation of the genders into public and private spheres.[8] She focused on a diverse range of selected examples taking in the presence of gender in the religious iconography of medieval English embroidery known as Opus Anglicanum, the rise of secular embroidery, domestic sewing and sampler making from the sixteenth to the eighteenth centuries, and the industrialization and commercialization of embroidery as well as the expansion of sweated labour and the parallel rediscovery and revival of medieval embroidery's aesthetics and techniques in the nineteenth century. She concluded her overview with an analysis of the role of needlework in the feminist movements in the opening and closing decades of the twentieth century. Parker noted that in medieval Britain 'men and women embroidered in guild workshops, or workshops attached to noble households, in monasteries and nunneries,' but by the Victorian age 'historians of embroidery obscured its past and instead suggested that embroidery had always been an inherently female activity, a quintessentially feminine craft.'[9] As embroidery became feminine it became amateur too.[10] 'Art of course has no sex,' but craft seemed to.[11] Victorian readings of embroidery as an essentially feminine pastime, Parker contested, prevailed unchallenged throughout the entire twentieth century. Within this, she further argued, 'embroidery and the stereotype of femininity have become collapsed into one another' yet, 'paradoxically, while embroidery was employed to inculcate femininity in women, it also enabled them to negotiate the constraints of femininity.'[12] If needlework became compulsory in the construction of 'women' as a social category, for men the opposite was true. Masculinity became defined through a conspicuous renunciation of needlework yet, predictably, men also retained the privilege of access according to demand or desire.

Concepts of masculinity as a 'constant, solid entity embedded, not only in the social network but in a deeper "truer" reality' seemed to resist, and continue to resist, analysis in terms of their construction.[13] But men (and certainly their relation to the culture of needlework) were unquestionably shaped by social and economic contexts that fixed genders as stable categories. Parker sees this as happening in tandem with the advent of modern capitalist society after the end of the eighteenth century.[14] This is the period in which the term 'masculinity' was first used.[15] As the Victorians cast women in the role of nature's needleworker, men were erased from its history. If we know that men stitched during medieval and early modern history, what, from the nineteenth century onwards, compelled Parker to claim, 'few men would risk jeopardising their sexual identity by claiming a right to the needle'.[16] Although Parker pays no attention to 'cissies' beyond the first page of *The Subversive Stitch*, gay men, in particular, have taken up needle and thread for its 'queer' subversion of the homophobic and heterosexist policing of gender and sexual identity.[17] Indeed, Parker and Griselda Pollock noted in *Old Mistresses* (1981), one of their major collaborations and very much a prequel to *The Subversive Stitch*, that once the masculine ideal was obliterated from embroidery's history 'it continued to be stitched by queens'.[18]

The examples of sewing by men, that Joan Jensen included in her study of needlework, draw on what could be called homosocial spaces, all-male arenas in which women are absent, where, it is believed, men's interest in needlework grew purely out of necessity. If then, as Jensen argues, and Parker concurs, 'Art. Meditation. Liberation. Exploitation. Needlework has been all these to women,' what, if anything, has it meant to men?[19] Jensen, like Parker, pressed the point that women's needlework could be a source of pleasure as well as oppression. Women, she noted, could take great pride in their work: 'whether for sewing on buttons or for taking the fine stitches that created the great women's art of quilting.'[20] For Parker 'all embroidery' has a capacity to offer 'comfort, satisfaction or pleasure for the embroiderer'.[21] Yet, when men stitched it is generally understood in terms of practicality over pleasure. Mary Beaudry in her more recent study of the 'material culture of needlework and sewing' makes brief reference to the sewing skills of tailors, as well as merchant seaman and working-class boys, but contends that such sewing was motivated 'both by necessity and for pleasure'.[22] Yet, labour over leisure, employment before enjoyment, forms the subtext of any man's needlework so as to not imperil his fragile masculinity by calling it into question through too close an association with the feminine.

Embroideries by sailors, one of the best-known types of needlework by men, have been dated by historians to c.1840–1900, the very period when embroidery became enduringly wedded to stereotypes of idealized femininity.[23] Yet, as Bridget Crowley argues, for sailors, 'their growing status as folk heroes apparently survived any accusation of "unmanliness" consequent upon this activity.'[24] Hypermasculinity, then, could actively negate the feminizing associations of needlework. Victorian representations of the masculine labouring body, especially those of working-class men such as sailors, tended to emphasize male power through physical spectacle. Paradoxically, one of the few known images of a sailor embroidering, published in 1867 in *The British Workman*, a Victorian Temperance periodical aimed at the working classes, challenges this conventional conceptualization of Victorian idealized manhood (Figure 1.1). The sailor, in this wood-engraving, is posed like Parker's archetypal female embroiderer in a Victorian drawing room: 'eyes lowered, head bent, shoulders hunched'.[25] Equally he seems to embody Parker's equation of embroidery and enjoyment. In this vein, Crowley has further argued that 'the tradition of sailors embroidering

*Only Sissies and Women Sew* 5

**Figure 1.1** 'Jack's Christmas Present.' *The British Workman*, no. 156 (2 December 1867): 141, © The British Library Board (LOU.LON 23).

for pleasure while at sea was strong' and 'just as the sedentary, confined life of the middle-class Victorian woman is reflected in the static representations and minute stitches of her craft, so the characteristics of life at sea are reflected in the work of the seaman'.[26] Like Crowley, Janet West suggests that sailors probably used materials that were produced for domestic consumption and may well have shopped for Berlin wools.²⁷ The sailor in this engraving is working a kit (which looks like a version of the popular Berlin woolwork 'birds of paradise' design), complete with the pre-designed canvas stretched in a tambour frame, with packs of wool on the table.

A group of surviving embroideries by an English sailor, Capt. Garrison Burdett Arey, are known to have been made from 'paper patterns' using popular Berlin wools. One depicting a *Bird of Paradise* (*c.*1865–9) (Figure 1.2) is strikingly similar to many of the designs sold to middle-class women, in the mid-late nineteenth century, for stitching at home. But another design by Arey, *Jesus Blessing the Children*, was apparently made after a painting he saw in Paris 'without any formal pattern or design'.²⁸ Clearly Arey, who also painted (more

**Figure 1.2** Capt. Garrison Burdett Arey, *Bird of Paradise*, c.1865–9, woollen yarn on canvas, 21.5 x 27.5 in. (54.6 x 69.8 cm), Courtesy of the collections of the Museum of Old Newbury.

conventional images of the ships on which he served), had artistic ambitions with needle and thread. Even so, there remains a resistance to accepting the relationality between the image of the embroidering Victorian housewife/damsel, explored by Parker in her book, and that of the hypermasculine sailor. The survival of Arey's embroideries is unusual as men's needlework generally goes unrecorded and uncollected. Few museums and galleries hold examples. Such embroiderers are, in terms of public display and discourse, not so much on the margins as beyond them. When an embroidery by a man surfaces it tends to be seen as completely unique.

Most people would agree that the feminine culture of needlework, seen to embody a set of binarized clichés (soft, domestic, submissive, amateur), is wholly irreconcilable with masculinity, as defined by its own set of clichés (hard, social, virile, masterful). But this assumes all men are the same; that masculinity as a dominating hegemony is homogeneous.[29] An example might illustrate the problem inherent in such assumptions. In the 1990s the American artist Elaine Reichek, one of the most influential embroiderers of modern times, embarked on a body of work that reflected on 'men who sew'.[30] Reichek's *Sampler (Hercules)* (1997) brings together images of once-celebrated male embroiderers from history (Plate 1). At the centre is Hercules, the personification of heroic masculinity from classical mythology to today's popular culture (Disney released its *Hercules* animated film the same year Reichek made her sampler), here subordinated to Queen Omphale, whom he helps with her needle and thread. The outrageously camp and charismatic Ernest Thesiger, the interwar English actor, artist, aristocrat and celebrated 'needleman', is on the left. Thesiger, author of *Adventures in Embroidery* (1941), was a widely acknowledged expert on embroidery as well as a pioneer in the teaching of needlework as occupational therapy to disabled veterans after the First World War. On the right is Rosey Grier, the American football player, actor, and later a popular advocate of embroidery and author of *Needlepoint for Men* (1973). Unlike the tailors, factory workers and sailors referred to by Jensen and Beaudry, or the professional male embroiderers working before the advent of the Industrial Revolution referred to by Parker, Thesiger and Grier were amateurs who saw needlework largely in terms of pleasure.[31] Equally important is the fact that Thesiger, as a gay man, and Grier, as a black man, existed outside culturally dominant inscriptions of normative masculinity.

Their perceived masculinity cannot, therefore, be read as the binary opposite of women as it was also defined in relation to other men. Thesiger and Grier, as men, were subordinated to prevailing models of hegemonic (white, heterosexual, middle-class) masculinity that occupied the dominant position in their specific historical and social contexts. As such it makes more sense to talk about 'masculinities', even the 'pluralities of masculinities' or 'multiple masculinities'.[32] R.W. Connell has suggested if we don't distinguish between men then there is a danger of 'multiple masculinities collapsing into a character typology', especially if some men resist hegemony and embody a 'symbolic blurring with femininity'.[33]

Given the fact that there is material evidence that men did embroider, knit, crochet, quilt, etc., why does it seem hard to accept that they invested something of themselves in it (time, pleasure, affection)? In the numerous studies, comparable to Parker's, of the history of needlework that have proliferated since the 1970s men appear to be omitted in entirety.[34] Occasionally, men are included by reference and inference, but they are widely perceived to be marginal to all of needlework's narratives.[35] Women's needlework, on the other hand, has been scrutinized from every conceivable angle. Needlework as a tool of domination and symbol of oppression, as well as a means to agency and activism or rebellion and subversion, in women's labour, education, leisure and consumption practices, continues to be widely investigated. Reference to needlework by men, in contrast, is fragmentary and reductive, elusive even. Men's needlework, much like men themselves, appears to have gone largely unexamined. Feminist historians have long acknowledged the necessity of studying 'both women and men' in countering representations of women as essentialized 'symbols of transhistorical femininity'.[36] Yet it is only recently that men in terms of gender have been exposed to any serious critical examination.[37] Parker's interest in men's needlework is striking but it remains exceptional. It is also more by implication than interrogation.

As the first quarter of the twenty-first century reaches a close such classifications of cis-gender in an age of hybridity, fluidity and non-binary identification may seem charmingly old-fashioned and completely redundant. Masculinity is, today, to some extent accepted as 'inherently relational', as something that 'does not exist except in contrast to "femininity"'.[38] There is, furthermore, a growing acceptance of 'female masculinity', of 'masculinities without men', even if 'male femininity' remains obscure and retains the power to unsettle.[39] But the age-old problems of patriarchy continually return to us in culture as much as in politics. Men seem just as defined today, by power and privilege, as they were in the past. Men are troubled too. Recent statistics (taking Britain as an example) reveal that men make up 76 per cent of adult suicides, 73 per cent of adults who are registered missing, 87 per cent of rough sleepers and 95 per cent of the prison population.[40] Misogyny, harassment and abuse by men seem endemic. Gender inequality is very real. Toxic masculinity thrives. Conversely, more men than ever before are believed to be taking up needlecrafts and many, over a much longer period, have used it to question personal, and political, meanings of the masculine. So a study of men and the culture of needlework may be, in some ways, timely and, further it may help us to better understand the construction of men as a social category rather than a biological entity.

* * * * * * * * * *

Needlework can be broadly defined as the surface embellishment of cloth (with pictures or patterns), the joining together of separate pieces of cloth or the mending of cloth. Rozsika Parker does not provide any definition or source for her use of the term 'embroidery'. She uses the terms 'embroidery' and 'needlework' interchangeably throughout *The Subversive Stitch*. She includes a range of activities under the embroidery/needlework rubric such as sewing, cross-stitch, knitting, lace-making and quilting. Whilst I am attentive to the important distinction between 'decorative' and 'plain' needlework, since the nineteenth century and after, I follow Parker's general example and include embroidery, needlepoint, cross-stitch, petit point, knitting, crocheting, quilting, patchwork, appliqué, tatting, lace-making, dressmaking and rag rug making.[41] Parker makes little distinction between handwork and machine work. I also follow her example here and include both in my discussion. And finally, like every other writer on needlework after Parker, I fully concur that what she 'theorizes about embroidery can in large part be extended to include any needlecraft'.[42]

2

# Needlework and the creation of masculinities: 'The prick' of patriarchy

In 2010, *The Subversive Stitch* was re-issued with a new 'Introduction' by Rozsika Parker in which she expressed some surprise at the presence of men within the contemporary culture of needlework.[1] Parker was hesitant to attribute this solely to the fact that 'embroidery practice seems to have become significantly less gender specific'.[2] In the intervening twenty-five years, since her book's original publication, much had changed but what was most striking, to Parker, was the early twenty-first century's revival of interest in 'homecraft' fuelled by the resonance of handmaking activities in yet another age of global recession. This impulse has been given a political edge, and voice, through the new DIY and Craftivist movements, even if much of this is mainstream, done in leisure time and in tandem with wider consumer trends. With this the centuries-old shame of men taking on feminine needlecrafts seems to have suddenly evaporated. This may be partly explainable through the extension of legal rights to gay men and women (in education, the workforce, marriage, family life), which no longer made them threatening to concepts of the home.[3] It is a very recent turn of events. In 1996, 'Only 3 per cent of men said they did dressmaking, needlework or knitting.'[4] Twenty years later, Hobbycraft, the largest arts and crafts retailer in Britain, estimated that sewing and knitting patterns sales were up 60 per cent and the sales of sewing machines were up 30 per cent and the Craft & Hobby Trade Association has estimated that 7.7 million people were making their own clothes, 6.8 million now knit and at least 1 million people had taken up sewing.[5] Women form the majority of this 'millennial makers movement,' but more and more men are visible.

In popular terms the presenters on the BBC's *Great British Sewing Bee*, including the Savile Row tailor Patrick Grant, have argued against the lazy 'sissy' stereotype of men's sewing and have given us several male contestants from the hypermasculine former soldier to the more middle-class and 'blokey' and the stereotypically gay. One male contestant now writes for *Patchwork, Essentials* and *Sew Magazine* and has authored his own book on sewing.[6] As part of research into the rise of the male needleworker, several male journalists have been inspired to take sewing classes and one has even written a book about his experience.[7] There are numerous websites run by men and for men, on sewing, knitting and other needlecrafts, and images of men with needles in hand are easily found on social media: on Facebook, Twitter, Tumblr, Flickr, Instagram, Pinterest and YouTube. However, as Parker contends, it would be a mistake to interpret this as simply a reflection of gender equality. Men who sew or knit are still feminized and they are, like women, routinely infantilized. The murderous threat of violence still persists against men who seem to repudiate the patriarchal and embrace the feminine.[8] At the beginning of the millennium, within the British education system, only 4 per cent of boys had any exposure to needlework classes, which were perceived as 'cissy' and out of bounds for 'real boys', even though other domestic-associated activities, such as cooking, saw an uptake.[9]

Since Victorian times there has been no perceptible shift in societal perceptions of needlework as anything but feminine. As such it is easy to overemphasize men's place within popular revivals of needlecrafts. For many to attempt a study of men's needlework may seem irrelevant, ridiculous, laughable even. To explore this through a historical survey could also be interpreted as the '"prick" of patriarchy', in which femininity is neutralized through its absorption into what men do.[10] The 'prick', as Jane Gallop suggests, denotes 'the male sex organ (the famous penis of penis-envy: attraction-resentment) and an obnoxious person – an unprincipled and selfish man who highhandedly abuses others, who capriciously exhibits little or no regard for justice'.[11] Yet, when used against itself, as in the 'prick of conscience', the term is divested of all its phallic symbolism and re-inscribed as a tool that can puncture prevailing power structures. This book, then, does not propose to map the progress of men's needlework, through a procession of canonical examples; instead it seeks to extend feminist debates; in that, it interrogates the culpability of social practices (the culture of needlework) in the construction of gender (the masculine) by troubling orthodox histories of both. This book's argument pivots on two key points. The first is how needlework operated in the making of modern masculinities through the exclusion, effacement and elision of men from its history. The second is the completely overlooked yet central presence of needlework in medical, legal as well as socio-cultural discourses that gave birth to modern homosexual identities, their subsequent mediation through mass culture and in various forms of subcultural resistance.

## Needlework and the making of the masculine: From monk to manbroiderer

Much of the initial inspiration for Rozsika Parker's book came from the realization that it was the Victorians who had deliberately repositioned women in needlework's history. For instance, although the makers of England's great medieval embroideries, known as Opus Anglicanum, are generally unrecorded it is acknowledged that men as well as women made such work. From the late medieval period up to the sixteenth century there was an increasing professionalization and organization, along capitalist logic, of embroidery workshops, which previously had been attached to the church and court. These were privatized and regulated, by the newly founded Broderers Company in the City of London, which was run exclusively by men. Within this men's prominence in terms of design and production was easy to overstate. The list of male embroiderers in C.H. Hartshorne's *Mediaeval English Embroidery* (1848) somewhat misleadingly includes, as Parker reveals, merchants, goldsmiths and even clerks.[12] Only when the economic and cultural value of embroidery began to diminish in post-medieval society was needlework aligned to ideas associated with the domestic and feminine. By the advent of modern industrial society, in the late eighteenth and early nineteenth centuries, which saw far-reaching transformations in all aspects of textile production, men were eclipsed in the narrative and women, increasingly divested of power, were framed as needleworkers by nature. The Victorian equation of femininity and needlework obscured men in its history so fully that any examples of men's needlework were relegated to the distant past. Modern conceptualizations of craft, emanating from the Arts and Crafts movement, were so dependent on Victorian interpretations of the past, in which needlework's alignment with the feminine was so complete, that the architect W.B. Lethaby could write, without accuracy or irony, 'down to the mid-thirteenth century we hear of women in connection with the production of such works' but before that 'I only know of men who are named as embroiderers'.[13] The textile historian A.J.B. Wace added: 'Monks have always been just as skilled in crafts and applied arts as nuns … To despise embroidery therefore as feminine is misguided as to reject it as an applied art.'[14] If anything, the image of the needleworker as medieval monk (as a point of origin) operated as a sign of male authority, re-aligned to religious revivalism in the nineteenth and twentieth centuries, co-opting needlework in moments when it seemed to be re-invested with some degree of cultural capital.

Parker established that it was the Victorians who dreamt up the image of the medieval monk embroidering in a cloister but she contended, much more significantly, that women's 'subversion' of their social, economic, political and cultural subordination can be traced through the symbolism of fertility and motherhood in images of the Virgin and St Margaret (the patron saint of childbirth) in the embroideries of Opus Anglicanum, through the seventeenth century when women seditiously stitched images of the Old Testament's 'female heroines', such as Ester, Judith and Jael, who murdered male oppressors.[15] But what can be said of men's work? Did a medieval monk ever speak through his needle and thread? What did it mean for the seventeenth-century embroiderer Edmund Harrison to depict the *Circumcision of Christ* from the New Testament (*c.*1687) (Figure 2.1).[16] Does it say anything about his masculinity? Sigmund Freud thought this specific biblical episode reflected the masculine fear of castration: the making of the male body like a woman's through mutilation.[17] If, as Parker argues, women in the seventeenth century turned to stitching the 'masculine' acts of violence by biblical heroines, during a period of gender instability, is it so implausible that men may have expressed similar feelings or anxieties? Parker's argument, as an interpretation of women's history, hinges on embroidery's duality – as the process of oppression and simultaneously the agent of subversion. Her conceptualization of the 'subversive stitch' was, also, part of a wider parallel drawn within feminism between needlecrafts and 'women's writing'. The French writer Hélène Cixous was first to formulate the concept of 'l'écriture féminine', but it was an American writer, Elaine Showalter, who argued that a distinct 'women's tradition of piecing, patchwork, and

**Figure 2.1** Edmund Harrison, *Circumcision of Christ*, c.1687, linen silk, gold thread, silver thread on linen, 43 x 28.5 in. (110 x 73 cm), © National Museums Scotland (A.1987.317).

quilting' was fundamental in the creation of female literary expression outside phallocentric discourse.[18] If the pen was a phallic signifier then the needle operated as both the sign and repudiation of female subordination.[19] As seventeenth-century women had embroidered biblical heroines so too did later writers excavate the history of women. Marie Cardinal's novel, *Le Passé empiété*, published just before *The Subversive Stitch*, links its protagonist, a contemporary embroiderer, with Clytemnestra, the classical god celebrated for her weaving and stitching as well as the murder of her husband. Cardinal employs embroidery as a process of self-exploration, a return to the maternal (through ancient history) and ultimately a rejection of male power.[20] The textile practices of the 'female heroines' of classical literature, Penelope, Medea,

Arachne, Athena and Clytemnestra, had often been evoked by male writers to stress the continuity of femininity through time. Yet for women they could be seen as disrupting narratives of feminine passivity. Men who had unfettered access to the high literary tradition did not have to search for a reflection or validation in the past. They could ignore their history in needlework, which was not, like women's, a pantheon of heroes but instead one of abject failures: the traumatized Oedipus, who uses the golden pins from his mother's dress to blind himself after the trauma of his betrayal. It is the heroic deeds of Hercules that are most often represented not his subjugation and emasculation through needlework.

In an interview with Elaine Showalter, Parker drew the conversation to a discussion of the presence of the 'male invalid – the prostrate, dependent man' in literary history.[21] Parker further speculated: 'It could be argued that the construction of masculinity – the process that turns boy babies into men with the characteristics valued by our culture – does "blind" them.'[22] More often than not invalided or suffering men in fiction were more than pitiable – they were deviant. In the hugely popular 'sensation' novels by Wilkie Collins, for example, the act of embroidery is often performed by male characters who have been emasculated and feminized through disability. Both the eccentric, wheelchair-bound Miserrimus Dexter who embroiders throughout *The Lady and the Law* (1875) and the ailing Abel Gracedieu who takes up knitting in *The Legacy of Cain* (1888) illuminate Parker's point that for the Victorians embroidery embodied a stereotype of a subordinate femininity, even when taken up by a man. Indeed, as Eve Kosofsky Sedgwick has suggested the disabilities, and by association the feminine pastimes, of such men (even if fictional) acted as 'the shadowy presence of a mysterious imperative', debarring them from embodying a full masculinity.[23] Showalter, in reply to Parker, suggested that 'most critics see them as castration scenes. For a man to suffer, to feel and to be helpless is in their sensibility to become castrated.'[24] The articulation of a man's identity through the symbolism of needlework entailed, then, some sort of literal (physical or psychological) as well as metaphorical (social or cultural) disempowerment.

However, since the early twentieth century many men seem to have openly embraced such stigmatization, symbolic or otherwise. Parker suggested that the recent increase in men taking up needlework could be understood not only as part of a wider reinvestment in the culture of domesticity but also as a conscious means of interrogating identity as well as an unconscious return to the maternal. Perhaps operating beyond the margins has left many men free to explore the pleasures and creative possibilities of needlework relatively undisturbed. Those men who have achieved a level of recognition for their needlework have often provoked speculation about their masculine credentials. After the Second World War James Norbury, for instance, wrote several books on knitting, and one on embroidery, and has been described as 'the strongest single influence on knitting during the 25 years after the war'.[25] Yet, 'Norbury the Knitter' was called the 'Rugged Type' by influential women's journalist Marjorie Proops deliberately satirizing his unashamedly camp manner in case anyone had missed it (Figure 2.2).[26] More recently,

**Figure 2.2** Ron Gerelli, *James Norbury Knitting*, c.1930s, © The Hulton Archive/Getty Images.

other men, such as Kaffe Fassett, Raymond Honeyman and Richard Box, have achieved similar professional and popular success as designers of needlepoint kits or authors of books on technique. Kaffe Fassett is perhaps the best known and has been embroidering, knitting and quilting for almost fifty years (Figure 2.3).[27] Grayson Perry has written of how his interest in textiles and his transvestism could be read as an 'unconscious renunciation' of the masculine archetype.[28] Mark Newport has employed knitting and embroidery in his work to purposely reflect on the social and cultural construction of the masculine ideal. He has also employed needlework in an exploration of how boys are inculcated with models of idealized masculinity through popular culture – such as comic books. Superheroes as symbols of hypermasculinity have been appropriated by Newport and refashioned into knitted bodysuits

**Figure 2.3** Portrait of Kaffe Fassett sewing by David Cripps on the cover of *Glorious Inspiration: Kaffe Fassett's Needlepoint Source Book* (London: Ebury Press, 1991), Reproduced by permission of The Random House Group Ltd/Penguin Books Ltd. © 1991 and Courtesy of the artist.

or embroidered bedcovers, such as the *Freedom Bed Cover/Zachary* (2006) (Figure 2.4). These objects have destabilized meanings, both male and female, and help expose the masculine as a complex struggle between hero identification and '"feminine" desire to create, love and nurture'.[29]

Other men have seen in needlework a means to explore issues of race or class in relation to constructions of masculine identity. In explaining his decision to make quilts, the artist Wendell Brown stated: 'I am interested in tracing the experience of black men working with textiles from Africa to this country.'[30] Kellie Jones contends that for several artists an understanding of a past 'vernacular' proved critical in the choice of why and how to 'make' art: 'The incorporation of sewing into the work of Al Loving, Sam Gilliam and Joe

**Figure 2.4** Mark Newport, *Freedom Bed Cover/Zachary*, 2006, hand-embroidered cotton thread and ribbon on comic book pages, 80 x 65 x 1 in. (203 x 165.1 x 2.5 cm), Courtesy of Greg Kucera Gallery Inc. Seattle, © Mark Newport.

Overstreet at this time evoked family traditions of quilting and tailoring. These were functional arts that African-Americans had used to earn a living and keep their creative juices flowing at the same time.'[31] Norman Willis, a former leading trade unionist and TUC general secretary, started doing cross-stitch after someone bought him a kit for 'a joke'. Yet from 1998 Willis wrote a regular feature in *Cross-Stitcher* magazine (Figure 2.5). Asked why he embroidered, Willis, slightly defensive of working-class masculinity so central to modern trade unionism, stated: 'The truth is that my cross stitch is neither therapy nor a crusade – it is total unadulterated pleasure.'[32] Men's needlework has been often characterized as amateur and there has been much interest in work which could be categorized as 'primitive' or 'outsider' such as that of the Scot Angus

**Figure 2.5** Norman Willis, 'How I Got Stitched Up…' *Cross Stitcher* 72 (August 1998): 74, Courtesy of *Cross Stitcher*/Dennis Publishing Ltd.

McPhee, the Brazilian artist Arthur Bisop Rosário and the Frenchman Jules Leclerq, who all turned to needlework during long incarcerations after being diagnosed with different forms of schizophrenia.[33] The miniature embroideries made by Ray Materson, who took up needlework whilst serving time in a high security prison, for its nostalgic, consoling and redemptive properties, have generated much interest.[34] Yet within the world of commercial embroidery as much as in the context of professional fine art men have engaged with a diverse range of needlework practices. In the fashion world there is much focus on the male designer but little on the male embroiderer – from the workshops of haute couture to the sweatshops of fast fashion. Alexander McQueen was often called 'Edward Scissorhands' for the way he cut fabric, but no-one ever mentioned his phenomenal sewing skills. The leading studios producing (and teaching) hand embroidery, such as the Atelier François Lesage, Hand & Lock and the Royal School of Needlework, all employ male as well as female embroiderers. Not only do these studios service fashion designers in couture houses and museum conservation departments, but they also provide sewing skills for contemporary artists. The elegant workshop of Penn & Fletcher, a 'custom embroidery company' founded in New York by Ernie Smith in 1986, for example, has worked for a diverse range of male artists including Matthew Barney – providing embroidery for his *Cremaster Cycle* (1994–2002). Many male artists have profited from the use of ironic and uncanny references to the domestic familiarity of needlework and from its novelty when authorized by the male hand. Luc Tuymans, for example, has received wide acclaim for his paintings that incorporated embroidery and Wim Delvoye cemented his *enfant terrible* status by having pigs (and later slices of ham) elaborately tattooed with needlework designs. Alighiero Boetti's embroidered wall-hangings and maps were made by women in Afghanistan and Pakistan, whose names he did not record but he had already employed embroidery, crochet and lace in his work made by his wife, the art critic Annemarie Sauzeau.[35] The significance and scale of sewing in these artists' *oeuvre* are significant and haven't gone unremarked on in assessments of their work. Boetti was recently called 'Signor Lazybones' by one critic.[36] Whether intentionally or not the assumed originality of such work has often garnered invitations to exhibit at prestigious international venues and participate in high-profile awards and prize competitions – such as Documenta, the Venice Biennale, the Whitney Biennial and the Turner Prize.

Many men in trying to understand their own desire to stitch have turned to researching the past for answers. Such research has often generated important archives of knowledge about the history of men's needlework. Clyde Olliver has published on sailor's needlework, Paddy Hartley on textiles of the First World War and Gavin Fry has conducted extensive research on the rise of the male embroiderer in Thatcherite Britain.[37] Mark Newport's short article on masculinity and 'fiber art' remains authoritative after two decades.[38] There are many other examples of this archiving the past and it should not be taken as a search for patrilineage as any man who engages with needlecrafts submits, whether consciously or not, to its associations with the feminine and the maternal. How else can we explain the American embroiderer Stephen Beal's use of the sampler format in the late twentieth century? Beal also wrote poetry, and prose, sometimes from a female perspective or about female experience. His collection of poems, *The Very Stuff: Poems on Color, Thread and the Habits of Women* (1995), comprises forty-three poems about embroidery thread colours manufactured by Dollfus-Mieg et Compagnie, and anticipates his largest sampler, entitled *Periodic Table of the Artist's Colors* (2004), which depicts ninety-five colours of embroidery floss each with a witty epigram (Plate 2).[39] Like the multitudes of historic samplers this one is deceptively simple – in its exploration of the technical through the tactile.

William Morris, perhaps the most famous male needleworker of the past two centuries, taught himself to embroider so he could decorate his bachelor quarters with the then fashionable tapestry-style wall hangings. However, he started by studying the humble sampler. A surviving fragment of Morris's first attempts at embroidery depicts a repeat pattern of fruit trees and stylized birds, believed to be drawn after a fourteenth-century manuscript by Froissart, and inscribed with the fifteenth-century painter Van Eyck's motto 'If I can' (Plate 3).[40] In the 1850s while Morris was still teaching himself embroidery he married Jane Burden who later recalled that he then taught her to embroider. No doubt Burden could plain sew but she soon became imbricated in Morris's project to rescue lost craft skills. Subsequently, Burden, and their daughter, May Morris, became the central figures in Morris's embroidery workshop.[41] These adult relationships echo those of Morris's boyhood. His father had died when he was fourteen and he developed an especially close relationship with his mother and his older sister. His biographer records that in order to appease his 'nervous manner' Morris was encouraged to 'seek relief from it in endless netting. With one end of the net fastened to a desk in the big schoolroom he would work at it for hours, his fingers moving automatically.'[42] Frederick Kirchhoff, in his study of Morris's masculine self-fashioning, has suggested that Morris's textile designs were like 'the "endless netting" of his schooldays' an 'activity [that] affirms the self only through its submission to a process with no internal mechanism of closure'.[43] Kirchhoff further argues that Morris's embroideries can be read as a 'retreat to childhood' and as symbols of the 'infantile mother-child relationship'.[44] Other examples of this abound in the Arts and Crafts movement. The embroidery designs of the architect and designer Ernest Gimson, for example, deliberately evoke the child's sampler (Figure 2.6). Some of these were stitched by his young niece, Phyllis Lovibond.

**Figure 2.6** Ernest Gimson and Phyllis Lovibond, *Sampler*, c.1890s, cotton thread on linen, 18.5 x 13.4 in. (47 x 34 cm), © Crafts Study Centre/University for the Creative Arts (T.81.54).

For boys to fully enter into the phallic order of the father they need to deny and repress identification with the mother and all things feminine. The maternal, then, is a central component in the 'construction of male domination'.[45] Failure or refusal to align with the father, or a return to the mother, marks the rejection or reconfiguration of masculine authority. Many men did just that and their relation to concepts of mothers and the maternal, although widely denied in culture, can be seen as a thread running through the history of embroidery. Fine Cell Work, an English organization set up in 1997 to help prisoners earn money through the making of embroidery, for Parker, was a key example of 'the mirroring function of embroidery'. Its founder, Lady Angela Tree, was inspired to set up a programme to teach prisoners to sew by her recollection of seeing a soldier sewing in a canteen during the Second World War.[46] Parker offers an interpretation of Fine Cell Work, and by implication men's needlework in general, by way of D.W. Winnicott's equation of the 'mirror' and the maternal in child development.[47] Parker studied the ex-prisoner testimonials that Fine Cell Work has collected that attest to the rehabilitative power of needlework. One man stated the embroidery teacher became 'like my mum', and another explained how the process of sewing encouraged him to reflect upon his background and made him consider his relationship with his own children.[48] Under the aegis of the scheme, between 2007 and 2010, fifty-two male prisoners at HMP Wandsworth made a quilt, using everything from cell bed sheets to prison officer uniforms, reflecting on masculinity and its relation to authority, all framed within the prison's distinctive panopticon design.[49] Using embroidery, patchwork and appliqué techniques the quilt stitched together individual stories of redemption through needlework, what Claire Smith has called the 'the continuing appeal of the needle as a tool of both subversion and salvation' (Plate 4).[50]

In her new 2010 'Introduction' Parker also seemed especially surprised by the contemporary phenomenon known as 'manbroidery'. The earliest instance of the 'manbroidery' term being used is online, in 2009, by the artist, Jenny Hart, who wrote on her blog:

> Man-brodiery. Boy-broidery. Guy-stitching. Bro-broidery. What you call it, guys are (and always have been) doing it. You know, embroidering! Wielding the needle! Marking the muslin! Poking the pillowcase! Splitting

the stich! Which is fantastically awesome. I say: there needs to be more men embroidering. And it seems that there are.[51]

About the same time there emerged a range of websites, blogs, Etsy pages and Flickr pools run by men who were embroidery enthusiasts, including: Johnny Murder's 'Manbroidery', Paul Overton's 'DudeCraft' and Jamie Chalmers's 'Mr X Stitch'.[52] Parker was especially interested in the dynamic Chalmers (Figure 2.7), the 'poster boy for a culturally diverse approach to embroidery; notably cross-stitch', who has, since 2008, run his own website, founded a magazine, published two books as well as lectured and exhibited extensively. Since 2012, his website has run a page, entitled 'eMbroidery', on which Chalmers interviews contemporary male embroiderers from all over the world. Parker was intrigued by the semantics of the (re)gendering of embroidery. She

**Figure 2.7** Jamie Chalmers aka 'Mr. X-Stitch.' © Jamie Chalmers.

noticed this in Chalmers's hypermasculine self-referential gesture to Marvel Comics 'X-Men' franchise, as much as its play on the phonetics of cross-stitch, in his name. She was also struck by how he countenanced the potential feminization of his embroidery by reference to his masculine physique: 'I'm six-feet tall yet I like stitching.'[53] Of the manbroidery phenomenon, in general, one contemporary female stitcher countered:

> I find this whole 'manbroidery' business patronizing. Why do they need a special term because they're men doing embroidery? It's still embroidery.
>
> In the world at large, men are always taken more seriously than women. Non-stitchers believe that, because we're women, we're born with the knowledge of stitch in our ovaries or something ridiculous. I learned the craft just as any man would have to. I've put in just as much effort. People will say, 'Wait, he's a man, but he's doing embroidery? He must be doing it for a real reason, as opposed to girls, who just do it "cause they all love it."'[54]

Parker pointed out that although the Women's Liberation movement of the 1970s had resulted in 'a greater flexibility in what is considered natural or normal behaviour for men and women' the 'associations of embroidery with femininity, triviality and domesticity still need to be warded off by the term "manbroiderer" – and by the build of the stitcher'.[55] Since the nineteenth century the history of embroidery may have elided the presence of men, but men did engage with needlework as a social practice irrespective of the interpretations it may have invited. Embroidery had its part to play in the making of the masculine.

## Needlework and the birth of the homosexual: From sexology to subculture

In 1984 reports of the deteriorating health of Hollywood actor Rock Hudson added an unexpected postscript to the publication of Parker's *The Subversive Stitch*. Hudson had been diagnosed with AIDS in June 1984, although this was not made public until a year later and a few months before his death in October 1985. Reports of Hudson's final weeks in hospital in the British tabloid press, in particular, seized upon his embroidery as somehow symbolic of his 'secret' homosexuality. By exposing his predilection for needlework the press sought to confirm Hudson's essentially feminine, rather than masculine, nature.[56] Newspaper reports implied that Hudson had taken up needlework as a sort of solace during his sickness but in fact knowledge of Hudson's needlework is dated to well before his AIDS diagnosis. In America many men (some gay, some not), from the immediate postwar years to the 1980s, took up embroidery, knitting, crocheting and quilting as part of the wider revival of needlecrafts. In Britain, Hudson's embroidery was first reported in the press in the 1970s when he and Henry Fonda (much better known for his needlepoint in America than Hudson), Hollywood stars perceived as paradigmatic of modern masculinity, were named by Richard Adler, as avid 'needlemen', in the promotion of his mail-order needlepoint kit business, which he had set up in England with his wife in 1976.[57] The focus on Hudson's needlework as a means to revoke his once-powerful manliness was not completely isolated. Other gay men who liked to sew received similar treatment in the popular press. When John Curry, the British Olympic figure skating champion, was dying of AIDS in the early 1990s his embroidery was taken as an emblem of the suffering and shame rooted in homosexuality – as a toxic set of emotions that propelled his destructive perfectionism: 'Curry's samplers were the product of the same tortured ambition to eliminate human error from art.'[58] Reports of the death of the radio and television star Kenny Everett from AIDS around the same time also focused on his embroidery as the tacit marker of deviance.[59] AIDS was not necessarily a requisite. When the actor John Inman, whose portrayal of Mr Humphries on the BBC's *Are You Being Served?* (1972–85) indelibly sissified the homosexual in the British popular imagination, was dying of cancer his needlework was evoked by the press as shorthand for his famously camp manner on and off the screen. Effeminacy and embroidery collapsed into one another.

Defining masculinity through an emphatic exclusion of needlework meant that any man who took it up needed to be pathologized. This process is often disguised by laughter. Indeed, in the course of her 1984 interview with Caborn, Parker admitted her own research initially 'provoked some laughter by choosing an area of art not normally taken so seriously'.[60] She was further conscious that images of men's needlework were so incongruous that they generated much stronger reactions: 'The laughter provoked by embroidery practiced "out of place" illustrates the strength of sexual divisions in society.'[61]

Images of men embroidering have consistently been seen in terms of a joke. Think of the cliché of a bachelor sewing on a button, a popular Victorian vaudeville act that has permeated mass culture such as cinema, television and advertising, throughout the twentieth century. Freud suggested that laughter gives expression to what is repressed and it allows us to overcome usually forbidden feelings and fears of ostracization. Laughter, then, as a 'sign of repression' threatens to expose what we desire or need to control.[62] For example, a Victorian image of a 'sewing match for men' on-board a luxury ocean liner seems innocent enough (Figure 2.8). But the fun and frivolity of the 'match' serve to mask the reality that Victorian wealth was built from the colonial exploitation of textile crafts such as embroidery, which was still made by men in India, the destination of these travellers (Figure 2.9).[63] More recent studies of masculinity have continued to suggest that 'truths about our deepest desires, fears, and fantasies are revealed through laughter.'[64] Images confirming men's natural inability to sew or their pathetically entertaining attempts to learn have

**Figure 2.8** Arthur Hopkins, 'Amusements on Board an Ocean Liner: A Sewing Match for Men.' *The Graphic* (10 November 1894): 549, Private Collection © Look and Learn/Illustrated Papers Collection/Bridgeman Images.

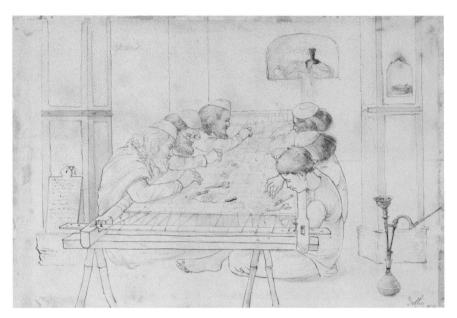

**Figure 2.9** John Lockwood Kipling, *Men at an Embroidery Frame for Jewelled and Spangled Cloth*, November 1870, pencil, pen and wash on paper, 10.4 x 14.4 in. (26.3 x 36.7 cm), © Victoria and Albert Museum (0929:31/(IS)).

proliferated since Victorian times and have been remarkably consistent. For example, when in *Modern Times* (1936) Charlie Chaplin is carted off to prison, after causing chaos in the factory where he works, he finds himself next to a brawny cellmate who to Chaplin's surprise passes the time embroidering. Yet, the incongruous image of the male prisoner with his embroidery hoop is rendered comic by his sheer physical presence and its projection of a manly stereotype (Figure 2.10).

Other examples of male needleworkers in cinematic history, used to stabilize normative gender stereotypes, include a remarkable opening shot of Sidney Olcott's *Monsieur Beaucaire* (1924) that shows the hands of King Louis XV busily embroidering. The film was a vehicle for its star Rudolph Valentino who played the more masculine Duke de Chartres (Beaucaire) to the foppish and decadent monarch. In Alfred Hitchcock's *Jamaica Inn* (1939) a gnarly, tattooed Cornish sailor/shipwrecker sews lace cuffs onto his jacket. In H.C. Potter's *Mr. Lucky* (1943), Cary Grant takes refuge from gangsters in a branch of the War Relief Fund and becomes involved in a knitting demonstration in

**Figure 2.10** Charlie Chaplin, *Modern Times*, 1936, film still, © The Estate of Charlie Chaplin/Roy Export SAS, Paris, 2018.

which his protestations, as well as his later sexual advances to the female staff, serve to affirm the authority of heterosexual masculinity during wartime. Even by the end of the twentieth century such images had little changed. Think of the laughter induced by macho man, such as the cop played by Bruce Willis in Renny Harlin's *Die Hard 2* (1990), or the cop played by Sylvester Stallone in Marco Branbilla's *Demolition Man* (1993), who disclose penchants for needlepoint and knitting, respectively.

During the twentieth century representations of masculinity in film were just as important as those in literature in the nineteenth century. In the paranoid era of post-McCarthy America, insinuation of a queer subtext in a man's behaviour was often underscored by the presence of, or reference to, needlework. In Hitchcock's *Psycho* (1960), for instance, in the scenes that build to the film's climax we are shown all the traces of Mrs Bates in her bedroom, including her clothes, her dressing table, her recently slept-in bed and a Victorian embroidery trestle table with an unfinished floral canvas, thread dangling. Did embroidery, like cross-dressing, feature in her son Norman's

Oedipal crisis? This is referenced in William Castle's *Homicidal* (1961) as during the opening credits as Castle introduces his film to the viewers (in direct homage to Hitchcock), he is pictured in the process of 'stitching a needlepoint sampler', with the title of film on it. Alexander Doty has read this as 'queering' the film's phallocentric symbolism. Doty contends that such a juxtaposition of symbols (feminine servility and masculine savagery) suggests 'that such traditionally feminine pursuits as needlework could be preferable for men as opposed to the violent masculinity the rest of the film critiques'.[65] A more recent Hollywood take on this can be found in Jonathan Demme's *Silence of the Lambs* (1991) in which the killer, 'Buffalo Bill', flays his victims in order to make a woman's outfit he can wear. In such films, sometimes drawn from real-life events, men's needlework becomes imbricated in the armoury of violence used against women.

The appropriation of a feminine-associated activity by men continues, more often than not, to signal a queer trace in a film's narrative. Benigno Martín, the shy, sensitive male nurse who rapes the comatose female ballet dancer in his care in Pedro Almodóvar's *Talk to Her/Hable con ella* (2002), is shown in one scene embroidering her name onto a pillow case. Patrick Braden, aka 'Kitten', in Neil Jordan's *Breakfast on Pluto* (2005), an adaption of Patrick McCabe's novel, discloses his otherness through not just cross-dressing but also his/her interest in the needlework class at school. The sexual deviance of both Martín and Kitten is mediated through their desire for women's clothes, bodies and activities. In children's films, in particular, needlework as gender-inappropriate behaviour has long been deployed to denote the stigma of effeminacy and homosexuality. Recent examples include the wizard, and headmaster of Hogwarts school, Albus Dumbledore in David Yates's *Harry Potter and the Half Blood Prince* (2009), who makes an oblique reference to 'knitting patterns' and who was, just a few years earlier, outed as the franchise's only gay character by the author of the original books, J.K. Rowling.

The symbol of male embroiderer as gay stereotype, as a visual means to reinforce the dominance of masculine authority and heteronormativity, has been widely deployed in the enormously popular television format of the sitcom. These almost always pivot around the nuclear family or comparable networks of kinship and community: from the son of the TV handyman taking a 'home ec' class at school, that will include learning to sew, just to meet girls in *Home Improvement* (1991), and Joey, the only macho male in *Friends* (1999), learning to knit under the influence of a new female roommate, whom he ultimately seeks to seduce, to the effeminate boy-men such as Kenneth, and his knitted-bikini, in *30 Rock* (2007) or Sheldon in *The Big Bang Theory* (2014) dressed up as 'Betsy Ross' stitching the first American flag with an embroidery hoop.[66] In Seth MacFarlane's animated sitcom *Family Guy*, in a highly acclaimed episode that parodies Hitchcock's *North by Northwest* (1959), we see the boy-man Stewie in bed, with the family's talking dog Brian, embroidery hoop in hand stitching 'die Lois' in a reference to his mother.[67] The matricide joke is part of the show's wider parody of Stewie's mirroring of his mother. In an episode of *Curb Your Enthusiasm* (2011) Larry buys a sewing machine as a birthday present for Greg, the flamboyant and fashion-loving son of his girlfriend. Clearly insulted at the insinuation that Greg is not 'a happy, healthy, normal seven-year-old' the boy's mother asks, 'What are you trying to turn him gay?'[68] There is a whole range of memorable examples from British television: from the flamboyant Mr. Humphries in *Are You Being Served?* who declares 'I don't do needlepoint! Not now I'm doing the lace mats' and 'My mother gave me this watch when I became captain of the embroidery team'[69] to the openly gay and melancholic character called Lukewarm whose campness is literalized through his knitting in the prison-set sitcom *Porridge* (1974–7) or the never-seen character Sheridan, son of the social-climbing snob 'Mrs. Bucket', on *Keeping Up Appearances* (1990–5) who is studying 'Tapestry and Advanced Needlework at the Poly'.

The most systematic use of needlework as a marker of queerness can be found in the groundbreaking gay sitcom *Will & Grace* (1998–2006). The show routinely evoked the homophobia inherent in seeing a man perform a female act that served to highlight just how actively mainstream culture polices notions of gender and sexual normativity. For example, Will's friend Larry is first exposed as a needlepoint devotee and in subsequent episodes Will reveals: 'My home ec teacher said I was a needlepoint prodigy. In fact, I was the only guy to have a piece in the state-wide needlepoint competition. Well, the only guy who is still a guy.' Later we hear more of Will's love of needlepoint and of his knitting, of the sewing machine and sewing trophies of Vince, Will's boyfriend, and in one episode we see the shady and sexually ambiguous character of Malcolm, Will's new boss, stitching 'Welcome Wi … ' on an embroidery hoop.[70] Perhaps the most remarkable example of the symbolic use of needlework in this sitcom is an episode entitled 'Looking for Mr Good Enough', in which Will, dressed in fifties-style housewife's apron that he has intricately embroidered with an image from a children's nursery rhyme, becomes enraged at being set up with a prostitute by his friends so that he would no longer be the 'sad' single person at a cooking class, stating 'Let me tell you something. Will Truman doesn't have to pay for it, okay? Will Truman just goes months and months at a time without it and then pours all his sexual energy into his embroidery.'[71] This is a play on Richard Brooke's *Looking for Mr Goodbar* (1977), a film version of Judith Rossner's novel that fictionalized the real-life murder of a New York schoolteacher in 1973. In the book needlework is evoked in the final murder scene as the killer 'couldn't get an erection' because 'his wife had castrated him', to which his female victim replies, 'Well, call me up when someone sews it back on.'[72]

Modern mass culture's preoccupation with linking the homosexual and the pathological has its origin in the nineteenth century. The emergence of medical and legal classifications of male sexuality rested largely on stabilizing definitions of masculinity and femininity. As Michel Foucault has contended homosexuality was historically understood as an 'abject act' but, by the late nineteenth century, it was transformed into a subjective identity: the 'homosexual became a personage, a past, a case history, a childhood … The sodomite had been a temporary aberration; the homosexual was now a species.'[73] The establishment of sexology in the late nineteenth century is important in the history of embroidery as men who expressed same-sex desire, and by doing so seemed to relinquish masculine authority over women, were feminized and thought to adopt the characteristics and traits of women and to appropriate their social habits including their hobbies. This was labelled 'inversion' and such men were thought to represent 'a female soul in a man's body'.[74] Foucault dates the origin of this to exactly 1869–70 and the publication of Carl O. Westphal's essay 'Contrary Sexual Feeling', the first medical text to attempt to describe the subjective life of the homosexual. Westphal through a series of clinical case studies endeavoured to show that men with an 'inborn reversal of sexual feeling' possessed a 'feminine essence' displayed through a range of behaviour from 'passivity' in sex to an ability, or appetite, for 'sewing, knitting embroidering, [and] crocheting'.[75] The 'birth of the homosexual' does not denote the emergence of a modern queer consciousness but rather a new visibility in medical and legal and, subsequently, social and cultural discourses. Almost every sexologist and psychiatrist since has designated needlework by men as the sign of the homosexual. The case studies in the work of Richard von Krafft-Ebing, Havelock Ellis and Magnus Hirschfield are peppered with references and inferences to the feminine hobbies of the 'invert'. David Halperin has more recently questioned the linkage of homosexual desire and gender inversion, suggesting that the latter does not necessarily specify a same-sex object-choice.[76] However, the equation of embroidery and effeminacy held firm. If for women embroidery became the tool of subversion, for men it became the apparatus of surveillance.

If, since the nineteenth century, needlework was seen to bear the stigma of homosexuality, by the twentieth century gay subcultures began to re-appropriate and invest it with new meaning. Indeed, as Foucault suggested: 'Homosexuality began to speak on its own behalf, to demand that its legitimacy or "naturality" be acknowledged, often in the same vocabulary, using the same categories by which it was medically disqualified.'[77] Needlework could, then, be used to carry 'secret' meanings to resist the dynamics of dominant discourses. It would be difficult to define a 'queer voice' in modern literary culture but in the twentieth century when gay men began to write openly of gay experience they embraced the language and culture of needlework as part of the 'conceptual framework of resistance'.[78] Truman Capote once described writing as 'like doing the finest needlepoint' and more recently writers such as Edmund White and Alan Hollinghurst have employed the symbolic language of needlework in their work.[79] White's trilogy of autobiographic novels, *A Boy's Own Story* (1982), *The Beautiful Room is Empty* (1988) and *The Farewell Symphony* (1997), contains numerous allusions to needlework:

> –I was conscious of the emblem of proud and tragic loneliness I was embroidering stitch by stitch before the eyes of the other boys;
> –a design of sorts, not a stencil but a weave, could be teased out of all these balls of yarn;
> –As I said those words, I felt the tension in my body knitting;
> –I once teased Butler by saying he was like a Victorian miss who'd been required to pick up all the accomplishments (sewing, music making, canning, painting on china) since she didn't have a dowry;
> –I was delighted when I imagined a room full of five hundred people who'd read my book and allowed their minds to be tattooed by my needles.[80]

Needlework as a site of emasculation through irony or metaphor has similarly been deployed in Hollinghurst's books, from *The Swimming Pool Library* (1988) to *The Stranger's Child* (2011): 'It was empty and orderly, with folded newspapers, a sewing-basket and a darning mushroom on a side-table – things that a masculine household must have'; 'my writing, which as one wit remarked looks like a man's attempt at knitting'.[81] Needlework expressions appear in gay slang from the allusions to 'embroidery' in Polari to the use of 'sewing circle' to denote 'orgies' or 'jack-off parties'. The first use (in print) of 'plain sewing' as a euphemism for gay sex was apparently in a review by W.H. Auden of J.R. Ackerley's memoir, *My Father and Myself* (1968). Much to Auden's delight it was subsequently published in the OED: 'Plain sewing, n. (a) Needlework which is functional or practical rather than decorative; (b) slang [popularized by W.H. Auden (see 1980)], a sexual activity of homosexuals involving mutual masturbation.'[82]

In the context of the Women's Liberation Movement in the 1970s men in positions of power and authority often disparaged any sort of women's work as a 'knitting circle', a term that was then re-appropriated by gay men.[83] Following the founding of the Gay Liberation Front (GLF), in America in 1969 after Stonewall and in the Britain the following year, there was a serious political investment in women's work as a site of repudiation of heteronormative values.[84] Rarely did this involve any actual needlecraft activities but at the South London Gay Community Centre in the 1970s, 'there was a wrestling group in the basement and, to counter the "macho" posturing of the group, a sewing bee and knitting circle was formed in the upstairs front room'.[85] The relation between the British Women's Liberation Movement, from which *The Subversive Stitch* grew, and the Gay Liberation Movement deserves to be much better known.[86] The emergence of gay liberation in Britain can certainly be charted on the pages of *Spare Rib* and Parker took at least one image for her book from *Gay Left*, the GLF's publication.[87] Gay men's activities could equally be dismissed through allusions to needlecrafts. Simon Watney recalls that at a meeting of the GLF in the early 1970s:

> Someone had intervened, saying that the group was no more than a 'knitting-circle'. At once a keen argument followed. Wasn't this a typical male sexist remark? Didn't the metaphor suggest that women are innately different from men? Didn't it reinforce a stereotype of women? And finally – what was so

*wrong* about being members of a knitting-circle, talking quietly while being involved in useful (if unpaid?) work? This may perhaps sound trivial when written down like this. What is important I think is that such a discussion could not have taken place between a group of socialist men in any other context than that of GLF. It also illustrates, I think, the practical sensitivity of the gay movement. This kind of discussion introduced a not inconsiderable number of women and men, like myself, to an altogether new and exciting idea of politics.[88]

Yet, for all this any impact of gay liberation on needlework itself has generated almost no discussion. Examples of how the social and political changes were registered on the early gay community range from the amateur sewing kits (commercially produced by companies such as the American 'Style Art Needlepoint'), which grew to encompass the era's political investment in homoeroticism and pornography (Figure 2.11), to the 'Make Yourself a Cuddly

**Figure 2.11** 'Style-Art Needlepoint Inc, (M502)', unexecuted needlepoint scrim, 1978, 18 x 12¾ in. (46 x 32 cm), Private Collection.

Clone' knitting pattern in David Shenton's *Stanley and the Mask of Mystery* (1983), the pioneering comic strip that had first appeared in Britain's *Gay News* and *Gay Capital* (Figure 2.12). In this spirit, the Tom of Finland Foundation recently released a series of four cross-stitch kits based on original 1970s designs (Figure 2.13). This convergence of the homoerotic and handwork can be found in numerous, disparate examples – such as early 'participatory' artwork by the Filipino artist David Medalla entitled *A Stitch in Time* (1968– ), which was initially installed in a series of London venues before it was shown at Documenta 5 (1972) (Figure 2.14). In this, Medalla suspended long cotton sheets in a gallery space onto which visitors were invited to embroider, with needles and threads provided, whatever messages they liked. The idea of the work has a history in which the act of stitching and gay subjectivity coalesced. Of its origin Medalla recalled giving two ex-lovers 'each a handkerchief (one black, one white), a spool of thread each, and a packet of needles. I told them to stitch anything they liked on the handkerchiefs.' The idea was to ask other

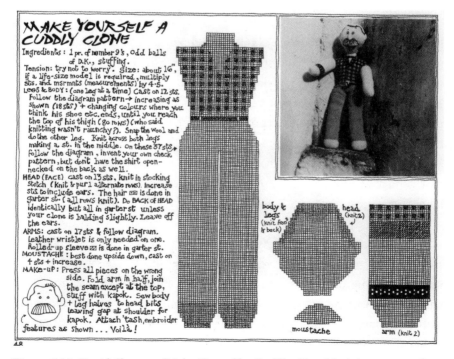

**Figure 2.12** David Shenton, 'Make Yourself a Cuddly Clone' knitting pattern from *Stanley and the Mask of Mystery* (London: Gay Men's Press, 1983), © David Shenton.

**Figure 2.13** Tom of Finland, 'Shipwrecked.' Cross-stitch kit, © Tom of Finland/Artists Rights Society (ARS), New York/DACS, London, 2019.

**Figure 2.14** David Medalla, *A Stitch in Time*, 1968–72, Arts Council Collection, © David Medalla.

lovers, friends and acquaintances to then add messages to the original 'simple message of love' Medalla had stitched.[89] Guy Brett had suggested that 'some years later, and presumably without any direct connection, the ideas behind Medalla's participatory works were put into practice on a mass scale by women protesting against nuclear weapons at Greenham Common US Air Force Missile Base in southern England' in the early 1980s.[90] And John Walker has added, 'For most men, sewing has feminine connotations. Medalla challenged that gender assumption and so made possible the use of sewing by male landscape painters such as Michael Raedecker.'[91]

More recently sewing as subcultural resistance can be seen in the work of the American artist Jim Hodges who has made work from mass-produced silk flowers – unpicking and re-stitching them and then assembling them in new hanging arrangements. Between 1995 and 1998 Hodges made ten curtains from these artificial blooms or from other domestic and feminine-associated fabrics. Hodges's 'disidentification' of the everyday object was initially encouraged by his friend, the artist Félix González-Torres, who had been working with similar hanging fabrics, but it was thinking of his mother's needlework that brought the process into focus for Hodges.[92] His mother, in fact, worked with him in sewing the earliest of the curtains.[93] As well as representing a 'paean to his mother and his great-grandmother, who taught him to sew', these deconstructed floral fabrics were, Hodges has also stated, a conscious attempt at 'queer expression', to capture a moment of 'coming out'.[94] In *Here's Where We Will Stay* (1995) the vast, floating wall of gauze-like silky and satiny fabrics, made from inexpensive women's headscarves, sewn together like a quilt by Hodges, evoke the emotion embedded in such ordinary, everyday, often overlooked feminine objects (Plate 5).[95] References to quilts stitched by men during this period, however, took on another meaning. The mournful and meditative dimension in Hodges's handsewing prompted more than one critic to suggest these works could be 'read as an oblique response to the AIDS epidemic'.[96] Queer affect and kinship also suffuse Richard Saja's *Diversity Quilt* (2009) in which he stitched directly onto delicately printed *toile de jouy*, marking out with thread, slight differences in the male figures to reflect upon how social exclusion has shaped, and still generates a need for, the gay community in the new millennium (Figure 2.15).

**Figure 2.15** Richard Saja, *Diversity Quilt*, cotton, 2009, 93 x 97 in. (236.2 x 246.3 cm), Photo. Andy Duback, Collection of the Shelburne Museum, Gift of Richard Saja.

## *From querying to queering* The Subversive Stitch

Today it is widely accepted that the pervasive and oppressive ideals of femininity prevalent since Victorian times have been inculcated through everyday practices such as embroidery. The legacy of this can be traced through first-, second- and third-wave feminism which reinvested needlecrafts with a renewed sense of agency subverting their association with the tropes of abjection, amateurism and absence in canonical histories of art and design. But what can be said of the social construction of masculinity – was it in any way shaped by men's apparent exclusion from needlework's history? No matter what way it is viewed men are generally perceived as the losers in the story. What an unexpected irony within the all-pervading structures of patriarchy that otherwise privileged all men in all arenas. But what's wrong with failure? Isn't success the measuring stick of phallocentrism, anyway? While all men who take up needlework are perceived to be less masculine, they become feminized, *queer* even, in the popular imagination, there has never actually been a study of men's relation to needlework, nor a study about the relation of needlework to homosexuality. Whilst the many men who took up needle and thread since Victorian times always did so in the shadow of female archetypes, such as the 'Angel in the House', many continued undeterred. Their work may sometimes be acknowledged, but it is very rarely subject to any serious interpretation or evaluation nor is it studied in collective terms. In contrast, the study of women's needlework has gone 'where angels fear to tread', interrogating the continued contradictory role needlework holds in women's lives from its pivotal place in the global exploitation of women's labour to the private pleasures of their personal sexual liberation.[97]

As vast and diverse as scholarship on the topic of women's needlework is the omission of men remains troublesome. Men's exclusion from the culture of needlework rests on essentialist and essentializing assumptions. I realize that there could be no more phallocentric act than inserting men into the narratives of women's history (as embodied in needlework), but it remains problematic that even though feminist discourse has long exposed the relationality of hierarchical constructions of gender and cultural production, needlework is continually (mis)read in gendered terms, regulating and stabilizing the very binary identities that feminism purports to deconstruct and dismantle. It was feminism that established: 'The omission of whole categories of art and artists has resulted in an unrepresentative and distorting notion of who has contributed to "universal" ideas expressed through creativity and aesthetic effort.'[98] Elaine Showalter has suggested (taking the example of literary history) that

> feminist criticism as a process as well as a set of ideas ... is not simply a mode of analysis which may be appropriated by men but a perspective on literature that comes out of the experience of marginality, negativity and exclusion, and that must begin with one's own life.[99]

This idea for this book began with this image of a young man knitting that I uncovered as part of my research into the Celtic Revival in early twentieth-century Ireland (Figure 2.16). The image, on a commercially produced postcard, shows a young man, 'John McNeil', who won first prize for the best 'hand-knitted pair of long stockings from homespun Irish wool', and then a 'Special Prize' for 'the best knitted cycling stockings', at a series of exhibitions

**Figure 2.16** 'Mr. M'Neil.' Postcard, June 1905, Private Collection.

of Irish craftwork held in 1904–5 that arose from the failed attempt to organize an Irish display the 1900 Exposition Universelle in Paris.[100] These local exhibitions are best known because Roger Casement, British diplomat and Irish revolutionary, not only attended but presented, and even sponsored, some of the prizes. When I first encountered the image, I wondered if there was any link between this young man and those Casement cruised in cities, from Belfast to London – especially given Casement's own interest in fashion and textiles. Whilst my search for the hidden history of homosexuality in the Celtic Revival proved extremely fruitful I still wondered about the image of the young male knitter.[101] The more I looked the more images like this I found. Together they suggested that there was perhaps some overlooked, hidden history of needlework by men. And further that the myth of the 'great masculine renunciation' of modern times (the historical moment when men apparently stopped having an interest in fashion and textiles) may have involved men not only ceasing to consume but also making things too.[102] I wondered if we could also rediscover the 'hidden producer' as we once did the 'hidden consumer', a concept that the design historian Christopher Breward has shown to be rich as a site for the exploration of modern masculinity.[103] I was further prompted to think of Donald E. Hall's speculation of how a 'query' can in some way 'queer' a discussion through its interjection of 'personal intrusions, theoretical provocations, and sometimes unanswerable complications'.[104]

In the early twenty-first century when gender seems less stable than ever before, is there even such a thing as masculinity as we previously understood it? In the last quarter of a century or so the study of the masculine has shifted from attempts to define it as a heuristic category to analysis of it in terms of performativity, as socially and culturally constituted and no longer authorized through essentialist notions of gender as biological destiny.[105] Even so, the discourses surrounding women's needlework, whether historic or contemporary, remain saturated with references to femininity as a binary position. By implication any study of men's needlework has been open to question as 'an act of penetration, violence, coercion, or appropriation', and further as the 'reproduction of domination'.[106] As the literary critic Margaret Higgonet memorably put it: 'Can a man implicated in patriarchy speak for a woman constrained by it?'[107] But is there really nothing to say about men in roles traditionally seen as feminine beyond accusations of impersonation, parody and mimicry, passing, cross-dressing, drag, and as 'a way of promoting the notion of masculine power while masking it'?[108] Such approaches risk perpetuating the argument that 'all women are victims and all men are unimpeded agents of patriarchy', and they also fail to take on-board the wider shifts in thinking about gender's taxonomic instability in the wake of queer theory.[109] As Judith Butler suggested, as long ago as 1990, gender is 'neither natural or innate' and that 'gender norms' are, in fact, 'regulatory fictions'. Gender, Butler has argued, is 'the repeated stylization of the body, a set of repeated acts within a highly rigid regulatory frame that congeal over time to produce the appearance of substance, of a natural sort of being'.[110] Gender is, therefore, 'always and only an imitation of an imitation, a copy of a copy for which there is no original'.[111] This, Butler has since added, is not a self-conscious ('voluntarist') process but constructed through a nexus of social and cultural contexts.[112] Needlework can perhaps, then, be understood as a set of acts that police and enforce gendered binaries and even related facets of normativity such as compulsory heterosexuality.

If hegemonic masculinity is a socially sanctioned construct, a contingent performance of what certain cultures at certain times believe constitutes the masculine, then subordinated and marginalized masculinities are potential sites of resistance. R.W. Connell has suggested that such resistance could be 'doing something outrageously unmasculine' and gives an example of a young man, interviewed in the course of Connell's early research, 'who moved from a stifling rural background to college in the city, [and] broke out by dying his hair, wearing hipster jeans, wearing nail-polish, and taking up knitting'.[113] Needlework by men, then, as an act of performativity not only disrupts 'heteropatriarchal sexual scripts' but also visualizes and legitimizes male-femininity by upending the fixed reference points of the heteronormative.[114] It offers men a profusion of transgressive and subversive possibilities to critique the social and cultural conceptualizations that authorize the masculine ideal. This troubling of the history of needlework began as a *query* with regard to the absence of men in *The Subversive Stitch* and has evolved into a *queering* of needlework as a history.

Parker gives several instances of women using the term 'pride' to describe their investment in needlework.[115] But what of men? What do they feel when they make it? A man may find pleasure, even solace, in needlework but engaging in a form of feminized labour could be read as repudiation of all things masculine. Masculinity has often been defined through a prohibition of feeling and Parker contends in *The Subversive Stitch* that it was during the nineteenth century that feeling became aligned to the feminine, and by association needlework. Feelings associated with women's needlework, as elucidated by Parker, such as patience, selflessness, devotion and love, were compounded when men took it up by wider cultural inscriptions of 'shame, loss, melancholy, trauma, and hate'.[116] Raymond Williams defined this process as the 'social formations of a specific kind which may in turn be seen as the articulation (often the only fully available articulation) of structures of feeling which as living processes are much more widely experienced'.[117] Eve Kosofsky Sedgwick suggested there was a special queer resonance in shame as a feeling, 'the proto-form (eyes down, head averted) of this powerful affect', links shame to performativity.[118] Ann Cvetkovich has further argued that 'affect and sexuality are not merely analogous categories but coextensive ones with shared histories'.[119] This book seeks to locate these 'structures of feeling' and in particular how men employed needlework to explore emotions such as pleasure, tenderness and mitigate against silence and shame. Throughout this book I also take up Parker's intimation that needlework can be understood through three types of emotional motivation: in the relation of artisan and activism, as self-interrogation and a return to the maternal. Even though *The Subversive Stitch* has been universally celebrated as groundbreaking, it has also raised concerns, like most other histories of needlework, for its 'transhistorical' approach to women's history, its exclusion of class-bound accounts domestic and plain sewing, its focus on 'white Western, particularly British women of the middle and upper classes', and its 'cis-gendered' delineation of femininity.[120] But, to query *The Subversive Stitch* from the perspective of its omission of masculinity and homosexuality has been taboo.

Parker suggests in *The Subversive Stitch* women's investment in needlework correlated with moments of 'transition' in their history. Men's engagement with needlecrafts must ultimately be seen in light of this. Women in the labour market, women's political enfranchisement, women's sexual liberation, all prompted seismic shifts not just in the cultural creation of the feminine about also in the making of the masculine. Masculinity and femininity only exist in relation to one another. Throughout the twentieth century women's encroachment on the preserves of male dominance generated a perception that men were somehow slipping into a state of crisis, becoming the 'new victims'. Historians have highlighted several historical moments when masculinity seemed to become unstable.[121] John Tosh has suggested, 'The crisis over women's suffrage between 1905 and 1914 was the latest and most dramatic stage in a destabilizing of gender boundaries that had been gathering pace since the 1870s.'[122] Robert Corber has pointed to a 'masculinity crisis' in Cold War America, which was precipitated by the rise of a new consumerist domesticity, dominated by concepts of the feminine, that generated a new surveillance of homosexuality.[123] And most recently there has been discussion of a renewed 'crisis in masculinity' on a global scale in the twenty-first century.[124] However, it is hard to see where one crisis ends and another starts. John MacInnes has suggested that 'masculinity is always in one crisis or another'.[125] The twentieth century's 'crises of masculinity' all stem from the moments when women make meaningful gains in gender equality. Susan Faludi, who has documented the more recent 'chronicles of the "masculinity crisis"', has speculated that they always function as part of the 'backlash' against feminism.[126]

For the large part, however, this theory has permitted masculinity go unexamined and my desire is to delve deeper into how such apparent crises materialized the making, unmaking and remaking of the masculine. Historical moments of so-called crisis, beginning in the early twentieth century, appear to be the very instances when masculinity was under scrutiny and men turned to, and invested, in needlework: before and after the First World War; during the Second World War and at the height of the Cold War; during and after the AIDS epidemic; and in the rise of extremism and populist politics before and after 9/11. These generally follow on from developments in first-, second- and third-wave feminism and moments of visibility and validation in the history of women's needlecrafts (the agitprop banners of the suffrage movement, the domestic craft revival of 1970s feminism and the interventions of twenty-first-century Craftivists). They also correspond to historical moments of homosexual panic as well as the ruptures of resistance and liberation. As such these periods form the organizing structure of the rest of this book. The following chapters consider: the legacies of Victorian needlework that shaped concepts of masculinity as well as homosexual panic in the early twentieth century; and the hidden history of needlepoint in the homosexual subcultures of modernism and their context in debates about popular culture in the postwar period up to the 1970s. The final chapter considers the presence of men's needlework in postmodern and post-millennial contexts and in light of the current re-investment in the politics of cloth and the continued influence of Parker's notion of the 'subversive stitch'. Historicizing men's needlework has allowed me to problematize its narrative trajectory. My periodization may seem arbitrary but it has been useful in revealing when, and how, concepts of masculinity and craft coalesce.

As Rozsika Parker and Griselda Pollock have argued, 'whilst women can justifiably take pride' in crafts such as embroidery 'it does not displace the

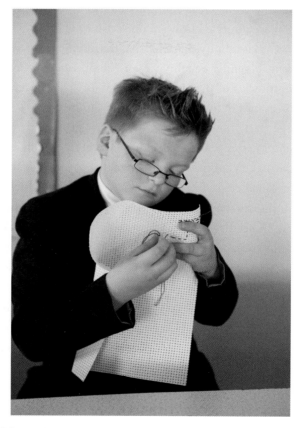

**Figure 2.17** Martin Parr, *Liam Moore, RSA Academy, Tipton,* 2010, © Martin Parr/Magnum Photos.

hierarchy of values ... [and] by simply celebrating a separate heritage we risk losing sight' of the base ideology that constructs and maintains systems of difference.[127] This book, then, is neither an uncritical celebration of men's needlework nor a recuperation of its notable figures and histories. Rather, it offers selective perspectives and insights into the social construction of the masculine through needlework as a paradigmatic social practice. The queering of narratives surrounding men's needlework might, I hope, stimulate further debate. This feels necessary as needle-wielding effeminate men and boys continue to face stigmatization, ostracism and even violence. The inculcation that sewing is still sissy holds firm even today and an image of a boy sewing continues to 'play and disrupt' fixed notions of gender-appropriate behaviour, as seen in this photograph of an English schoolboy by Martin Parr (Figure 2.17).[128] The only other thing I would like to add is the case for the teaching of needlework to boys in schools. Recent research has suggested boys are engaging with the haptic pleasures, historically associated with crafts such as needlework, in the form of gaming.[129] This may be true but what better way to explain the interrelation of history and gender than through a social practice used to shape both.

3

# 'Killing the angel in the house': Victorian manliness, domestic handicrafts and homosexual panic

At the outbreak of the First World War Queen Mary wrote to her third-born son, Henry, who was away at school: 'All you write about is your everlasting football of which I am heartily sick.'[1] When Henry returned home his father, King George V, began to focus his attention away from sport and to drill him for a military career, but at the Queen's insistence Henry also 'learnt to knit with ordinary needles so he was able to turn out more comforts for the Queen's collection for sailors and soldiers'.[2] The Queen taught all of her children, her five sons, David, Bertie, Henry, George and John, as well as her only daughter, Mary, to sew, knit and crochet at an early age. Only Henry, who became the Duke of Gloucester in 1928, and his brother David, who would become the HRH Prince of Wales in 1911, King Edward VIII in 1936, and the Duke of Windsor upon his abdication, kept up needlework as a hobby. In his memoirs the Duke of Windsor recalled:

> As a small boy I enjoyed making these things more than did my sister or brothers. Many years later, during an enforced period in bed while recovering from a riding accident, I became quite proficient with a crochet-hook. When at the beginning of the last war I was attached to a British mission with the French army and was obliged to make long motor trips through the zone of operations I returned once again to my gentle diversion, as a means of killing time … I was understandably discreet about my hobby at first. It would hardly have done for the story to get around that a major-general in the British Army had been seen bowling along the roads behind the Maginot Line crocheting. Nevertheless, crocheting did for me what detective novels do for statesman.[3]

Indeed, in January 1932 when he invited the shipbroker Ernest Simpson and his wife to Fort Belvedere, his home in Surrey, for a weekend, they were more than surprised upon arrival to find the prince engrossed in embroidery in the drawing room. He told them it was his 'secret vice', the 'only one I am at pains to conceal', he added, proudly showing them the several antique chairs in the dining room covered with his work. The sense of 'feminine feeling' lurking in the prince had an immediate effect on Simpson's wife, Wallis, who later recalled: 'I decided then and there that he must have a really sweet and tender side to his nature.'[4] Such anecdotes help excavate something of a hidden history of needlework by men. As a hobby for men, a vestige of the Victorian boyhood perhaps (the princes were born between 1894 and 1905), it would become more discernable in the context of the two world wars.

We know something of the Duke of Windsor's experiences through the luxury of published autobiographical writing but across the strata of other classes in society evidence is harder to locate. It is not known what survives of the needlework by the Duke of Windsor, or the Duke of Gloucester for that matter, but occasionally embroideries by men or boys do surface. When they do they are often seen as incongruities and oddities. Take the sampler made in 1828 by a twelve-year-old boy who stitched the words: 'James Wilson is my name, And with my Needle I make the same, And by work you may see, What Pains my Parents took with me' (Figure 3.1). This is in a museum collection and was recently made into a DIY kit and an internet blogger, who came across a digitized image of it, pondered, 'I wonder if he enjoyed or hated every stitch?'[5] It is difficult to say as such samplers have never been studied and remain obscure. Yet surviving examples, although rare in museum collections, are easily found (often for sale) on the internet. Many of the major studies of the history of samplers include at least one or two by boys. In Marcus Huish's authoritative *Samplers & Tapestry Embroideries* (1913), for example, there is one illustration of a sampler by a boy, a Scot named Robert Henderson, dating from 1762, and there are details of several others. Reflecting on the novelty of the boy sampler Huish was prompted to recount 'canvas and Berlin wool-work having been one way of passing the tedious hours a wet day' during his own boyhood.[6] In *The Subversive Stitch*, Rozsika Parker includes one sampler by a boy named John Nichols Hackleton, made in 1858 when he was aged six. The text on the sampler reads, 'Who was it took such pains, To teach me very plain,

**Figure 3.1** James Wilson, *Sampler*, 1828, cotton thread on linen, 13 x 16.7 in. (33.5 x 42.5 cm), Courtesy of Haslemere Educational Museum.

With care to mark my name, my Aunt'. Parker was prompted to speculate, 'Despite the art's role in the construction of femininity since the Renaissance, there have always been a few men and boys who practiced the art for the pleasure it provides and the artistic possibilities it offers.'[7] Would John have taken up a needle if not for his aunt? Probably not. Although samplers often mention both parents the proximity to the feminine through the maternal, the thread tacitly linking the boy to his mother, could imperil masculine identification that was so dependent on disavowal of all things feminine.[8] As some Victorian girls used samplers to voice their anxieties so did boys.[9] One undated sampler (but from the mid-nineteenth century), by a boy named Isaac Lomas, records:

> When other boys play and lark
> Then I sat down to needle work
> If they did laugh I did not shame
> For laughing was just all their Gain.[10]

Clearly a boy's interest in anything feminine marked him out as different from other boys and it was in the nineteenth century, during the heyday of sampler making, that 'the pathologization of the sissy boy' first emerged.[11] Yet, even in the face of societal disapproval boys did stitch samplers and grown men did embroider. Maureen Daly Goggin has speculated that men as well as boys made samplers for 'pleasure'. She contends that 'it has been largely, and unquestionably, assumed that surviving unsigned samplers have been solely the work of women. Given the history of needlework practices [that are often anonymous], this assumption seems at the very least open to question.'[12] Sailors, we are told, stitched because of confinement. Perhaps men who experienced social, physical or psychological constraints turned to embroidery, much like women in the confines of bourgeois domesticity or within the precincts of sweated labour. Certainly, the association of the sedentary act of sewing and Victorian women's social subordination meant needlecrafts were often linked to the concept of invalidism. Throughout the nineteenth century needlework was recommended to women as a treatment for a range of physical and psychological conditions. As Parker points out Sigmund Freud's linkage of women's 'day-dreaming over embroidery' to 'dispositional hypnoid states' suggests that needlework in the nineteenth century, somewhat paradoxically, was seen as both cause and cure of 'hysteria'.[13] During and after the First World War, needlework gravitated closer to debates about masculinity through its use in occupational therapy. Here embroidery was deployed in the treatment of wounded soldiers initially to help strengthen or repair damaged motor skills but eventually to treat 'hysteria' (termed war neurosis or neurasthenia when diagnosed in men). Although historically prescribed to women as a 'rest cure' there is evidence that needlework was also recommended to convalescing men during the nineteenth century. A rare surviving sampler by a man, named John Glazbey Crumpler, dated 1841, composed of simple floral sprigs that frame his name and birth date, is believed to have been made, during a period of convalescence, after he lost his job at Portsmouth docks due to an injury (Figure 3.2).

Until the end of the nineteenth century the education of some boys included needlework. Orphans and working-class boys, for example, were taught to sew within the state school system established by the Elementary Education Act of 1870. Schools (much like prisons) exercise control through the nurturing language of the maternal. Parker suggests it was not until the start of twentieth century that the practice of teaching boys to sew was eliminated from the national curriculum, pointing to the decisive moment of the Education Act of 1902. Some historians have disputed this date and suggested by the 1870s the teaching of needlework to boys began to be eradicated as part of the new

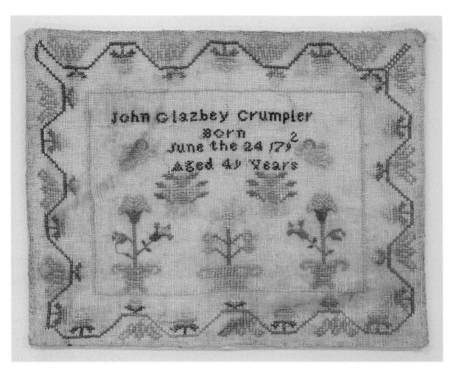

**Figure 3.2** John Glazbey Crumpler, *Sampler*, 1841, cotton thread on cloth, 7 x 8.46 in. (17.78 x 21.5 cm), Private Collection.

provision of state education.[14] The Metropolitan District Schools of London set up in the wake of the 1870 Education Act, which established mandatory education of children between the ages of five and thirteen, saw needlework for working-class, or orphaned, boys as a means to instill a sense of finer 'feeling'. The Metropolitan District Schools had been established to rescue young children from the workhouse and curtail careers as 'thieves, paupers and prostitutes'. The Metropolitan District School in Sutton, southwest of London, housed some 1200 children drawn from some of the city's worst slums, and here young boys were taught rudimentary sewing skills (Figure 3.3). These children were being prepared for life in domestic service or factory work; and needle skills, although essential for young girls to become maids, were for boys an exercise in patience, self-discipline and obedience: 'The real demand is simply not for labour, but trained labour, efficient labour, intelligent labour.'[15] The tightening of the strictures of the masculine stereotype evident in the Victorian

**Figure 3.3** 'Instruction of Pauper Children in the South Metropolitan District School, Sutton.' *The Illustrated London News* LX (4 May 1872): 425, © DEA/Biblioteca Ambrosiana/GETTY Images.

decision to fully remove needlework from the curriculum for boys was, in fact, mediated through women. But when, in 1889, the Metropolitan Board Mistresses' Association moved to discontinue the teaching of needlework to infant boys it was not without protest: 'Women's work will never be rated at its true value till men have to try their hand at it themselves.'[16]

However, as men and boys were pushed outside the margins of the culture of needlework women and girls became imprisoned within it largely through 'the oppressive Victorian stereotype of "The Angel in the House"'.[17] From the highly commercialized textiles of the nineteenth century, such as Berlin woolwork, to the 'art needlework' of the Arts and Crafts movement, the angel seemed inescapable. The lovely angel, needle in hand, could be a middle-class housewife or a working-class seamstress, or even a consort like Queen Mary, but it turned a 'social myth' into a 'prevailing ideology'.[18] Many of the women who couldn't sew, didn't want to, or who objected to its symbolic sexism, sought to rid themselves of her 'phantom' and her 'spectre'.[19] Needlework was so central to the 'Angel in the House' fantasy that when the battle for women's political and economic enfranchisement gathered pace during the suffrage campaigns of the early twentieth century women turned the symbolic 'self-denial' of embroidery into a form of 'self-defence' in the banners made in prison or for protests.[20] It has been argued that men, in the historical moment of first-wave feminism, 'helped with the stitching, [and] tailoring of a new cultural fabric', but there has been almost no analysis of whether men did any actual sewing or not.[21] When men's needlework started to be noticed by the public and the popular press, before and after the First World War, it seemed to arrive fully formed out of nowhere. But as Parker herself acknowledged needlework as 'reparative', as a 'maternal craft', did not exclude men and, indeed, some were 'wrestling with their own version of the angel'.[22]

Victorian concepts of masculinity embedded in all-male spaces (like sports and the military that King George desired to induce the young princes into) depended on qualities of strength, aggression and resilience that had evolved into a 'cult of manliness' and 'established itself as a moral code and as a widespread social imperative'.[23] Yet, 'manliness' was also secured through an ongoing 'process of differentiation, denigration and appropriation' of the feminine.[24] So for men the retreat to the 'Angel in the House' was both comfort and conflict. Whether their interest in the angel was to consume her or to become her they were perceived to be in 'flight from masculinity'.[25] Feminized labour, much like male intimacy, could re-inscribe as well as demarcate normative and transgressive masculinity.[26] By the 1930s when Virginia Woolf felt able to publicly say, and commit to writing, 'Killing the Angel in the House was part of the occupation of a woman writer', there was increasing public interest in needlework by men, such as the Duke of Windsor, stimulated by events such as the *Exhibition of English Needlework (Past and Present)*, held in the spring of 1934, the largest exhibition of historic and contemporary embroidery in the period.[27] By taking up needle and thread men, perhaps, helped expose femininity as a construction of (often) arbitrary social practices and in doing so played some part in the dismantling of the angel fallacy. This chapter, then, is not so much concerned with the origins of Victorian manliness but rather its effect and impact on men who were boys in the late nineteenth century, and came of age in the early twentieth century, when there was increased public focus, for the first time, on the male needleworker.

## The beast in the sewing box: Needlework and the circle of Henry James

In March 1869, the young aspiring American writer, Henry James, visited the London workshop of William Morris, at Queen's Square in Bloomsbury, during the English leg of the family's European tour. In a letter to his sister, Alice, James wrote of his surprise to learn that Morris was a 'manufacturer of stained glass windows, tiles, ecclesiastical and medieval tapestry, [and] altar-cloths'. Until then he thought of Morris primarily as a poet. James especially admired the designs for 'tapestry' he saw at Queen's Square. These were, in fact, embroideries that Morris worked, James recounted in his letter, 'stitch by stitch, with his own fingers'.[28] In his later prolific career as a novelist, and after he became a permanent resident in England, the image of, or reference to, such a 'male embroiderer' would not feature again in any of his own writings. Yet, it was to become a *leitmotif* in the lives and work of the circle of male writers that later surrounded James: 'the coterie of clever, literary-minded younger men whose company the ageing novelist relished'.[29] Within this band of young bachelors two writers in particular, 'Howard' Overing Sturgis and E.F. 'Fred' Benson, captured something of the age's social and sexual non-conformity through the language and culture of needlework that borrowed much from the Victorian 'Angel in the House' archetype. Both Sturgis and Benson had met James as young boys as he had been a friend of both their families. And James was also to read important manuscript versions of pivotal novels for both these young men at critical points in their careers.

Howard Sturgis was the youngest son of an affluent Boston banker, Russell Sturgis, and his third wife, Julia Overing Boit, who had settled in London in the 1850s. Howard's parents had certainly been encouraging of his artistic interests even if they had expressed concern at his interest in 'feminine habits and arts'. However, 'they were Bostonians; and would it have been *right* to correct dear little sweet Howard for his girlishness, when girlishness wasn't *morally wrong*?'[30] To instill some manliness into Howard he was sent to Eton and then onto Cambridge. But by the 1880s his artistic inclinations took him to the Slade School of Art. He was, however, forced to abandon his studies to nurse his dying father and then his mother. The American writer Edith Wharton, one of the few women who frequented this literary circle, suggested since

Sturgis had been his mother's 'devoted slave' in life that her death left him 'a middle-aged man, as lost and helpless as a child'.[31] Arthur Benson, Fred's older brother, who knew Sturgis at both Eton and Cambridge, recalled that caring for his parents not only curtailed his artistic ambitions but it also weakened his health and left him 'in the condition of a nervous invalid, suffering from the long strain as well as from the shock of the double bereavement'. For Arthur Benson, Sturgis had to perform the role of 'not only the son of the house, but, so to speak, the daughter as well'.[32]

The feminine, even maternal, side of Sturgis's nature was further revealed to visitors to his home, Queen's Acre (known as 'Qu'Acre') in Windsor Great Park, in his devotion to needlework. In contrast to his more manly, cigar-smoking, companion, William Haynes Smith, known as 'The Babe', Sturgis was the lady of the house plying his needle 'with modest contentment and unremitting application'.[33] Edith Wharton remembered 'his legs covered by a thick shawl, his hands occupied with knitting-needles or embroidery silks,' and the novelist Mary Cholmondeley noted 'people thought him original and odd, but also very domestic, very cosy, as he hooked at his woolwork or stitched at his silken embroideries'.[34] Arthur Benson recorded, in his memoirs:

> One of his pleasant tastes was for a kind of fine embroidery with silk upon a canvas ground. He used to say that it was no doubt thought an effeminate occupation; but he did not smoke to speak of, could not read or write continuously, and liked to have his fingers occupied while he talked; and so it became one of his most characteristic aspects to see him drawing out and matching the silks, or delicately inserting them; and it was a pleasure to watch his small, firm, expressive hands, and the little hampered gestures were a real comment on his talk, growing out of it and not superimposed upon it.[35]

Sturgis's cousin, the American writer George Santayana added: 'As if by miracle, for he was wonderfully imitative, he became, save for the accident of sex, which was not yet a serious encumbrance, a perfect young lady of the Victorian type':

> This was not all he imbibed from his mother's circle. He was not only imitative, but he also had a theory that there was nothing women did that a man couldn't do better. Pride therefore seconded inclination in making him vie with the ladies and surpass them. He learned to sew, to embroider,

to knit, and to do crochet; these occupations were not only guiltless of any country's blood, but helped to pass away the empty hours. He became wedded to them, and all his life, whether he sat by the fire or in his garden, his work-basket stood by his low chair. His needlework was exquisite, and he not only executed gorgeous embroideries, but designed them, for he was clever also with the pencil.[36]

Henry James, however, was openly dismissive of the 'the spell of Berlin wool' he found at Qu'Acre.[37] Although the two men had known each other for many years by the turn of the century, it is believed that James fell 'briefly but passionately in love' with Sturgis.[38] Not only was this marked by a period of intense correspondence but Sturgis also appears to have made embroidery for James. 'It will in its inveterate intimacy, remind me as repeatedly of your elegant hand & generous heart,' James wrote of one of these gifts.[39] Sturgis had published two novels and in 1903 James agreed to read a draft of his latest manuscript, *Belchamber*. A nostalgic Edwardian meditation on the decline of English aristocratic life, the novel recounts the story of Charles Edwin William Augustus Chambers, Earl of Belchamber and Viscount Charmington, known as 'Sainty' because of his sweetness, sensitivity and all-round goodness, the heir of a great house who strives to keep his family line alive. The effete Sainty is bullied and deceived by his manlier and more virile brother, Arthur, and cousin, Claude, and in his disastrous marriage to the unfaithful Cissy, whose very name serves to underscore his manifest femininity. The key to Sanity's character lies in his boyhood in which he renounced the privileges incumbent with his class and sex by rejecting sports, hunting and other forms of male bonding in favour of sewing. Arthur taunts: 'You're jolly bad at games, and you like to sit and suck up to an older governess, and do needlework with her, like a beastly girl.'[40] Sainty's sewing, which he is forced to give up as an adult, also hints at his hidden homosexuality. Somewhat surprisingly, given the intimacy between the two men (or maybe unsurprisingly as gay men tended to police each other for queer signs) James was harsh in his criticism of Sturgis's draft. In particular, the effeminacy of Sainty troubled him. As the novel's only embodiment of the 'Angel in the House', James felt Sainty was '*all* passivity & nullity', was too obviously a homosexual and his 'once forbidden needlework' was too literal an allusion to Sturgis himself.[41] Sturgis was devastated by the criticism and considered withdrawing the novel from publication but, as Edith Wharton recalled, 'he accepted James's verdict' and allowed the book to go to print but gave up writing and 'relapsed into knitting and embroidery'.[42] Likewise, E.M. Forster thought that the criticism had ended James and Sturgis's intimacy and compelled Sturgis to give up 'the practice of literature' and devote 'himself instead to embroidery, of which he had always been fond. His life wore away in quiet occupations.'[43]

Needlework's function as the emblem of effeminacy, deflecting yet disclosing a character's homosexuality, lurks in the novels and short stories of another of Henry James's young acolytes, Fred Benson. James had read Benson's first novel *Dodo* (1893), in its manuscript form, but his polite and evasive response Benson suspected was actually damning criticism.[44] James advised Benson to find a 'style' and Benson's subsequent novels, especially those that include male embroiderers, are a parody of the stylish and frivolous in contemporary society (which would have appalled the high-minded James). Benson's novels are social comedies that satirize the manners and mores of the upper-middle class, often in caricaturing the social climbing and cultural aspirations of women, in which effeminate men serve to further highlight the construction and constraints of the feminine ideal. Drawing very directly on Sturgis's novel, and in many ways an obvious pen portrait of him, Benson's dramatization of the male embroiderer, however, goes much further than Sainty's sewing as a vestige of boyhood or the various accounts of Sturgis's own needlework as somehow benign and neutralized. In Benson's *Paul* (1906), Theodore Beckwith's dislike of sports and games and preference for working at his embroidery frame or crocheting give him an air of ambiguity rather than menace.[45] And Oliver Bowman in *The Countess of Lowndes Square and Other Stories* (1920), who declares 'I ought to have been a girl', is often pictured embroidery in hand but is sweet and angelic: 'His unerring needle made daffodils or lambs.'[46] However, in *Dodo the Second* (1914) Seymour Sturgis (a barely veiled allusion) takes 'a piece of needlework' everywhere, which

> he often produced when he was staying with friends, in order to irritate them. He seldom worked at it when at home, but to-night he got it out in order to irritate his sister into going to the ball without delay, for Esther was always exasperated to a point almost beyond her control by the sight of her brother with his thimble and needle. So before long she took her departure, leaving Nadine to follow (which was Seymour's design), and he put the needlework back into its embroidered bag again.[47]

Unlike Sainty, Seymour does not renounce his needlework, nor his effeminacy, when he agrees to marry Nadine, daughter of the novel's eponymous character. *Dodo the Second* was published on the eve of the First World War and Seymour's embodiment of male-femininity reflected something of the current 'crisis of masculinity' that had been gathering pace since the turn of the century. In the wake of the rise of the socially and sexually liberated 'New Woman', and women's subsequent campaign for the vote, the economic and political decline of absolute male privilege and the increasing scrutiny of men's minds and bodies by sexologists and psychiatrists engendered a panic about the impact of decadence and degeneration upon the male stock.[48] In an age of the mass mobilization of manliness in the service of militarization, young men, in particular, who were unable to go to war or who refused to go, were seen as in flight from masculinity. Withdrawing to all things womanly and motherly these effeminate boys were often shown sewing or knitting. Edmund Blampied, who illustrated some of Benson's work, such as his boyhood novel *David Blaize* (1916), produced several images of this 'phenomenon' for the popular press, such as *The Sketch* (Figure 3.4). Yet, masculinity could be recovered through the recuperation, or absorption, of the feminine, as Seymour's marriage to Nadine demonstrations: 'He isn't a lady any more than he's a gentleman: he's just a phenomenon.'[49]

During the war Benson took the potent image of an effeminate embroiderer, 'eyes lowered, head bent, shoulders hunched', to the extreme in the creation of Aunt Georgie in his *The Freaks of Mayfair* (1916).[50] Georgie, although born 'a male boy', grew up very much like any girl did, playing with dolls, wearing dresses, until 'Public-school life checked the outward manifestation of girlhood, but Georgie's essential nature continued to develop in secret'. Growing into spinster-like 'auntishness', his 'essentially feminine' nature was symbolized not just by his physical appearance but also through his hobbies, 'impromptu piano-playing' and 'tittle-tattle', and especially his love of 'working at his embroidery' every day. Georgie was daringly visualized by the American George Wolfe Plank, known for his covers and illustrations for *Vogue*, in a *recherché* Beardsleyesque style that reeked of decadence and the yellow nineties (Figure 3.5).[51] However, Aunt Georgie as well as the other fey, young aesthetes in Benson's novels, with their embroidery silks, coloured wools, tambour frames and embroidery bags, serves as a preface for Benson's

**Figure 3.4** Edmund Blampied, 'Everybody Can Help.' *The Sketch* (9 December 1914): IV, © The British Library Board (MFM.MLD52).

**Figure 3.5** George Plank, 'Aunt Georgie.' From E.F. Benson's *The Freaks of Mayfair* (London: T.N. Foulis, 1916), facing p. 40, Private Collection.

greatest and most enduring male embroiderer, Georgie Pillson, in his *Mapp and Lucia* novels. The six novels published between 1920 and 1939 that make up the series recount the competitive and comic battles of two middle-aged snobs set in the fictional seaside town of Tilling that was based on Rye, in East Sussex, where Henry James lived. 'Mallards', the Tilling house occupied by Miss Mapp and then Lucia in the novels, is based on Lamb House in Rye where James lived and which was subsequently home to Benson himself. Throughout the novels Georgie is depicted as camp, silly and frivolous, a sexless appendage to Lucia, her confidant and conspirator but also her subordinate. Aside from his docility, passivity and submissiveness, it is the needlework that performs his femininity for readers: 'His house was full of the creations of his needle, woolwork curtains, petit-point chair seats, and silk embroideries framed and glazed.'[52]

The fictional characters of Thomas Beckwith, Seymour Sturgis, Oliver Bowman, Aunt Georgie and Georgie Pillson are all thought to be fashioned after Howard Sturgis, but there were also other models some to be found much closer to home. Benson was the third son of E.W. Benson, who was the Archbishop of Canterbury, the most senior role in the Church of England, and therefore one of the most distinguished and important public figures of the Victorian age. In spite of their father's pivotal role 'in the interpreting and teaching doctrines of manliness', and his place in the debates about Victorian masculinity in the context of domesticity, Fred, his older brother Arthur and their younger brother, Robert 'Hugh', all pursued 'lives in an all-male, homoerotic setting'[53]: Arthur through his teaching roles at Eton and then Cambridge; Fred in fashionable society and literary circles; and Hugh, after a failed attempt to join the Indian Civil Service, became a priest and entered an Anglican celibate community but converted to Roman Catholicism in 1903.[54] Their father may have been distant and authoritarian but Fred's recollections of their childhood are filled with memories of his 'mother's needle' or their nurse, Beth Cooper, who 'spent most of her time sewing'.[55] Needlework as a cipher for the maternal can be seen in the first story Fred wrote, when he was aged ten, penned especially for his mother, entitled, 'The History and Adventures of the Needle!'[56] Their mother, Mary (née Sidgwick) Benson, was devoutly religious, like her husband, but a much more complex and controversial figure, who set up house with another woman, after the bishop's death. She was a powerful influence on her sons and several of the family's biographers have suggested it was a relationship that shaped the boys' closeted homosexuality.[57] Of the three boys Hugh was the only one who did needlework and was certainly in Fred's mind when he formulated his secession of sissy stitchers.

Both Arthur and Fred, in their memories of Hugh, recalled his 'skilful hand' at embroidering, even as a child.[58] As an undergraduate at Cambridge, Hugh decorated his rooms with 'Gobelins tapestry,' but these were probably woolwork copies after well-known religious paintings.[59] The 'fantastic weird tapestries, which he later designed and made and put up with his own hands' for his home, Hare Street House, Buntingford, in Hertfordshire, are believed to have been inspired by the brief but intense relationship Hugh formed with the artist and writer Frederick Rolfe who by the early 1900s was writing under the Italian affectation 'Baron Corvo'.[60] Soon after Hugh's religious conversion he read Corvo's *Hadrian the Seventh* (1904), a novel about an Englishman, once denied entry into the priesthood but who later ascends to the Papal throne. Corvo was also a Catholic convert but had failed to enter the priesthood and by this stage he was already living an erratic and peripatetic life. Inspired by Corvo's book Hugh wrote to him and instigated a meeting. Their friendship was immediate and Hugh suggested they work together on a collaborative book: 'I propose the story be told by a monk … That no female enters into it … That the monk has strong and vivid artistic perceptions and is occupied by his community in some branch of handicraft.'[61] It was a vision that fitted with both their lives but the two men, as quickly as they fell in love, fell out and their book was eventually completed by Hugh alone. However, Hugh remained devoted to Corvo's writing and he had been deeply moved by a short story, entitled 'About the Penance of Paisalettrio', published in Corvo's *In His Own Image* (1901), a book Hugh referred to as 'the fifth gospel'.[62] The story, loosely derived from Italian folklore, recounts how St Gabriel appears in an impoverished village seeking an embroidery to be made in his image. Particular emphasis is placed on the process by which the needlework is eventually made by celestial power through mortal hands. It was part of a series of 'Italian peasant lore' that Corvo had originally published in *The Yellow Book*, which he later collected and expanded into two separate volumes.[63]

At Hare Street House, Hugh, assisted by his friend, Gabriel Pippet, an ecclesiastical artist and illustrator, designed and made a series of embroidered wall hangings. Two sections are known to have depicted 'The Quest for the Holy Grail' made for a downstairs room and the 'Danse Macabre' for an upstairs bedroom.[64] These were made by appliqué whereby the figurative designs are cut out and then stitched onto a canvas background.[65] These 'tapestries' took visual and thematic influences from Lord Tennyson's poetry, Richard Wagner's *Parsifal* and more directly from William Morris and Burne-Jones's 'San Graal' arras tapestries made for Stanmore Hall, which had recently been on display at the Arts and Crafts Exhibition Society. Hugh had also studied historic needlework and tapestry and was especially interested in the textile collection at Oxburgh Hall in Norfolk, then owned by Sir Hugh Bedingfeld, which included important Mortlake tapestries, embroidered wall hangings by Mary, Queen of Scots and Bess of Hardwick, as well as one of the celebrated Sheldon tapestries. The scheme may have had, however, some direct input from Corvo who had, in the 1890s, integrated needlework into his paintings and made his own 'tapestries' by stitching designs in appliqué onto 'Arras of pure flax'.[66] An embroidery by Corvo depicting 'St. Michael, the Archangel' was made, his friend Charles Kains-Jackson recorded in *The Artist and Journal of Home Culture*, after a photograph of an 'Italian boy of 17 years, yellow haired and blue eyed and of the most exquisite physical development, was instantaneously photographed in mid-air, when leaping into the lake of Nemi near Rome'.[67] Although he had successive careers as a painter and writer Corvo retained a lifelong interest in photography and produced many homoerotic images.

The relation between effeminacy and homosexuality was something that concerned rather than amused Fred Benson. For his male characters embroidery is the brazen badge of queer self-identification but Benson also recorded, as a schoolboy, his abhorrence at such sissiness: 'I put out my lights and showed a stony blackness to flutterings from one mincing walk or elegant gestures or a conjectured softness of disposition.'[68] Equally Arthur recorded his shock and revulsion at witnessing 'a long and loverlike kiss' between Howard Sturgis and the writer Percy Lubbock, when they were Cambridge undergraduates.[69] Ross Posnock has suggested that Sturgis's mimetic femininity and 'his maternal presence embodied in the emblem of his workbasket of embroidery', although 'reminiscent of the knitting of James's own mother' as an 'emblem of his nurturing sympathy', incited conflicting emotions in James, and his circle, on a sliding scale from amusement to anxiety.[70] It is widely believed that about the time he read the draft of *Belchamber* the suggestiveness of Sainty's sissy stitching sent James into a 'homosexual panic', which ended his intimate relationship with Sturgis. In 1903, James also published a short story 'The Beast in the Jungle' in which a male character, John Marcher, is tormented by 'the secret of his life', which threatened to disclose the 'real truth' about him.[71] The secret is only hinted at but at the end of the story when Marcher is unable to find redemption through heterosexual love, and conventional marriage, he finally accepts 'the jungle of his life' and 'the lurking Beast'.[72] Needlework may have operated in James's circle, then, as code not for the secret in itself but for the open anxiety of having a secret that could be discovered and disclosed at any moment. Many of these men may have been innocent of same-sex acts but their desires, fantasies, longings and their mere imaginings were what was under threat of exposure. In her reading of James's story Eve Kosofsky Sedgwick has suggested: 'The secret of having a secret, functions, in Marcher's life, precisely as *the closet*. It is not a closet in which there is a homosexual man, for Marcher is not a homosexual man. Instead, however, it is the closet of, simply, the homosexual secret – the closet of imagining *a* homosexual secret.'[73] For these men, and for many others like them, the mere hint of a 'homosexual secret' was the 'beast' lurking out of sight, where no one thought to look, in the sewing box.

## Masculinity as feeling: Berlin woolwork and the boys of Bloomsbury

Whilst men, such as Howard Sturgis and Hugh Benson, certainly did not make embroidery for exhibition but rather as amateurs crafting for private personal consumption, there remained an underlining sense of display or performance of 'feeling' (patience, comfort, selflessness, devotion, love) embedded in such objects that ran counter to the tropes of Victorian masculinity. Not all gay men, however, had an interest in, or knowledge of, needlework. When E.M. Forster visited Qu'Acre for the first time he was mortified by his inability to differentiate between one of Sturgis's fine embroideries and a commonplace 'cloth kettle holder'.[74] The reason for Forster's *faux-pas* can be explained, in part, by the visual similarity between the kind of delicate needlework Sturgis pursued and the commercially produced needlecrafts (manufactured in kits) that continued to perpetuate the aesthetics of Victorian cross-stitch or Berlin woolwork. The latter, in particular, proved especially enduring. In contrast to the fine silks and high skills of late nineteenth-century 'art needlework', Berlin woolwork was created from skeins of thick, brightly coloured wool and pre-prepared canvas complete with the design punched or printed in grid form. It enjoyed immense popularity in the early-mid nineteenth century largely because it could be applied to 'virtually anything: chair backs, cushion covers, even slippers, and bookmarks', and represented 'craft as a modern pursuit, an easy and recently invented hobby, inexpensive and fashionable'.[75]

Victorian handicrafts such as Berlin woolwork are generally studied as part of the consumption habits of middle-class women. Within this historians have been confounded by its popularity and its longevity. And beyond this historians have been perplexed as to why artists (especially the male artists) of the Bloomsbury group, allied to the European avant-garde as agents of a formalist modernism, took up Berlin woolwork before the First World War, and then again throughout the interwar decades, with such wild enthusiasm.[76] This is often explained through Roger Fry's setting up of the Omega workshop in 1913 to provide employment for his friends but also as a response to the Atelier et École Martine established by the Parisian couturier, Paul Poiret, a few years earlier. However, in November 1910, following the Manet and the Post-Impressionists exhibition organized by Fry, a damning review by Robert Ross summed up the wider reaction to Fry's promotion of modernism as a new way of seeing and feeling – drawing on the 'primitivism' of Post-Impressionism that had inspired many of Bloomsbury's other sources from Poiret to the Ballets Russes. In a stinging invective about the import of continental modernist tendencies, in general, and the work of Vincent Van Gogh, in particular, Ross stated it was the territory of the psychiatrist (and by implication the sexologist) and argued: 'The only primitive he [Van Gogh] resembles are the woolwork trophies of our great grandmothers.'[77] In a period of increasing jingoistic paranoia, which would lead to war, the disparagement of European modernism became a common occurrence in the English press, especially in the wake of Fry's 1910 exhibition and its sequel two years later. A review of the New English Arts Club exhibition in 1911, for example, reduced the formal technical developments of Post-Impressionism to the cult of Victorian domestic handicraft, feminizing and infantilizing its defenders: 'The epidemic of painting in skeins of Berlin wool has not yet caught on over here as yet, except in British nurseries and play-rooms.'[78] Prevailing Victorian ideas of painting, still gendered as a masculine space, meant that any man who embraced modernism's craftiness must be not only emasculated but effeminized. Conversely, embroidery's popularity in contemporary women's fashions, largely emanating from Parisian couture houses, encouraged the English press to re-colonize and bizarrely search for the essential 'Englishness' of needlecrafts such as Berlin woolwork.[79] Fry was acutely aware of the experiments in textile design by European modernists and in this wider context he deliberately sought to harness and subvert the popular enthusiasm for, and critical condemnation of, domestic hobbycrafts such as Berlin woolwork.

In March 1913, Fry organized an exhibition, under the title of the 'Grafton Group' and aside from paintings by Fry, Vanessa Bell, Duncan Grant and other artists, the show contained the group's first attempts at needlework. Criticism echoed that of 1910 with references made to 'the ghastly grin of the lunatic or the imbecilic' and, with some sarcasm, to the embroidered 'firescreen, bed-screens, woolwork chaircovers and tablecovers, all in the most approved modernist design', within this a chair cover by Duncan Grant was singled out and compared to 'an Early Victorian beadwork bag'.[80] Subsequently, that summer, at the exhibition held to officially launch the Omega workshop, Fry pre-emptively drew the press's attention to the workshop's 'Post-impressionist Berlin wool-work': 'It seems quite a mid-Victorian idea, but it is not treated in a mid-Victorian manner. The colours and designs are full of colour and rhythm as the others were full of dullness and stiffness. I like Berlin woolwork. It is so durable and strong, and it is a particularly good medium for us.'[81] Fry's wry amusement at the expense of the press has, in some ways, coloured all subsequent readings of Bloomsbury needlework as being arrived at by expediency and nothing else: 'He [Fry] did help revive Victorian cross-stitch and Berlin wool-work, the latter because it was strong and durable. His approach was essentially pragmatic, appropriateness and practicality determining the choice of process.'[82] The correspondence between Bloomsbury's search for 'pure form' in the aesthetics of abstract painting and Berlin woolwork, which was essentially a commercial 'stitch-by-numbers kit', seems irreconcilable especially given the gendered nature of such textiles which would have marked men like Fry and Grant out as dilettantes, aesthetes and even inverts. In some ways there was very little distance between the needlework produced in the 'cosy and chatty, rather than outspokenly gay' atmosphere of Qu'Acre and Bloomsbury's 'society of buggers', as Virginia Woolf called it.[83] Indeed, even the embroidery of 'peacocks' by Theodore Beckwith described in E.F. Benson's novel *Paul* (1906) could have been on sale at the Omega:

> This was stretched on a frame in front of him, and was certainly a wonderful, if slightly barbaric piece of work. It represented a group of peacocks with tails spread, so that the gorgeous-coloured feathers filled the entire background. From the whole canvas flamed the green and vivid blue of their eyes, and they stood in a meadow starred with brilliant flowers. The design was his own, and now as it approached completion, the daring success of it was apparent, while not less successful was the exquisite workmanship of its execution.[84]

After the war Grant's painting was increasingly described by the press in feminized terms, particularly in the language of needlework often thinly disguised as allusions to Post-Impressionism. One review, for example, described Grant's work 'as honest as needlework'.[85] Writing on the eve of the First World War, Fry suggested that even though such 'fancy work' reflected for his generation the 'peculiar little earthly paradise' made up 'of the boredoms, the snobberies, the cruel repressions' of the Victorian age, conversely, Victorian handicrafts could offer comfort in an age of conflict and chaos.[86] The men of Bloomsbury were not completely isolated in the paradoxical collapsing of modern art and modern craft into one another. Other male artists within Europe's modernist avant-garde took up needlework as an idea or as an activity. French Cubists, Italian Futurists and Russian Suprematists all designed or made embroidery before the First World War. Man Ray made a patchwork quilt, Giacomo Balla and Fortunato Depero designed *arazzi*, Kazimir Malevich sought inspiration in peasant embroidery and Jean Lurçat was taught to embroider by his mother after he was sent home from the front during the war and subsequently abandoned painting in favour of tapestry design. Jean Arp embarked on a collaborative body of work with the artist Sophie Taeuber that resulted in small embroidery panels that could be read as in terms of the sampler or abstract painting.[87] Men's decision to engage in an activity so saturated with feminine associations was most certainly linked to their feelings about war. Many such artists opposed the war, were injured or traumatized in it, or were conscientious objectors. In the case of Arp, Bibiana Obler has speculated: 'It would seem that a draft-dodging male artist flaunting his engagement with women's work would be a flagrant declaration of antiwar sentiments, [but] the critics made no mention of this apparently obvious point.'[88]

Grant was a conscientious objector, although Fry was slightly too old to go to war being nearly fifty when it had started, but as a Quaker he shared the pacifist beliefs of other Bloomsbury men, who were often seen in terms of 'effeminacy and aestheticism'.[89] Eve Kosofsky Sedgwick has argued that Lytton Strachey's play on the effeminacy of the conscientious objector, envisaging himself knitting a muffler for the troops or interposing his body for his sister's in the fantasy of her rape by a German soldier, was 'not gay self-knowledge' but the flaunting of fear.[90] Grant's apparent disinterest in taking up a needle himself, even as he was becoming deeply engaged in embroidery as an art form, can perhaps also be understood in terms of 'homosexual panic'. At the Omega needlework designs were stitched by nearly every woman who came into contact with workshop. Paul Nash later remembered the Omega as a feminized space, as 'an exceptional species of sewing "bee"', which was revived by the central artists associated with the group, Fry, Bell and Grant, in the early 1920s, and continued as 'a kind of' women's 'guild or bee'.[91] Yet by the mid-1920s some of Grant's designs were being made by Angus Davidson following their brief love affair. Over the Christmas holidays in 1924, Virginia Woolf wrote to her friend Jacques Raverat about Davidson, a young Cambridge graduate who she and her husband had recently employed at the Hogarth Press: 'He is working in cross stitch at a design by Duncan Grant for a chair.'[92] This may have been to cover furniture as part of the interior scheme of Davidson's London flat that Grant and Bell had recently decorated.[93] But Davidson also stitched covers for a pair of Victorian chairs for Grant that remain at Charleston. Other members of Bloomsbury remembered visiting him and 'chatting while Angus did his petit point'.[94]

Conventional readings of Grant's 'particular affection for embroidery and wool-working' as dependent upon his close relationship with his mother, Ethel Grant, who worked the majority of his designs, as nothing more than the exploitative power of his 'masculine prerogative',[95] seem especially reductive.[96] It also occludes any discussion of the collaboration with his former lover, Davidson. Perhaps Ethel Grant's encouragement of her son's interest in embroidery carried some implicit approval of his homosexuality, freeing her from ever having to acknowledge his 'secret', freeing him from the 'panic' of discovery, and equating the masculinity of her only son not with sexuality but with sensitivity and 'feeling'.[97] After all she wrote to Lytton Strachey, as her textile collaboration with Duncan was about to begin: 'I suppose there are certain things that boys cannot speak to their mothers about.'[98] In this scenario, for Ethel and Duncan, he becomes less the exploiter than the safely infantalized boy, like the young nobleman, in Woolf's *Orlando* (1928), who seeks comfort in his 'old writing book, stitched together with silk from his mother's workbox'.[99] As Rozsika Parker intimated, the observations by D.W. Winnicott on 'transitional objects' in his studies on child development, especially those about 'string' (much like thread) being used by young boys to maintain connections to their mothers, perhaps can shed some light on the mother-son needlework dyad. Winnicott argued that 'playing with string' allowed a boy to 'symbolically communicate with his mother in spite of her withdrawal' and further that 'sewing' could allow boys to experience 'maternal identification' through acts associated with mothering.[100] Carol Mavor has, more recently, read the string/thread play in boys as 'a sign of their queerness', and she has criticized the hidden homophobia of Winnicott's pathologization of 'the effeminate boy' in the conclusion of his study, which argues that over-identification with the mother in a boy could 'develop into homosexuality' as a form of 'perversion'.[101] Certainly from her son's perspective as Ethel Grant grew closer and more central to his life through their 'collaboration', withdrawal and separation were avoided by her active participation in his art. The effeminacy of embroidery and its place in the queer subcultures of the period may have been masked by silence, but it underscores a wider critique of the hypocrisies of Victorian heteropatriarchy within Bloomsbury.

Not only men, of course, sought the stability of the past, and reverted to the cosy securities of childhood. Mary Hogarth the professional embroiderer and prime mover behind the revival of Bloomsbury's needlework in the early 1920s was described by the artist Ronald Grierson as a sort of throwback in 'a Victorian poke bonnet'.[102] In reviewing the work of the group at the Embroiderers' Guild's exhibition in 1923 for *Vogue*, the first such show since the outbreak of the war, Hogarth focused on the significance of 'feelings' for the modern artist and the need to 'understand the thoughts of the present young generation which has just passed through the disturbed years of war'

(Figure 3.6).¹⁰³ This the first display of Bloomsbury needlework since the closure of the Omega saw Grant submit seven embroideries for chairs and screens and one needlework panel, worked by Vanessa Bell, Marie Moralt, Lady Ottoline Morrell, Mary Hogarth and Ethel Grant; Fry showed a design for a chair embroidered by Winifred Gill; and Wyndham Tryon showed one panel stitched by Mary Hogarth and another of a surreal cacti landscape that he embroidered himself.¹⁰⁴ Grant, in particular, submitted to every other major embroidery exhibition that took place in London during the interwar years. At the *Exhibition of Modern British Embroidery*, held at the Victoria and Albert Museum in the summer of 1932 and organized by Mary Hogarth, Grant showed a firescreen, a mirror frame and a needlework panel embroidered by Bell, Hogarth and his mother.¹⁰⁵ At the 1934 *Exhibition of English Needlework (Past and Present)* Grant showed eight designs for chairs, stools, cushions and needlework pictures embroidered by Morrell and his mother.¹⁰⁶

In 1925 the *Modern Designs in Needlework*, at the Independent Gallery, was the group's only collective show. Reviewers generally agreed that the embroideries possessed 'a peculiar significance at the present moment'.

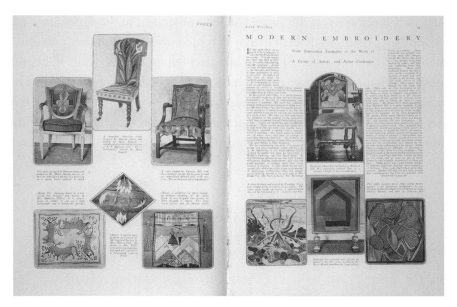

**Figure 3.6** Mary Hogarth, 'Modern Embroidery.' *Vogue* (London) (late October 1923): 66–7, Courtesy of *Vogue* © Condé Nast, Photo. © The British Library Board (Zc.9.d.565).

Clive Bell, writing in *Vogue*, pointed out that the work was the 'fruit of the seed sown in the Omega Workshop' but remained puzzled by their uncanny application of modern embroidery to Victorian furniture.[107] One chair seat by Grant showing a fashionable 'Pierrot' was fitted onto an eighteenth-century chair; Bell called such furniture 'repulsive'. Some of the work made for this show was large and complex and clearly referenced historic models, including seventeenth-century tapestry and Opus Anglicanum. The largest surviving work by Grant, still unfinished by the show's opening, is the appliqué banner depicting angels and symbols of the Eucharist, which was cut out by Vanessa Bell and stitched with silk and wool threads as well as pearls and beads by Bell, Mary Hogarth, Mary Simmonds and 'Miss Elwes', who was the companion of Ethel Grant (Figure 3.7). It was subsequently shown at the Arts and Crafts Exhibition Society.[108] The last major display of Bloomsbury needlework was the contributions of Grant and Tryon to the *Exhibition of 20th Century Needlework* held at the Leicester Galleries in January 1935.[109] By the early 1940s Bloomsbury artists seemed to have ceased designing and making embroidery. In preparing the large *Needlework and Embroidery* touring exhibition in 1943 Rosamund Willis had some difficulty locating examples of work by Bloomsbury artists.[110] But there was still interest in, and awareness of the significance of, Bloomsbury needlework. In one study of contemporary British taste published in the 1930s, by the design historian Margaret Bulley, Duncan Grant's 'Pierrot' design for a chair seat cover was contrasted with a Berlin woolwork 'picture of a boy', designed as a stool cover, to demonstrate the ('masculine') merit of the artist's vision over the ('feminine') design of the mass-produced commodity but paradoxically it served to highlight, if anything, their similarities and interdependence (Figure 3.8).[111]

## Ernest Thesiger and the queer sewing circle: Embroidery as effeminacy

In the early 1920s Weldon's, the pioneering Victorian manufacturer of embroidery, knitting, crocheting, and dressmaking patterns and magazines, published a series of booklets on *Tapestry* and *Antique Tapestry* in their 'Needle-Arts Series'. Within these designs after original Elizabethan, Stuart and Jacobean tapestries for contemporary chairs and cushions, Queen Anne and Georgian

*Killing the Angel in the House* 73

**Figure 3.7** Duncan Grant (designer), Vanessa Bell, Mary Hogarth, Miss Elwes and Mrs Antrobus (embroiderers), *Ecclesiastical Banner*, 1925, appliquéd fabrics, wool and silk threads, pearls and beads, 72 x 36 in. (182.8 x 91.5 cm), © Estate of Duncan Grant. All rights reserved, DACS 2018, Photo. © Victoria and Albert Museum, London (T.52.1935).

**Figure 3.8** '27. Embroidered Chair Seat. Duncan Grant. Worked by Mrs. Bartle Grant. The Property of Mrs. Maynard Keynes / 28. Embroidered Footstool Cover. Victorian.' From Margaret H. Bulley, *Have You Good Taste? A Guide to the Appreciation of the Lesser Arts* (London: Methuen & Co., 1933), Private Collection.

designs for Hepplewhite and Chippendale reproduction furniture, Victorian designs for a baby's pouffe, ladies bags covered in daffodils, tulips, pansies, roses, poppies and foxgloves, a 'Victorian nosegay' panel, tapestry pictures of English gardens and the Scottish highlands, patterns for eiderdowns, wall hangings and fire screens, all battled to evoke an 'essential and eternal' English femininity. The designs were further endorsed by the leading manufacturers of embroidery threads and knitting wools, including Pearsall's, Wm Briggs, Dollfus-Mieg et Cie, Viyella and Patons & Baldwins. The needlework designer, Julia Cairns, writing in Weldon's *Tapestry* booklet, suggested that such patterns for the revival of domestic 'needlework tapestry', although they may have looked suspiciously like Berlin woolwork, were in fact evocations of a once-great English textile tradition stretching back beyond Elizabethan times that allowed the modern needlewoman 'to recapture much of the glamour of yester-year'.[112] However, what marked this publication as distinct was Weldon's employment of male fabricators from the Disabled Soldiers' Embroidery Industry, a workshop of wounded veterans founded in 1918 by the glamorous society figure Ernest Thesiger, to make up several of the products photographed for its pages. Reproductions of sixteenth- and seventeenth-century English tapestry in petit point, gros point, and cross-stitch or gobelin stitch were faithfully 'copied by the men' from valuable originals. The second booklet in the series had a double-page spread of a range of more modern designs, again made up by the Disabled Soldiers' Embroidery Industry, including twee country scenes, with titles like *Pride of the Pack* or *Vixen on the Alert*, a rather Wildean church banner of 'orchids and passion flowers', and a modern floral design for a stool cover in primary, almost Post-Impressionist, colours (Figure 3.9).[113]

Men in the 1920s and 1930s became acutely visible as fabricators of embroidery and needlework was increasing talked about in relation to men's hobbies.[114] Needlework by disabled veterans, aristocrats, captains of industry, politicians and artists was seen in the numerous embroidery exhibitions of the period and was featured in newspapers and magazines. The male needleworker suddenly appeared as a character in the theatre and in the popular middlebrow fiction of the interwar years and was often discussed in relation to women. For instance, Ralph Lion, husband of the painter Flora Lion, was a well-known artist, but he also appeared in the press as a 'stitchery expert' who embroidered his wife's dresses.[115] His emasculation and subordination came

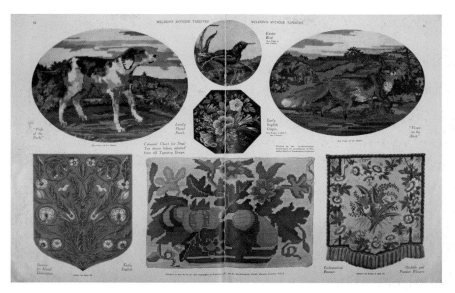

**Figure 3.9** *Weldon's Antique Tapestry. Part 2* (London: Weldons Ltd., Fashion, Pattern and Transfer Publishers, n.d. [c.1920]), pp. 10–11, Private Collection.

through public knowledge of her suffrage sympathies and activities (he took her name when they married). The fashionable Warren Gallery in London, run by Lady Ottoline Morrell's niece Dorothy Warren, was central in showing work by several such men including John Craske, a former deep-sea fisherman from Norfolk who had been injured at the beginning of the war and who was prescribed embroidery as part of his recovery.[116] *Beach Scene: The Foreshore* (1931) is a typical example of his work, in its large panoramic format depicting the teaming life of a seashore town, stitched while he lay prostrate in bed (Figure 3.10).[117] Embroidery for an 'invalided' man was perhaps, like for the Victorian housewife, bound up with 'stifled emotion'.[118]

Other men felt differently. The writer D.H. Lawrence, for instance, who exhibited his paintings at the Warren Gallery, thought sewing was not effeminate but rather a sign of virile self-sufficiency.[119] Lawrence designed and stitched several embroideries, sometimes in collaboration with his wife, Frieda, or friends; he also mended clothes.[120] One surviving example made with Frieda shows an *Etruscan Figure*, in a frozen balletic pose, recalling images from the ancient Etruscan frescoes and pottery that were being rediscovered in the 1920s and that so fascinated Lawrence (Figure 3.11). Beyond its art

**Figure 3.10** John Craske, *Beach Scene: The Foreshore*, 1931, wool and silk threads on canvas, 15.7 x 46.7 in. (40 x 118.5 cm), © Britten-Pears Foundation (5-9400060).

**Figure 3.11** D.H. Lawrence and Frieda Lawrence, *Etruscan Figure*, cotton threads on unbleached linen, *c.*1920s, 10.6 x 12.9 in. (27.5 x 33 cm), Courtesy of The University of Tulsa, McFarlin Library, Department of Special Collections & University Archives (1976.013.3.2.4).

historical accuracy, the figure's exposed phallus suggests that the sexual charge of sewing, itself, played a part in the creation of such work. Indeed, Lawrence's friend Juliette Huxley recalled: 'Touched by the subtle but definite influence of Lawrence, I wanted to embroider Adam and Eve in their Paradise ... Lawrence finished Adam's genital organs which I had fumbled, adding a black virile business to a perfectly sensible phallus. He obviously enjoyed the last touch.'[121] Lawrence was conscious of the nurturing connotations not only of needlework embedded in its association with the feminine but also of its potential for erotic pleasure. In Lawrence's *Sons and Lovers* (1913), a novel very much about masculinity as feeling, the protagonist Paul Morel, a young, sensitive aesthete in the industrial wasteland of coalmining country, designs a '*portière*, beautifully stenciled with a design of roses', for his beloved mother to embroider.[122] As an act of love it is tinged with sadness as their poverty forces Paul to consider selling it – to 'Liberty's' as it is so fine. In the same scene in the novel, Paul then gives Miriam, the young woman he has romantic feelings for, 'a cushion cover with the same design' of which he says 'I did that for you'. As Lawrence explored men's emotions through the mother-son dyad in his writing, as Duncan Grant did in his embroidery designs, similarly Craske's stitching as part of his care-giving and convalescence had a wider history and significance in interwar Britain.

The men who fabricated the designs for Weldon's did so through the Disabled Soldiers' Embroidery Industry, which had been established at the war's end to provide employment to severely disabled ex-servicemen. Many men had returned from the war with such severe physical and psychological injuries that they were unable to return to their previous jobs. In the absence of a welfare state, and with only a diminutive statuary pension, most men needed to work in order to survive. For those with life-changing disabilities finding a job was a challenge and there was no guarantee of employment or legal protection from discrimination. The Disabled Soldiers' Embroidery Industry was the idea of Ernest Thesiger, who himself had been injured during the war, to help such disenfranchised men (Plate 6). After studying at the Slade School of Art, and a stint on the West End stage, Thesiger had enlisted in the Queen Victoria Rifles in 1914. With his characteristic arch-campness, that made him famous in his day, when asked at the start of the war by a senior officer what he did at home (i.e. his job) he replied 'fancy needlework'.[123] During the early stages of the war whilst Thesiger's battalion advanced toward the Western front he was injured in a bomb blast. He was formally discharged after a medical examination in 1915 following operations to remove shrapnel from the metacarpal bones in both his hands. By the end of the war Thesiger was once again embroidering and whilst visiting a friend convalescing in Charing Cross hospital he 'found men busily making needlework' and it occurred to him that they would be 'better employed copying some really good designs'.[124] He started to teach some of the men, lending them examples of old cross-stitch from his own collection and taking them to the Victoria and Albert Museum to look at historic embroideries, tapestry and other textiles. Thesiger first tried to formalize his teaching through the Ministry of Pensions but, he claimed, they thought needlework was 'too effeminate an occupation for men'.[125] In the end he turned to his numerous society connections to help set up a charity scheme to teach men to make needlework (in a central London workshop or through the post as many men had injuries that left them housebound) and to sell it for them through exhibitions and retail outlets in the capital.

The Disabled Soldiers' Embroidery Industry went on to become one of the great success stories of the interwar embroidery revival and brought much visibility to the male needleworker.[126] The workshop produced a vast array of needlework and achieved widespread success. In a curious inversion of the sexual division of labour, so central to Victorian notions of embroidery, women in the workshop assumed the roles of managers, designers and teachers whilst the men did all the sewing. Thesiger remains exceptional in that he was the only male teacher. He sometimes gave embroidery demonstrations at exhibition openings, was photographed for *Vogue* and *House & Garden*, and filmed for the Pathé News, in his elegant Knightsbridge home, at 6 Montpelier Terrace, showing off his embroidery. He was often seen in newspapers and society magazines partying with the Bright Young People but also in more honourable pursuits, such as teaching disabled ex-soldiers 'petit point' (Figure 3.12), and he was given the title 'Hon. Sec. Cross Stitch' by the men in the workshop. Thesiger's social contacts brought both the press and patronage from popular celebrities and aristocrats. For example, in 1922, Fred Benson commissioned the workshop to restore an embroidery for Lamb House in Rye into which he had moved after Henry James's death: 'Mr. E.F. Benson (who was another admirer of the soldiers' work) told me he had just ordered to be

*Mr. Ernest Thesiger teaching petit point to two disabled men.*

**Figure 3.12** 'Mr. Ernest Thesiger Teaching Petit Point to Two Disabled Men.' From 'Embroideries by Disabled Soldiers.' *The Queen* (27 May 1931): 19, © The British Library Board (MFM.MLD45).

worked in "petit point" a seat for his wonderful mother o' pearl inlaid Charles II chair.'[127] And in 1929, the Prince of Wales ordered a set of needlework maps 'of Berkshire and Middlesex', made in 'petit point', which were 'replicas of old maps made by John Speed during Elizabethan days'.[128] Each map took a single embroiderer fifteen months to stitch. These were exhibited in London in 1931 before being installed in the hall at Fort Belvedere.

Work by the Disabled Soldiers' Embroidery Industry was also shown at several of the major embroidery exhibitions of the period. At the *Exhibition of English Needlework (Past and Present)*, in 1934, for instance, alongside work by the Bloomsbury group and other male embroiderers such as John Craske, the Disabled Soldiers' Embroidery Industry showed several embroidered bedspreads, tapestry panels and quilts. One cushion cover in 'petit point' was copied after one of the surviving Sheldon tapestries. Several exhibitions specifically of 'masculine needlework' were also mounted to coincide with display of the workshop's goods. In 1924 at the *Exhibition of Modern Embroideries and Decorative Art*, hosted by Lady Mary Morrison, at her home, 9 Halkin Street in London, a special men's display included work by Thesiger, several other 'gentlemen', such as Edgar Lister, Henry Hoare and Hubert Astley, and the 'peers' Viscount Ennismore, Lord Gainford and Lord Carmichael. One review jibed: 'We need no proof that in some of what we incline to consider essentially feminine industries men can meet us and sometimes beat us.'[129] Another asked, 'Is "needlework for men" to be one of the new slogans?'[130] Clearly, the work of the 'mere males' on display recalled the pre-war flurry of embroidered banners made during the suffrage campaign. At this exhibition a competition for men's needlework was announced, for the following year, that would include a special 'Golden Thimble' prize.

It is often thought that Thesiger only began embroidering just before the war through the encouragement of his friend, the Scottish painter William B. Ranken, who was an accomplished and avid needleworker.[131] But in an interview Thesiger claimed to have started embroidering whilst at the Slade in the 1890s, a period in which he had tea with Oscar Wilde, was sketched by John Singer Sargent and met Henry James.[132] Yet, in some ways Thesiger's taking up needle and thread, to 'the surprise of many & the horror of some', occurs at the junction of two important events in his life, the death of his mother, Georgina Stopford Sackville, and his meeting Ranken (at the Slade) with whom he fell in love.[133] Of his childhood, Thesiger later recalled not only his fascination with his mother's court dresses but also his mother's needlework and her eldest sister, who was 'fanatically religious', and who was always embroidering.[134] Ranken, however, was the catalyst who spurred Thesiger to search for and archive examples of needlework by men finding inspiration in books such as Daniel Rock's *Textile Fabrics* (1870). Rock was a Roman Catholic priest and ecclesiologist, a well-known antiquarian and a widely acknowledged authority on textile history who is known to have made embroidery himself. His book catalogued the vast textile collection of the Victorian and Albert Museum and was the source for many subsequent books on the history of embroidery by not only women such as Lady Marian Alford and Grace Christie (key works cited by Rozsika Parker in *The Subversive Stitch* as helping establish an essentially female history of needlework) but also Oscar Wilde's descriptions of 'decadent' textiles that so appealed to the male aesthete in *The Picture of Dorian Gray* (1890).[135]

Thesiger is well known for his anecdotes of his evenings embroidering with Queen Mary, comforting her after the King's death and through her long widowhood, or gossiping with his friend the novelist Ivy Compton-Burnett and her companion Margaret Jourdain. But he also spent much of his time in a sewing circle made of his most intimate gay male friends.[136] This included Ranken as well as William Lygon, 7th Earl Beauchamp, a Liberal politician whose career would be destroyed by the threat of homosexual scandal in the 1930s.[137] In the interwar years as embroidery became increasingly associated with effeminacy it also became more closely linked to homosexuality than ever before. Examples in the popular imagination that capture something of the reaction to Thesiger's needlework are the various characters in stage-plays and novels, which portray the male embroiderer as decadent and dangerous. These are very likely pen portraits of Thesiger. In Mordaunt Shairp's play *The Green Bay Tree* (1933), which exposes a 'hedonistic and elderly bachelor's ruination of a young man', the 'wicked sybarite' of the decadent older man, Dulcimer, is visualized through his embroidery.[138] The young man's life and future are secured when he renounces needlework: 'I'm glad to say he won't want to embroider,' his fiancée tells Dulcimer.[139] In Nancy Mitford's novel, *Love in a Cold Climate* (1949), the sexually voracious Harvey 'Boy' Dougdale embroiders with Lady Montdore, seducing her sister and then her daughter behind the scenes, and eventually runs off with the needle wielding, 'awful effeminate pansy', Cedric Hampton, heir apparent to the Montdore house.[140]

Ideas that surfaced in the popular press were clearly derived from sexologists such as Havelock Ellis whose controversial *Sexual Inversion* (1897) suggested that men with homosexual feelings had an innate aptitude for 'simpler forms of needlework', whereas female inverts found sewing 'distasteful'.[141] In one of Ellis's case studies a middle-aged man's 'inversion' was simply inferred from his interest in women's popular magazines. Thesiger read the work of sexologists, he makes explicit reference to Freud in his published and unpublished memoirs, and he certainly read women's magazines. Yet, he resisted the pathologization of the 'invert' and by performing femininity through his embroidery he somehow satirized the essentialist assumptions of sexology. Thesiger's embroidery seemed innocent enough. He often based his floral, and occasional ecclesiastical, designs on historic models. As late as the 1940s he was still making small samplers to teach basic stitches to men (Figure 3.13).[142] Yet, the writer Beverly Nichols described Thesiger as 'embroidering little wickednesses' that hinted at disturbing, sexualized, 'phantasms' and 'nightmares'.[143] Anxiety about male-femininity and female-masculinity seemed omnipresent in the period. Thesiger's close friend the writer Radclyffe Hall explored such ideas in her novel, *The Well of Loneliness* (1928), in which the protagonist Stephen Gordon is born female but identifies as 'masculine'. Hall's story draws a great deal on the work of Richard von Krafft-Ebing and she even asked Havelock Ellis to pen the foreword.

**Figure 3.13** Ernest Thesiger, *Sampler*, signed and dated 1946, cotton thread on linen, 12.2 x 14.1 in. (31 x 36 cm), Private Collection, © John S. Thesiger, Photo. © Jake Shaw, Courtesy of Bearnes Hampton & Littlewood.

It is within this context that Thesiger published a defence of the male needleworker in a popular women's magazine. 'Happy is the man who can sink into a comfortable chair and pick up his work-basket, select his strand of gaily-coloured wool, and forget his troubles in the engrossing pursuit of needlework,' he wrote in the 1926 spring issue of *The Home Magazine* (Figure 3.14). Masquerading as a personal ode to needlework, an innocuous relaxing and rehabilitative occupation, Thesiger used the article to point out that the feminine identification of embroidery was socially constructed and neither natural nor essential:

> When the complete history of needlework comes to be written, I suppose the first chapter will deal with the story of the couple who sewed fig leaves together and made themselves aprons. And it is worthy of notice that the gentlemen in question did not say to his wife: 'Look here, Eve, this is a women's job; just you make me a nice little costume!' but did his own plain sewing, and it is not on record that she thought any the worse of him for it. In later years I suppose Adam travelled eastwards and boasted of his prowess as a needleman – for in the East all the best work has been done by men. Eve, presumably, took her bodkin westwards, with the result that in Europe it has always been considered that needlework was entirely a feminine business.[144]

Written in the sardonic tones of his characteristic camp voice there was also a very serious side to Thesiger's article and also to his embroidery. There is a much-overlooked legacy of his work in the development of needlework as occupational therapy. His influence can be seen in the Government's *Needlecraft for H.M. Forces by Penelope* kits of the Second World War; the Royal School of Needlework's *Needle-Work in War-Time* teaching guide (Figure 3.15); and in the speech delivered by Albert Spencer, 7th Earl Spencer, as President of the Embroiderers' Guild, entitled 'In Praise of the Needle', that stressed the pivotal role of needlework in occupying men in hospitals or internment camps throughout the war.[145] The Disabled Soldiers' Embroidery Industry was acknowledged as a pioneering venture in this.[146] During the period sewing as a physically and psychologically reparative act came to be seen as emanating from the concept of 'mothering' but not necessarily, particularly in the context of war, as essentially 'feminine'.[147] Historians of modern warfare have increasingly stressed the importance of 'emotion' in men's experiences

**Figure 3.14** Ernest Thesiger, 'Needlework as a Hobby.' *The Home Magazine* XXXIV(119) (March 1926): 27, Photo. © The Bodleian Libraries, The University of Oxford (Per. 2705 d.45).

**Figure 3.15** From Lady Smith-Dorrien, 'Convalescing Soldiers.' In *Needlework in War-Time: Suggestions for Teaching Beginners and Convalescents* (London: The Royal School of Needlework, n.d. [*c.*1940]), p. 3, Private Collection.

of combat and civilian life and have started to consider, what Michael Roper has termed, 'mothering men'.[148] Other writers have gone much further in the possible meanings of 'mothering', symbolic or actual. Carol Mavor, using Eve Kosofsky Sedgwick's concept of 'effeminophobia', the culturally 'pervasive fear of the effeminate boy', has suggested that we may 'encourage girls to be tough, to play the man's game' but 'we rarely encourage our boys' to be 'feminine, maternal, soft caring', as embodied in acts like sewing.[149]

In her various essays on Henry James, Eve Kosofsky Sedgwick further suggested that the moment a child feels emotions such as sadness, following the break in the mirroring process with their mother, is for the queer child a moment of 'melancholia' that develops into 'mourning, disidentification, and shame' and eventuality is only resolved through 'performativity'.[150] She interprets the prefaces that Henry James wrote for the editions of his collected work, towards the end of his life, for instance, as a form of 'parenting his own past' (to combat his 'melancholia'), and she further suggests we understand James's explicit use of the language of nursing and childbirth in this process 'quite simply as male parturition'.[151] Sedgwick argues that this, like 'homosexual panic', is a kind of 'queer performativity'. Perhaps we can read the needlework of men like Howard Sturgis, Duncan Grant and Ernest Thesiger (men who were the products of Victorian boyhoods) as a kind of 'queer performativity'. Men as caregivers, as nurturers and mothers, as subversives and failures in the mechanisms of phallic power surely had some part to play in exposing the 'Angel in the House' myth.

# 4

# 'The mesh canvas': Amateur needlecrafts, masculinity and modernism

In 1947, in a terse review of a slim volume of essays on the role of art in modern society by Herbert Read, the English poet, art critic, museum curator, exhibition organizer, all-round man of letters and champion of modernism, the American critic Clement Greenberg stingingly dismissed Read's idea that 'manual crafts' could somehow unify 'the mind and the senses' in the production of art. For Greenberg, Read's 'argument falls flat' in that the optical is infinitely more expressive than the tactile, the abstract communicates more than the sensual: 'Mr. Read's handicrafts will exist only as hobbies, and hobbies have too precarious a place to enable them to defend sensuous intuition against abstract rationality.'[1] Greenberg's insistence on the autonomy of the visual arts, defined, in part, through a repudiation of the pleasures of mass culture, meant that modern art must 'confine itself to what is given in visual experience and make no reference to any other orders of experience'.[2] Subsequently, in a review of the first American exhibition of Ben Nicholson, the avant-garde painter Read had avidly supported, Greenberg sought to distance Nicholson's work from the pure abstraction of Piet Mondrian, whom Nicholson had been much influenced by and had encouraged to come to London from where he moved to New York, levelling at Nicholson's work the accusation of an essentially English problem of 'prettiness'.[3] To hammer home the abnormal nature of such an approach, which Greenberg clearly perceived as unnatural for the male artist, he added, in a tone of religious rectitude that recalled the pathologizing language of nineteenth-century sexology, that 'prettiness' had been 'the besetting sin of English pictorial art'.[4]

Nicholson by this time was far down the road of a severe and ascetic abstraction made of minimal tonal ranges of white that makes Greenberg's comments somewhat puzzling. Certainly, by the 1940s there had been flourishes of colour in Nicholson's work and, if anything, what Greenberg was hinting at is that the tactility of Nicholson's constructed surfaces betrayed an interest in, and knowledge of, textiles. Nicholson, like Read, had more than just a passing interest with the craft world, he had direct connections. In the 1920s along with his first wife, the painter Winifred Roberts, and their friend Mary Berwick, Nicholson had experimented with rag rug making (Figure 4.1) and, as Chris Stephens has suggested, 'through his implicit reference to domestic vernacular, one might see Nicholson articulating a feminised national tradition and a feminised modernism'.[5]

Herbert Read, however, just like Greenberg, was keen to distance himself from the strands of academic and figurative art, and their decorative qualities, that existed within modernism. Indeed, in a public debate, on the eve of the Second World War, about 'abstraction' versus 'realism' in British painting, Read rejected 'realism', as defended by Anthony Blunt, the art historian, labelling it 'the effete and bastard offspring of the Bloomsbury school of needlework'.[6]

**Figure 4.1** Ben Nicholson and Mary Berwick, *Animal Squares*, 1925–9, rag rug, 42 x 67 in. (106 x 170 cm), Photo. Whitworth Art Gallery, University of Manchester, © Angela Verren Taunt, All Rights Reserved, DACS 2019.

Read's equation of effeminacy and embroidery, especially in reference to how they were strategically conflated in the work of artists such as Duncan Grant, reflected the wider misogyny and homophobia of what had become the established hegemony of modernist discourse. Several artists echoed Read's panicky tone. The English sculptor Henry Moore, for instance, cautioned that Eric Gill's attribution of value in modern sculpture to 'workmanship' could 'degenerate into a most awful mental laziness, like knitting'.[7] The collapsing of masculinity and modernism into one another has meant that dissent from the orthodoxy proposed by male art critics such as Read and Greenberg, who shared essentialist and binarized notions of gender, was akin to patricide. Needlework existed, then, beyond the threshold (in the closet) of modern art. Certainly, in the British context its traces can be found in the queer domestic experiments of Howard Sturgis or the Bloomsbury group or in the nurturing charity work that masked the queer subcultural sewing circle that surrounded Ernest Thesiger, instances of investment in amateur handicrafts that remain beyond the margins of modern art. In the American context where needlework was equally associated with effeminacy and homosexuality, its presence can also be traced at modernism's seams.

In early twentieth century Britain public knowledge of, and interest in, the male embroiderer was directly stimulated by the teaching of needlework as occupational therapy to convalescing servicemen during the First World War, which continued throughout the interwar decades. Subsequently, in America needlework was taught to the wounded in military hospitals and there was much interest in developments in Britain.[8] As a consequence sewing as a therapeutic activity would feed its way into the wider revival of needlework in America and helped popularize it as a hobby, especially for men, following the war's end. Although the National Society for the Promotion of Occupational Therapy (which became the American Occupational Therapy Association) was established in 1917 many hospitals and medical schools dropped such programmes after the war but several important centres for occupational therapy were established.[9] American pioneers of occupational therapy, such as the psychiatrist William Rush Dutton, were interested in all sorts of needlework from the making of quilts and hooked-rugs to needlepoint and cross-stitch.[10] Sewing as a reparative act, helping restore physical dexterity as well as mental and emotional equilibrium, suggested to Dutton that commitment to such a hobby, recuperative in the immediate aftermath of injury, could also, if kept up, help sustain physical and psychological well-being in the longer term. Dutton's interest in needlework was inspired by his reading of Marie Webster's *Quilts: Their Story and How to Make Them* (1915) and, like many men of his generation, he continued to see sewing as essentially feminine despite its effectiveness as a therapy or the pleasures it offered to men. As a hobby its troubling associations with effeminacy and homosexuality never seemed to dissipate.

By the time of the Second World War needlework was again widely used as a form of occupational therapy in hospitals and internment camps. Displays of work by men were reported in the press. From First World War veteran H.B. McDermott's winning entry in a 'fancy needlework contest' at a St. Paul hospital, Minnesota, in 1925 (Figure 4.2), to the vast nationwide display of

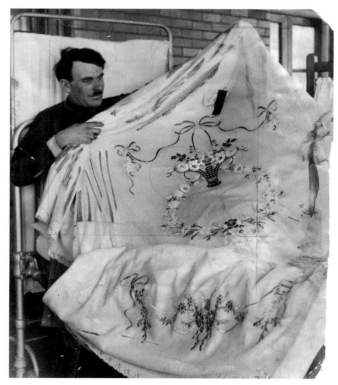

**Figure 4.2** First World War veteran H.B. McDermott's winning entry in a 'fancy needlework contest' at a St. Paul hospital, Minnesota, dated 27 April 1925, unidentified press photo, Private Collection.

'the hobbies of members of the armed forces, war workers and participants in civilian defense', organized by the American Hobby Association in 1942, emphasis was often placed not so much on the therapeutic efficiency of needlecrafts but on the pleasures men found in them and their transformative effects on masculinity turning the phallocentrism of the combatant into nurturers and caregivers themselves. In the latter exhibition, for instance, 'the best example of fancy needlework' was that of a soldier, who was formerly a boxer and sailor, who was 'on hand to teach the fine points of silk-thread embroidery and knotting on pillow covers'.[11] Softening and feminizing, as needlework was perceived, it was often necessary for any man who took it up to re-assert his essential masculine nature. One American serviceman in a German POW camp at the end of the war, for example, 'made knitted dresses and pocketbooks for use when impersonating a woman to escape the guards'.[12]

Outside of the new interest in needlework as occupational therapy the rise in popularity of needlework as a hobby was also evident by the close of the interwar years.[13] Historic examples of American needlework traditions, in quilts and samplers, were collected and studied and European needlework was widely admired. By 1950 *Vogue* estimated that some 18 million Americans, 'like Britain's Queen Mary and Sweden's King Gustav, are skilful and devoted needleworkers'.[14] In 1950 Queen Mary sent a large carpet (twelve panels in 'gros point' needlework designed for her by the Royal School of Needlework after examples of eighteenth-century textiles in the Victoria and Albert Museum), on which she worked for most of the 1940s, to America to be sold and raise funds for the British nation that was so economically depleted by the war. It was eventually sold to the Imperial Order Daughters of the Empire who donated it to the National Gallery of Canada in Ottawa. The tour, which ran from March through June 1950 started and ended in New York, taking in some sixteen cities on the way, generated much enthusiasm.[15] Like that of Queen Mary, the needlework of King Gustaf V, who was the reigning Swedish monarch from 1907 until his death in 1950, stimulated much interest with the American public. Images of King Gustaf embroidering that appeared in the American press are rare instances of the representation of a man actually sewing rather than in the role of connoisseur or an occasional competition winner.[16] King Gustaf's embroideries were widely admired;

**Figure 4.3** King Gustaf V of Sweden's final embroidery (left unfinished), silk threads on linen, c.1950, 19.3 x 15 in. (49 x 38.1 cm), © Livrustkammaren/The Royal Armoury, Stockholm, Photo. Erik Lernestål.

he was especially knowledgeable about the Italian 'bargello' technique, but he was also seen as 'eccentric' and helped perpetuate the association of needlework and aristocratic taste in the postwar American imagination (Figure 4.3).[17] However, he was not seen as unique. Other aristocratic men who had an interest in needlework were reported in the American press. Embroidery, as well as knitting and crocheting, as hobbies of Queen Mary's eldest son, the Prince of Wales, was widely discussed in America during the interwar years.[18] The very idea of embroidery as an act, of covering a mesh canvas completely, of rendering 'every element, every part of the canvas equivalent', in which 'the formal unity is contained and recapitulated in each thread', is in fact how Clement Greenberg described modern painting.[19] Needlework was the 'spectre' that haunted modern art becoming, in many ways, the 'bad dream of modernism'.[20]

## Sewing as surveillance: Needlework in the circle of George Platt Lynes

In May 1949, during E.M. Forster's second and final trip to lecture in America he visited, and stayed with, the writer Glenway Wescott at Stone-blossom, a renovated eighteenth-century farmhouse in Hampton, New Jersey, that Westcott shared with his partner, Monroe Wheeler, the publisher and curator who was by then director at Exhibitions at the Museum of Modern Art (MoMA) in New York.[21] Aside from socializing with their intimate circle of friends, whom he had met on his previous trip to New York, including the art critic, collector, curator and ballet impresario Lincoln Kirstein, the photographer George Platt Lynes, and the painters Paul Cadmus and Jared French, Forster recorded little else about his stay at Stone-blossom. But here, he undoubtedly saw the remarkable daybed depicting a male and female nude (almost life-size) in a post-coital position that had been embroidered by George Platt Lynes. Wheeler recalled 'George and Jared' devised the design together at Stone-blossom as a love seat: 'Jared was choosing the pattern and colours and George was sewing it together.'[22] Lynes is better known as one of twentieth century's great photographers of the male nude, but he was also an enthusiastic, committed and accomplished embroiderer. Lincoln Kirstein may have felt able to do a little 'plain sewing' backstage at the ballet, but disclosure of Lynes's needlework as a full-blown hobby may have attracted unwanted attention to his homosexuality, so it remained secret.[23] Knowledge of Lynes's needlework comes largely from the references made, often fleetingly, in the private exchanges of Wescott and Wheeler, frequently in the context of Stone-blossom. In 1939 when Lynes's friend, the writer Katherine Anne Porter, wrote asking for news, her impression that he was 'stitching away in Stone Blossom' sounds fanciful but was probably accurate.[24] Lynes also lived at Stone-blossom, for a period, in a sort of *ménage-à-trois* with Wescott and Wheeler, for whom the house had become an important country retreat from the city. Although Lynes is now largely unknown as a needleworker his surviving unpublished diaries record his serious investment in it as a hobby: 'up early stitching', 'do needlepoint and go to bed early', 'work for 2 or 3 hours on big needlepoint', 'stitch most of morning & afternoon', 'stitch all morning', 'a long evening of reading & stitching'.[25]

Other men, of course, did embroider and in New York's pre- and postwar world of glamorous artistic, literary and theatrical circles for a gay man to sew hardly seems exceptional. For example, Jack Cole, the queer choreographer from the golden age of musicals on Broadway and in Hollywood, who was Lynes's exact contemporary, was well known for 'his hobby' of 'creating pornographic needlepoint'.[26] Friends recalled, 'He'd just sit there and do needlepoint. Needlepoint, needlepoint, needlepoint!'[27] Like Lynes, Cole favoured the popular needlepoint technique in which yarn (wool rather than silk) is used to stitch a pre-drawn pattern or design (very much like nineteenth-century Berlin woolwork and also sometimes confusingly referred to as 'tapestry') onto a piece of open mesh canvas covered in the design and that could, once finished, be easily made into functional objects or applied to furniture as coverings. Like Cole, Lynes also made 'X-rated needlepoint'.[28] For example, about 1950 he is recorded as making a pillowcase embroidered with roses. To make each individual flower head, and to heighten their phallic symbolism, he 'requested clippings of pubic hair from each of his male acquaintances and wove the contributions of each into a rose dedicated to him'.[29] Although nothing of Cole's needlework is known beyond anecdotes some work by Lynes that was seen by visitors at Stone-blossom, or in Lynes's New York studio, has survived.

After leaving Stone-blossom and while in New York, E.M. Forster was painted by Cadmus, drawn by Bernard Perlin and also photographed by Lynes in his studio. It is tempting to wonder what Forster might have made of the needlework that he may have encountered there; would it have struck him as possessing any similarities to the needlework in the Bloomsbury interiors he frequented?[30] Mina Kirstein, the older sister of Lynes's friend Lincoln, studied in London during the 1920s and was certainly familiar with Bloomsbury's artists. She had met the writer David Garnett and through him was introduced to the wider Bloomsbury circle. In March 1923, when Garnett invited Kirstein, who was the focus of his current romantic infatuation, to his birthday party in the London studio of Duncan Grant, his former lover, she was immediately struck by Grant's work.[31] Before she returned to America, Kirstein sat for a portrait by Grant.[32] In the studio she admired Grant's paintings and drawings and she may have seen some of his needlework designs intended for display at the upcoming Embroiderers' Guild exhibition later that year. Grant's embroideries lingered in her mind as she wrote to him from Smith College, in Massachusetts, the following year: 'David has sent me the copy of the Vogue with the picture of your and Vanessa's things in it and I was so enchanted by the two lovely chairs that you designed that I am actually learning to do tapestry.'[33] There is little record of Kirstein's needlecrafts after that but her comments register something of a growing interest in Bloomsbury needlework, and other examples of English embroidery in America. In 1925, for instance, American *Vogue* reported on the 'wool craze [that] has captured London' society:

> The hostess has her needlework frame. The guest brings hers or his. Perhaps, the War Industries and the sock knitting of all those sad years have had something to do with it. The priceless family petit-point has gone Christie's way to pay income taxes or has been given to the moths, and the Chippendale or Sheraton needs fresh covering. Lady A is doing seats for dining-room chairs, from early Georgian designs she bought from the Royal School of Art Needlework, now presided over by the Duchess of York. Lady B is making a cushion cover of a shepherd and shepherdess in French taste. The happy couple is surrounded with Marie Antoinette garlands of bow-knots and roses. Lady A's mother who is religious, is doing part of a vestment, after a Henry VIII piece in her Chapel. Lord C, her son, who is artistic and was wounded in the War, is repairing a Charles II vanity box. He learned the trick in the hospital when he was shell-shocked.[34]

The work of Ernest Thesiger, the Disabled Soldiers' Embroidery Industry, the 1924 'masculine needlework' exhibition and subsequent 'Golden Thimble' prize were all reported in the American press.[35] The *Modern Designs in Needlework* exhibition showcasing work by Bloomsbury artists, held at the Independent Gallery in November 1925, was also praised for its application of the 'fresh and vital' and modern 'expression' of painting to embroidery. It was hoped that American 'artists will not consider it beneath their dignity to do likewise.'[36] There is very little mention in society and lifestyle magazines, such as *Vogue*, or in commercial publications like *Needlecraft: The Home Arts Magazine*, of comparable needlework by American men. Male needleworkers seem to have been routinely atomized in the American press. By the 1950s *The New York Times* reported that in the needlework section of Brooklyn's Abraham & Straus department store men were sending in their wives for supplies because they were too embarrassed to publicly admit such a hobby.[37] Although one teacher of needlework recorded having several male pupils register for her class, one 'a psychiatrist who is working on a sweater' was 'an exception to the rule [as] he knits unashamedly', most men, such as 'a retired sea captain who is hooking a rug and a fisherman who embroiders cloths during the winter months', remained conscious of the feminizing effect of such a pastime.[38] Only occasionally were men named in the press if they won at prestigious events such as the National Exhibition of Amateur Needlework of Today, founded in the mid-1930s in aid of the New York Association for the Blind known as the Lighthouse.[39] The fact that a special division was set up for 'men's work', at this national competition, sometime after the war attracted almost no comment.

As the First World War had done much to transform attitudes to, and perceptions of, masculinity so too did the Second World War. In the postwar years as men became more exposed to the pressures and demands of consumerism (previously targeted largely at women), there emerged growing concerns about the erosion of masculinity through men's subjugation in the workplace and in home life. *Life* magazine declared 1954 the year of 'the domestication of the American male' as it was 'the climax of a decade of dedicated fatherhood and husbandry'.[40] As masculinity became increasingly housebroken, within the postwar consumer revolution, it was also widely perceived as being under threat of feminization. Men who exhibited interest in feminine pastimes, associated with the pleasures of domesticity, came to be seen as in 'flight from masculinity'.[41] Needlework throughout this period was seen as historically the preserve of women and for men it became resonant of effeminacy.[42] The new study of sociology imported the ideas, and language, of nineteenth-century German and British sexology and psychiatry, and the equation of embroidery and 'inversion' in men was quickly absorbed.[43] One such study from the mid-1930s, by Lewis Terman and Catherine Cox Miles, expended immense effort in verifying that 'inverts' had an interest in 'housework, sewing and playing with dolls', from childhood, often instilled by an overbearing mother figure, and retained into adulthood an innate capacity for 'sewing and doing fancywork'.[44] In popular books such as Philip Wylie's *Generation of Vipers* (1942) mothers, or maternal figures, were seen as the cause of a boy's descent into homosexuality.

Effeminacy and homosexuality took on a new political meaning in these years as not only did they reflect an erosion of male dominance but, further, in their marginality, like other groups such as communists, homosexuals became 'subversives' and were widely believed to be a 'national security risk'.[45] This 'homosexual panic' reflected, Robert Corber argues, 'the politicization of same-sex eroticism in the postwar period [which] called into question the stability of male heterosexual identities and precipitated a crisis in the dominant system of representation'.[46] During the increasingly heightened tensions of the Cold War, in particular, homosexuality as a marginal identity appeared to threaten the very essence of hegemonic notions of the masculine and became embroiled in the era's witch-hunts and show trails.[47] Men's bodies and men's behaviour came under increasingly powerful 'systems of surveillance'.[48] Anything seen as effeminate and by implication homosexual was pathologized (homosexuality was to remain a registered mental illness until its declassification by the American Psychiatric Association in 1973). Hobbies such as needlecrafts may have been considered acceptable in that they were perceived as an 'arty' choice for men, but they remained associated with the 'swish' of effeminacy and the insinuation of homosexuality. Yet some men, even when faced with social opprobrium continued to take up needle and thread. They remained beyond the periphery of the art world, which was itself being re-masculinized through the rise of modernism as embodied in the male artist and the male critic. The male needleworker was also marginalized in the increasingly professionalized and commercialized craft industries that perpetuated Victorian notions of needlecrafts as domestic and stereotypically feminine.

Against this backdrop needlework was to surreptitiously emerge as part of New York's gay subculture in a similar way as it had done in early twentieth-century London. Lincoln Kirstein had spent some time in London, during the 1920s and 1930s, and had met some of his sister's Bloomsbury friends.[49] Kirstein was to become a central figure in a not dissimilar community of artists, writers and thinkers in the circle around Wescott, Wheeler and Lynes. This group of men has often been dismissed as 'a gay cabal' and seen as a tangent, even an irrelevance, to modernism proper as embodied in the rise of American painting during the postwar decades.[50] However, it was in these years that Kirstein co-founded an American ballet company (bringing George Balanchine, of the Ballets Russes, from Paris); Paul Cadmus, Jared French, Bernard Perlin and George Tooker sought to reinvigorate modern painting through the representation of the human figure and by reviving the historic egg tempera technique; and George Platt Lynes established a successful photographic studio – achievements that were hardly peripheral to local or national culture. Yet indifference to their accomplishments (from the standpoint of the highbrow and avant-garde) perhaps masks repudiation of what these men shared and what in some ways brought them together – an investment in the homoerotic and the decorative.

Like many of the men in this group George Platt Lynes's interest in homoerotic imagery was 'virtually unknown to the public in the artist's lifetime'.[51] Lynes, who had been a protégé of Gertrude Stein in 1920s Paris was, a decade later, a successful fashion photographer working for high-profile fashion and lifestyle magazines such as Condé Nast's *Vogue*, *Harper's Bazaar* and *House Beautiful*, or society publications like Hearst's *Town & Country*, as well as in publications associated with queer subculture such as the short-lived *Bachelor*.[52] Although Lynes's reputation rested largely on his fashion, celebrity and ballet photographs, a great deal of his career was spent photographing the male nude. These photographs share many formal features with his portraits of literary and bohemian figures and his images of ballet dancers. Shot exclusively in black and white, they are sharply focused, with 'high-keyed light and deep shadows'.[53] In their play on the dynamics of fantasy they partake of a range of contemporary art forms from Surrealist painting to film noir. After being introduced to the American sexologist Alfred Kinsey in 1949, through Wescott and Wheeler, Lynes began to supply Kinsey with photographs of male nudes. Kinsey's *Sexual Behaviour in the Human Male* (1948) had revealed that 37 per cent of the men interviewed had engaged in same-sex activity, to the point of orgasm. He concluded that homosexual desires and behaviours were, therefore, more widely prevalent than people believed, or wished to accept, although he retained some of the rhetoric of nineteenth-century European sexology suggesting that often when homosexual men displayed effeminate tendencies they did so through passivity in sex and taking an interest in domestic activities including sewing.[54] Kinsey amassed some six hundred prints and over two thousand negatives by Lynes to help illustrate his findings.

Like his erotic photography George Platt Lynes's needlework was secretive, only to be shared amongst his close circle of friends. Lynes's needlework, it could be argued, should be read like his 'aestheticizing [of] the male nude', in an age of moral purity, as evidence of his 'active participation in the burgeoning gay subculture in New York'.[55] One surviving small embroidery by Lynes was made for Wheeler as a Christmas card in 1944 (Figure 4.4). It is a small figurative design copied after the humorous and camp images of angels in the paintings, prints and drawings of Paul Klee, some of which had been on display at MoMA during 1944.[56] Lynes also made for Wheeler that year a set of cushions showing two reclining male nudes, thought to be modelled on the erotic male nudes in Pavel Tcheltichew's illustrations of Wescott's *A Calendar of Saints for Unbelievers* (1932).⁵⁷ Worked in brightly coloured wool yarns these cushions have many affinities with Victorian cross-stitch and Berlin woolwork not just in the materials used but also in the use of tight stitches and the overall finished aesthetic. In other embroideries by Lynes, such as the panel copied after Jared French's tempera painting *Elemental Play* (1946), there is clearly a reciprocity between the brushstrokes on the surface of the painting and the individual stitches on the embroidered canvas.

Other men in Lynes's immediate circle also made embroidery. Allen Porter, who Lynes met through Wheeler as he also worked at MoMA, was an avid needleworker. A surviving needlepoint by Porter directly references, in its subject matter, Lynes's photographs of groups of two or three male

**Figure 4.4** George Platt Lynes, *Embroidered Christmas Card for Monroe Wheeler after a Design by Paul Klee*, wool on canvas, 1944, 6 x 6 in. (15 x 15 cm), Monroe Wheeler Papers, Photo. Yale University Collation of American Literature, Beinecke Rare Books & Manuscript Library, Yale University (YCAL MSS 136), © The Estate of George Platt Lynes.

nudes. Porter's panel shows two men lying, one reading, the other reclining (Figure 4.5). Lynes also made embroideries that directly relate to his homoerotic photography. Before his death he began to stitch a cushion cover with naked male figures arranged to spell out the initial letters of his name (Figure 4.6). Bernard Perlin drew the design but the idea was based on a series of male nude photographs that Lynes had already started planning that would illustrate the letters of the alphabet. Louis Gartner was a more minor figure on the periphery of the Lynes's circle, but who was also an embroiderer. Gartner is best remembered today for his role as the 'creative crafts' editor at *House & Garden*, and for publishing the first book on needlepoint in the period by a man, *Needlepoint Design* (1970). Although the inclusion of ideas for needlepoint projects would have appealed to the stereotypically, effeminate interior designer there is also an overt eroticism of the male body (a Pompeiian satyr, a centurion's helmet, Michelangelo's *David*) that obliquely references

**Figure 4.5** Allen Porter, *Untitled*, c.1955, wool on linen, 27 x 33 in. (68.5 x 84 cm), Courtesy of the Leslie-Lohman Museum of Gay and Lesbian Art, New York, Gift of Timothy Stuart-Warner.

**Figure 4.6** George Platt Lynes (and Russell Lynes), *Cushion Cover*, wool on canvas, c.1955, 6 x 6 in. (15 x 15 cm), Bernard Perlin Papers, Photo. Yale University Collation of American Literature, Beinecke Rare Books & Manuscript Library, Yale University (YCAL MSS 849), © The Estate of George Platt Lynes.

Lynes's photography. In his needlepoint, Gartner advocated a move away from prepared designs and suggested such practices existed in a liminal space, at an intersection of art and craft:

> Needlepoint is a fabric, and a fabric that you invest with your personality. A work of needlepoint begins, like an oil painting, as 'canvas.' The canvas of needlepoint is an open-mesh scrim, and there are varieties of scrim to accommodate projects large and small, ambitious and simple. The scrim is the canvas on which you 'paint' with wool. Needle and yarn are your brush and paint. The comparison ends right there. Needlepoint parts company with actual painting because the color is applied with the repetition of a single basic stitch rather than with strokes of color. The stitches may be varied in size and in sequence, but the object of needlepoint remains the same – to

cover all the canvas with wool stitches in such a fashion that you have a finished fabric of your own design, as tough as it is a proud possession.[58]

Although Gartner cautioned against using painting as the literal inspiration and source for needlework design, in 1960 he made a needlepoint copy of Paul Cadmus's painting *Inventor* (1946), one of a group of three paintings described as among 'the most beautiful' and 'the most refined of all Cadmus's work'.[59] Cadmus's use of a historic craft medium, egg tempera, for this painting, a technique often disparaged and dismissed in modernist art discourse as ornamental, possessed an apparent decorative surface quality much like needlework. Writing about his embroidery, entitled *Facsimile of a Painting by Paul Cadmus* (Figure 4.7), Gartner was guarded and reluctant to disclose the

**Figure 4.7** Louis Gartner, *Facsimile of a Painting by Paul Cadmus*, signed and dated 1960, petit point needlepoint tapestry, 27 x 30.75 in. (68.58 x 78.11 cm), Photo. Courtesy of the Canvassed Gallery, Los Angeles.

reasons why it was so important for him to copy this specific work, and, if anything, he offered a layer of critical distance.[60] Although, Gartner gives little interpretation and reduces meaning to a description of materials and facture, his silence is suggestive of signification in another way. Initially, Gartner had moved to New York after the Second World War to work as a photographer's assistant, working notably with Irving Penn, who introduced him to the circle of artists and friends around Lynes. Gardner's embroidery is in the tradition of Lynes's work, in its codification of sexual desire, fusing the homoerotic and the decorative. As Eve Kosofsky Sedgwick has suggested this relationality between the 'explicit and the inexplicit', and the self-enforced performative 'act of silence' itself, is something more than just a desire to resist scrutiny and censor.[61] For men, such as George Platt Lynes, Allen Porter or Louis Gartner needlepoint, so ensnared in debates about effeminacy and homosexuality, perhaps operated as a sort of 'closet', surreptitiously and subversively drawing and deflecting society's gaze.

## From 'penis envy' to 'oppression envy': Men and the 1970s 'needlepoint boom'

When George Platt Lynes died in 1955 he left unfinished his alphabet cushion cover. His younger brother, Russell, who was an art critic, pioneering design historian and managing editor of *Harper's Magazine*, completed it. Russell was also a 'secret needlepointer', and also like George, one of his earliest memories was of his mother's 'church sewing group'.[62] However, by the 1960s Russell's needlepoint, rather unexpectedly, was to be thrust into the spotlight in debates about the relation of needlepoint to postwar painting. Lynes often stated that he started embroidering in the 1950s as a sort of therapy and then for pleasure replacing his Sunday painting.[63] He did, however, later note the influence of visiting his brother during the 1940s in his New York studio, or at Stoneblossom, and watching him as 'he worked on his needlepoint'.[64] Although Lynes often played down his interest in needlepoint he must have felt committed and confident enough as he entered and won first prize in the 'men's class' of the National Exhibition of Amateur Needlework of Today in November 1957.[65] This panel, which depicted a 'peacock', had already been reproduced in Mary

Brooks Picken and Doris White's *Needlepoint Made Easy: Classic and Modern* (1955). In 1970 he penned an introduction to Picken and White's *Needlepoint for Everyone* (1970), which included a chapter 'Men and Needlepoint', surveying the work of a range of contemporary male practitioners by way of reference to historical precedents such as work by sailors and even the Duke of Windsor who 'learned the art from his mother'.[66] By 1970 Lynes was one of most high-profile male needleworkers in America and was approached by the literary agent Gloria Safier asking if he would be 'interested in doing a book on needlepoint for men?'[67] Safier explained she had brokered deals for other 'celebrities', such as the actor Sylvia Sidney, to publish such books that were proving remarkably popular with the public.[68] Lynes declined the offer but later reflected:

> A year or so ago I was asked to do a needlepoint book for men. I was tempted, but I'm deep in writing another book. It occurred to me that it should include sckrimshaw [*sic*] and crocheting and macramé (all traditionally done by sailors) plus a chapter on tattooing … one of the older needle-crafts, surely.[69]

Not long after this Lynes was also asked to review the re-issue by the Arno press of a well-known volume on Victorian needlework – Sophia Caulfeild and Blanche Saward's *Dictionary of Needlework*.[70] As an amateur Lynes was less enthusiastic than the publishers, but he was struck by some unexpected parallels: 'What today is called needlepoint [today] was called "Berlin Work" in Victorian times.' As a self-confessed 'Victoriana buff and one-stitch needlepointer', Lynes found the volume's technical instructions largely 'incomprehensible', but he remained curious as to the timing of the publication with the popular surge of interest in needlecrafts, what he termed, the 'needlepoint boom'. Lynes expanded his book review to include an overview and analysis of the phenomenon with particular emphasis on his own experience, as a man, within it: 'There is an increasing handful of men who have no self-consciousness about plying needles and who are willing to look you straight in the eye while they do it.'[71] He concluded, 'The reprinting of a Victorian how-to-do-it book suggests that there may be a closer affinity between the Americans of the nineteen-seventies and those of the eighteen-seventies than we think.'[72] In postwar America leisure activities became 'a mass phenomenon', in a comparable way the Industrial Revolution had ushered in a similar movement in nineteenth-century Britain.[73] Hobbycrafts although hugely popular are often elided in historical studies of the postwar and postmodern cultural landscape. Women's art, and by implication any form of feminized craft, was emphatically excluded from the conceptualization of a new monumental and hypermasculine art. Known under the banner of Abstract Expressionism this loose group of largely male painters eschewed the feminine, and effeminate, and contemporary critics often talked about their work with reference to the language of sexological and psychoanalytic discourse. Clement Greenberg's 1946 statement that 'emotion' in the paintings of Jackson Pollock 'does not have to be castrated and translated in order to be put into a picture' accepts masculinity as 'feeling' so long as it is in no way feminine.[74] The construction of modern painting as essentially masculine re-positioned women, and women's activities, as defined through their 'lack' (of penis/phallic power), reductively collapsing the feminine with the notion of 'penis envy'. If critics, such as Greenberg, worked hard to diminish the mundane trivialities of everyday domesticity from housework to shopping to indulgences such as novels and needlepoint then advocates of popular culture, such as Lynes, sought to counter the hegemonic masculinity embedded in such thinking by destabilizing the binary structure of painting/craft, highbrow/kitsch, masculine/feminine.

In several essays and articles Lynes made direct reference to many of Greenberg's ideas and sought to parody the arid formalism of his approach. For instance, Lynes's 1949 article, 'Highbrow, Lowbrow, Middlebrow', directly satirizes the elitist posturing of Greenberg and specifically his comments on the aggressive expansion of middlebrow culture whose 'avenues of penetration have become infinitely more difficult to detect and block'.[75] By the 1960s the increasing social prominence of hobbycrafts saw Lynes's article reprinted and he was inspired to devise a project to highlight the prevalence of and authority ascribed to Greenbergian ideas that continued to prevail undiminished. Under the aegis of the magazine *Art in America* Lynes arranged an exhibition at the FAR Gallery in New York, during May 1968, of small needlepoint panels made after designs by thirteen contemporary artists.[76] The artists included Gene Davis, Leonard Baskin, Walter Murch, Carol Summer, William Copley, Richard Anuszkiewicz, Chryssa, Frank Stella, Lorser Feitelson, George Ortman, Cleve Gray, Alfonso Ossorio and Roy Lichtenstein, who 'were selected not only for their distinction, but because of the variety of their approaches – op, pop, hard edge, abstract expressionism, poetic realism, figurative, assemblage and light'.[77] Each design was to be fully made up for the exhibition and then ten were selected to be sold as pre-designed kits that could be made up at home. Lynes commented:

> For many years needlepoint has unfortunately been considered a suitably genteel pastime (like china painting and pyrography a century ago) only for otherwise unoccupied ladies – a sort of parlor version of occupational therapy. It deserves better than that. It is a medium exacting in its precision but relatively subtle. Wool has a built-in luminous quality that cannot be imitated in any other medium, and the colors in which it is dyed or which it can create (it can be mixed almost like paint) are limitless.[78]

For the exhibition, pointedly entitled *The Mesh Canvas*, Lynes embroidered several of the designs himself with 'some of the canvases left unfinished to show the process' of fabrication.[79] He was helped in making up the designs by three women, the writer Mary Jean Kemper, the collector Vera List and Antoinette 'Toiny' Fraissex du Bois, an art dealer who was married to gallery owner Leo Castelli. Leo Castelli represented several of the artists involved in the project, such as Frank Stella, who had a series of important one-man shows at Castelli's Gallery in the 1960s. Stella only agreed to supply designs for cushion covers, after his *Concentric Squares* series (1961), if they were made up by Toiny Castelli and afterwards remained in Castelli's private collection (Figure 4.8).[80] Toiny Castelli also made cushion covers after Andy Warhol's 'flowers [but] in gros point', but these were not included in the exhibition.[81] Writing in *Art in America*, Lynes further suggested the exhibition could be seen as transforming prevailing stereotypes of needlework: 'If this display of distinguished modern needlepoint designs helps to shoo out some of the cute and genteel nonsense that clutters the wool shops (and hence the living rooms) of America, that would be almost justification enough.'[82]

Following the exhibition Lynes was consulted by organizations such as American Needlepoint Guild and the Embroiderers' Guild of America for advice about men's needlepoint; he was offered solos shows, invited to select, judge or submit work to various 'men's divisions' or 'gentlemen's corners', and the countless 'Golden Thimble' competitions. One invitation even tried to tempt him with the promise that his work would be displayed 'in good

**Plate 1** Elaine Reichek, *Sampler (Hercules)*, 1997, hand embroidery on linen, 22 x 17¼ in. (55.9 x 45.1 cm), Collection Melva Bucksbaum, Photo. Adam Reich, © Elaine Reichek.

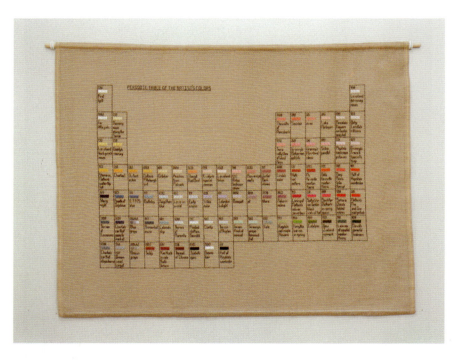

**Plate 2** Stephen Beal, *Periodic Table of the Artist's Colors*, 2004, hand-embroidered cotton floss, cotton canvas, 30 x 36 in. (76.2 x 91.4 cm), © Museum of Arts and Design, New York, Collection of Mr and Mrs Robert Lipp, 2007, Photo. Ed Watkins, 2008.

**Plate 3** William Morris, *If I Can*, 1857, wool and cotton thread on cloth, 66.3 x 73.5 in. (168.5 x 187 cm), Photo. Courtesy of Bridgeman Images. © Kelmscott Manor, Oxfordshire/Society of Antiquities of London.

**Plate 4** Fine Cell Work/Inmates of HMP Wandsworth in collaboration with the Victoria and Albert Museum, *HMP Wandsworth Quilt*, 2010, pierced, appliquéd and embroidered cotton on linen, 76.7 x 102 in. (195 x 260 cm), acquired with support of the Friends of the V&A, © Victoria and Albert Museum, London (T.27–2010).

**Plate 5** Jim Hodges, *Here's Where We Will Stay*, 1995, printed nylon, painted chiffon and silk head scarves with thread, embroidery, sequins, 216 x 204 in. (548.6 x 518.2 cm) overall, Photo. Mark Bower, © Christie's Images/Bridgeman Images, © Jim Hodges, Courtesy of Gladstone Gallery, New York and Brussels.

**Plate 6** Ernest Thesiger embroidering at home, 6 Montpelier Terrace, Knightsbridge, London, undated press photo, *c*.1920s/30s, EFT/000161, Ernest Thesiger Archive, © The University of Bristol Theatre Collection/ArenaPAL.

**Plate 7** Russell Lynes embroidering at home, 427 East 84th Street, New York, published in 'The Pleasure of Making It.' *House & Garden*, 142(1) (July 1972): 51, © The Estate of Russell Lynes, Photo. Courtesy of Dean Brown/House & Garden, © Condé Nast.

**Plate 8** Charles LeDray, *Army, Navy, Air Force, Marines*, 1993, fabric, wire, vinyl, silkscreen, zipper, 26¾ x 54 in. (67.9 x 137.2 cm) overall. Photo. Courtesy of the artist and Peter Freeman, Inc. Private Collection, Houston, TX. Photo. Tom Powel, © Charles LeDray.

**Plate 9** Grayson Perry, *Turner Prize Dress*, 2003, silk, lace, polyester and cotton, 38 ⅝ x 36 x 4 ⅜ in. (98 x 66 x 11 cm), Courtesy of the artist and Victoria Miro Gallery, London/Venice, © Grayson Perry.

**Plate 10** Nicolas Moufarrege, *Untitled* (detail), 1985, thread, pre-printed needlepoint canvas, fabric and needlepoint canvas 18 x 31 in. (45.7 x 78.7 cm), © The Artist's Estate, Courtesy Nabil Mufarrej and Gulnar 'Nouna' Mufarrij, Photo. Neil Johnson for Visual AIDS, New York.

**Plate 11** Nick Cave, *Soundsuit #5*, 2010, mixed media – knitted fabric with appliquéd found flowers, embroidery, sequins, metal armature, © Nick Cave. Courtesy of the artist and Jack Shainman Gallery, New York.

**Plate 12** Jochen Flinzer, *53 Wochen Glück (53 Weeks of Happiness)* (detail), 1994–5, embroidery thread on silk, 169 x 12.7 in. (430 x 32.5 cm), Photo. © MMK Museum für Moderne Kunst Frankfurt am Main, Photo. Axel Schneider, © Jochen Flinzer, Courtesy Thomas Rehbein Galerie, Köln.

**Plate 13** Francesco Vezzoli with an embroidery hoop in front of a display of his *Crying Divas from The Screenplays of an Embroiderer*, 1999, thirty black-and-white laser prints on canvas with metallic embroidery, each frame 13 x 17 in. (33 x 43.2 cm), overall 39 x 194 ⅞ in. (99.1 x 494.9 cm), Photo. Giorgio Lotti/Archivio Giorgio Lotti/Mondadori Portfolio/Getty Images.

**Plate 14** Chan-Hyo Bae, *Existing in Costume 1*, 2006, C-print, 31.1 x 25.1 in. (79 x 64 cm), Photo. © Chan-Hyo Bae.

**Plate 15** James Merry and Björk, *Moth* headpiece for *Vulnicura* tour, 2015, Photo. © Santiago Felipe.

**Plate 16** Nicholas Hlobo, *Macaleni iintozomlambo*, 2010, ribbon on tea paper, 30.3 x 41.3 in. (77 x 105 cm), © Tate London, 2018 © Nicholas Hlobo, Courtesy Stevenson Gallery, Cape Town, South Africa.

**Figure 4.8** Frank Stella ('and Mrs. Leo Castelli'), *Cushion Covers*, wool on needlepoint canvas, 15 x 15 in. (38 x 38 cm), originally published in Russell Lynes, 'The Mesh Canvas'. *Art in America* 56(3) (May/June 1968): 43, © The Estate of Russell Lynes.

company with Queen Mary's famous carpet'.[83] But aside from this Lynes's *Mesh Canvas* project seemed to have stimulated little interest. Mostly letters and enquiries were about where to purchase the pre-designed kits. Reaction largely came from women. The tapestry artist Gloria F. Ross wrote 'a straight fan letter' in which she suggested her work, translating the designs of painters into large tapestries, was analogous to Lynes's project. She also disclosed that she had made, for private use, a few small needlepoint objects herself from designs drawn after the large abstract canvases by her sister, the painter Helen Frankenthaler.[84] However, other reactions bordered on the hostile:

> –Your featured designs by artists who obviously had no knowledge of the work done in this country and cared less … Your illustrations were really insulting to the many women who are working in the medium;
> –I must admit to considerable disappointment that your experiment was on so elementary a level … It may be that you are not aware of the revolution that has been happening in the field of needlework

–By your suggestions of someone else executing another artist's designs you are putting needlepoint right back where it was a few years ago. A skill, not a craft.[85]

A few men wrote to Lynes including one who started needlepointing in his seventies and had recently entered a 'needlepoint foot stool' in the Kentucky State Fair for which he 'won a Blue Ribbon'.[86] Clearly, Lynes had hoped the project would bring some attention to the feelings of shame, as much as pleasure, experienced by the male needleworker. In an earlier interview he stated: 'No man who does needlepoint is, I suspect, entirely unself-conscious about engaging in a branch of what a century ago was called "fancy work." I am no exception.'[87] In 1972, Lynes was photographed in his East 84th Street home embroidering for an interview in *House & Garden* (Plate 7) in which he stated: 'It still takes a certain amount of gall, however, for a man to do needlepoint in public in America.'[88]

In 1974 Lynes received an invitation to write something more substantial on 'men in needlework' for a proposed special issue of new trade paper entitled 'National Needlework News'. The issue was to be dedicated to the subject of 'Men's Lib', a play on the Women's Liberation Movement, the editor, Sherry Baker, informed Lynes.[89] The idea humorously referred to the growing response, from straight men, to the critique of hegemonic masculinity offered by civil rights, feminist and the gay liberation movements. Men seemed suddenly alert to the fact that sex roles oppressed not only women but men too and that they were equally defined and measured against proscribed ideals and stereotypes. Men's liberation was initially formulated from feminist groups but soon splintered into a feminist-inspired men's movement and another that reverted to conservative and patriarchal models of preserving male power and privilege, which they felt had been eroded. The latter has been characterized as 'a curious mixture of a social movement and psychological self-help manual', and even, at times, as a kind of 'oppression envy'.[90] In the 1970s the various studies of masculinity turned from a trickle to a flood. Whilst such studies probed the masculine subject from every conceivable angle they perpetuated an essentially Victorian idea of men's needlework.[91] Sewing remained domestic labour and retained its historic feminine associations. 'Only sissies or "fags" play with girls', stated one author while another gave over a whole chapter to 'No "Sissy Stuff"'.[92]

The feminist reclamation of culturally devalued practices associated with domesticity and women's history, such as needlework, is well known but the many needlecraft books published in the 1970s by men remain obscure. Acknowledgement and analysis of men's needlework were far from absent in feminist discourse. From the 'castrated' husband who covets his wife's professional success but redeems his phallic power when his knitting is revealed as a triumph in Carol Shields's novel *Small Ceremonies* (1976), to the open acknowledgement of the men who supplied labour, including sewing skills, to Chicago's *Dinner Party* project (1974–9), feminists were attuned to the gendering intrinsic to craft.[93] One of the most influential needleworkers of the period Nina Mortellito, who established the enormously successful Nina Needlepoint store and mail order business in 1970, observed by then that needlepoint 'is no longer considered strictly a "women's hobby" (many men have evinced great interest and aptitude in doing it)'.[94] It was the popular appeal of women such as Mortellito or Erica Wilson, the self-styled 'Julia Child of Needlework', which was responsible for stimulating the revival of interest in needlework in the 1960s and 1970s.[95] Wilson was British-born and had trained at the Royal School of Needlework, and established a needlework empire in America that encompassed stores in New York and elsewhere, a dozen 'how-to' books, a show on PBS, a national syndicated newspaper column entitled 'Needleplay' and dozens of mail-order needlework kits, which brought in an estimated $1 million annually. By the 1970s, like many other women who taught, sold or simply made needlepoint, Wilson's example was encouraging a 'younger generation of women (and a few men)' to take up embroidery 'as self-expression and as defiance of a machine-made consumerscape'.[96] Wilson's first book, *Crewel Embroidery* (1962), sold over 1 million copies and quickly became a bestseller.[97] It was the first fiber craft book issued by her publisher, Charles Scribner Jr., who later recalled that it was Wilson's example that initiated the 'how-to' craft book 'bandwagon' that 'amounted to a literary revolution'.[98]

However, the 1970s needlework books by men are today largely forgotten. Possibly indefensible, and largely opportunistic, they seemed to bypass contemporary feminist debates about needlework as women's history and instead, at times, reflect back something of the phallic charge of modernism. Yet in a curious inversion of the gender hierarchy that characterized modern art, it is men who go footnoted in the narrative of needlework's popular revival in the period. Even in criticism of the 'how-to' craft book phenomenon all critique and commentary were directed at women as consumers and authors.[99] In reassessing the feminist interest in needlework in the 1970s Rachel Maines detected a dichotomy where women working with such crafts fell into two distinct categories, that of artists positioned as oppositional, vanguard and modern, such as Judy Chicago or Miriam Schapiro, and the 'quieter but firmer voices of the mainstream', or the middlebrow 'like the embroiderer Jacqueline Enthoven', author of several popular books.[100] Any man who took up needlework in the 1970s may have aspired to the first but definitely belonged to the second camp. Maines, with her encyclopaedic knowledge of needlework, suggested a few, including 'art critic Jonathan Holstein, weaver-writer Jack Lenor Larsen, sculptor Claes Oldenburg, quilter Michael James, bannermaker Norman La Liberté, football player Roosevelt Grier, and actor Henry Fonda'.[101] Nearly all of these men designed and made their own work and some, such as the actor Henry Fonda, prompted discussion as to the transformative meaning of a feminized craft upon masculinity. Fonda was the embodiment of the 'honesty' and 'morality' at the heart of the concept of modern American masculinity and unlike contemporaries, such as Rock Hudson, he was vocal in his support of male needleworkers.[102] Other men, such as the theatre and film director Morton DaCosta, who after a string of hit Broadway shows in the 1950s was ordered to take up needlepoint for his 'nervous disease'. His subsequent book, *Morton DaCosta's Book of Needlepoint* (1974), was predicated on helping men see the potential of needlepoint as not just a relaxing hobby but a reparative practice.

However, for many male artists the desire to incorporate needlework into their practices relied on women's skills, and labour, to make their work. For example, Patty Mucha, who was married to Claes Oldenburg from 1960 to 1970, made his soft sculptures on a portable Singer sewing machine; and Jonathan Holstein in his selection of work for the hugely influential *Abstract Design in American Quilts* exhibition at the Whitney Museum of American Art in 1971 was criticized for reinforcing the essential femininity of traditional needlecrafts, by marginalizing the role of his partner Gail van der Hoof in terms of his collecting and curation practices.[103] Joan Scobey and Lee Parr McGarth's *Celebrity Needlepoint* (1972) catalogued several other instances: from Louis Nizer known at one time as the 'highest paid lawyer in the world', representing everyone from Salvador Dalí to Mae West, who made needlepoint designs after famous modern paintings, which were then stitched by his wife, Mildred Nizer, to Aline Saarinen, the art critic, who made a pair of needlepoint sleepers 'designed in geometrics' by her husband, Eero Saarinen, the modernist architect.[104] As Lucy Lippard suggested in her analysis of the amateur needlecraft movement of the 1970s (written very much as a response to exhibitions such as Holstein's quilt show at the Whitney), when a man involved himself with the 'fripperies' of domestic craft that 'as well as dignifying the frippery by his participation', in the end it 'tends to raise the sphere rather than lower the man'.[105] Writing of this same context Rozsika Parker concurred: 'The effort to overthrow the hegemony of the fine arts by merging them with the applied arts tended to benefit painting rather than embroidery; to modify masculinity rather than to transform femininity.'[106] However, Scobey and McGrath pointed to another group of men, typified by Russell Lynes, who designed and made their own work.

Men like Russell Lynes or Rosey Grier may have been vocal in their support of men's needlework, but by the 1970s anxiety surrounding the feminizing potential of needlecrafts neither disappeared nor dissipated. So men devised strategies to justify working with domestic crafts – from associating sewing with painting, as in Inman Cook and Daren Pierce's *Pleasures of Needlepoint* (1972) (issued as part of the Betty Crocker Home Library), to play with 'soft' and 'hard' language as in Mark Dittrick's *Hard Crochet* (1978), or remasculinization of the male image as in Dave Fougner's *The Manly Art of Knitting* (1972), with its cover image of a cowboy on horseback looking *über* macho but who is, in fact, knitting. Indeed, in supporting or validating a feminine craft in any way, men needed to assert not just their masculinity but their heterosexuality. Erica Wilson's husband, the furniture designer Vladimir Kagan, when asked by a journalist at *People* magazine about his interest in his wife's needlework, replied: 'It took my mind off sex.'[107] Such assertions in reference to men's needlework could assert the masculine but also suffuse it with coded homoeroticism. In Robert Illes's *Men in Stitches* (1975), with its title page drawing of football players, in a locker room, stitching on an embroidery trestle table (Figure 4.9) but inside in a later description of a baseball game (all within the context of discussing needlework), Illes eroticizes 'the jock':

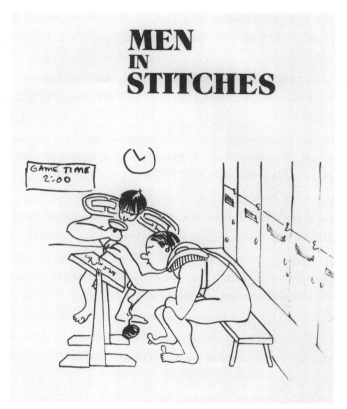

**Figure 4.9** Frontispiece from Robert E. Illes, *Men in Stitches* (New York: Van Nostrand Reinhold Co., 1975), Courtesy of John Wiley & Sons.

When you take up stitchery, you can still log plenty of TV-sportscast time. What you are doing is *something* while the guys on the field *ain't* … what is there to see while the pitcher looks at his shoes, kicks the dirt, inspects his cleats, looks at first base, checks left field, cases the hot number in the third row, looks at his fingers, spits in his mitt, wonders why miniskirts went out of style, pulls down his cap, adjusts his scrotum, leans over, looks at the catcher, shakes his head, nods his head, stands up, bosoms the ball, and gets set to pitch – just in time for the batter to step out of the batter's box, spit on *his* hands, kick around in *his* dirt, pull on *his* cap, sneak a look at the third-row cutie, lean over, pick up dirt, hate pantsuits, get the stickum bag, step up to the plate, adjust *his* scrotum, wave his bat, glare at the pitcher, stand there, and watch a strike go whistling by? … you [can] continue to stitch through all this choreography.[108]

The allegation that men were appropriating what women had earnestly been rediscovering is implicit in the press blurb for Illes's book cover, which states: 'Good-bye samplers and antimacassars – stitching lib is here!' This use of needlepoint to soften the stereotype of an aggressive, sexualized masculinity embodied in the archetype of the sportsman was not isolated. Mikel Shulman, the so-called Picasso of sports needlepoint, founded a business making needlepoint designs, of sports logos and sporting imagery, and successfully marketed them to men in the 1970s, many of them professional football players or their devoted fans.[109]

Of all these books by men perhaps the most popular, and best known even today, is Rosey Grier's *Needlepoint for Men* (1973) (Figure 4.10). Unlike nearly all the books encouraging men to take up needlepoint, in the wider revitalization of 'how-to' craft books, Grier's remains exceptional in that it does not reflect an image of a middle-class, middlebrow white male. Raised on a farm in Georgia in the late 1930s Grier later recalled that like the exploitation of women's domestic labour 'racial suppression was woven into the fabric of life'.[110] The imperatives in Grier's book are subtler and stress a sense of the collaborative and the wider societal benefits of craft. Grier, a former professional football player (for the New York Giants and the LA Rams), includes a full section entitled 'Other Men in Needlepoint'.[111] Grier looked to history, to the '*Opus Anglicanum* [which] was developed in medieval England by men', to confirm needlepoint's masculine lineage.[112] He also countered the equation of the male needlepointer with the 'sissy'. Grier recalled how and why he first decided to take up needlepoint affirming not just his masculinity but his heterosexuality: 'If you are going to "jive" with the ladies ... you had better learn how to do needlepoint.'[113] Grier only agreed to write his book after a feature in the *New York Times* showing him in the act of needlepointing brought him to the attention of a publisher.[114] Images of Grier sewing appeared also on the covers of the *Saturday Evening Post* and as a centrefold in *Look*.[115] In May 1971, *Life* magazine ran a feature, to tie-in with Holstein's quilt exhibition opening at the Whitney, on how men were 'invading the sewing circle' and in which they interviewed several men who had taken up needlecrafts, from embroidery to dressmaking (Figure 4.11), as well as an example of a dressmaking class, operating under the name 'the Executive Sewing School for Men run by the McCall Pattern Company', and

114     *Queering the Subversive Stitch*

**Figure 4.10** *Rosey Grier's Needlepoint for Men* (New York: Walker and Co., 1973), Private Collection.

**Figure 4.11** 'Man That Needle'. *Life*, 70(20) (28 May 1971): 80–1, Images by Yale Joel and Michael Rougie, © Time Inc. All rights reserved. © 1971 Time Inc. All rights reserved. Reprinted/Translated from LIFE and published with the permission of Time Inc. Reproduction in any manner in any language in whole or in part without written permission is prohibited.

a knitting class taught by a social worker, Mandy Nix, from her Manhattan apartment both having all male pupils.[116] In an accompanying editorial as well as reference to the contemporary male needleworker, Ralph Graves, *Life*'s managing editor, pointed out that the English grandmother of Nina Moertellito and Jebba Maes, the sisters who both ran their own highly successful needlepoint business, 'used to sit and do needlepoint with the Duke of Windsor, who learned from his mother Queen Mary'.[117]

## Amateur needlework and avant-garde masculinity: From studio to factory

In 1967, writing in *Vogue* Clement Greenberg stated that the real achievement of modern art was its ability to escape 'madeness', to erase the mark of the hand and reference to the body.[118] Certainly, in the postwar era the 'finish fetish' that subsequently evolved into minimalism eradicated any sense of human touch or emotion and pushed artistic production, paradoxically, closer to the mass-produced, the consumerist, the very 'Kitsch' and 'ersatz culture' that Greenberg had earlier admonished. Ironically, then, Greenberg's valorization of 'inspiration, vision, intuitive decision' over 'manual skill', exemplified in the paintings of Jackson Pollock, aligned the apparent progressiveness of avant-garde art with the bourgeois values of mass culture in their shared desire to stabilize masculine identity. It could be suggested, then, that at this juncture the concept of the modern artist and the notion of hegemonic masculinity seemed to collapse into one another. This may well not have been Greenberg's intention, but looked at in another way the desire to remove the body from the production of art was also a desire to obviate any reference to the everyday, the ordinary and by implication the domestic and the feminine. Even if described as being made with 'skeins of liquid' Pollock's paintings were so codified in hypermasculine rhetoric, emanating in a large part from Greenberg's criticism, that a needlework analogy (as obvious as it is when you begin to look closely) failed to register any impact on the discourses of postwar art.[119] However, more recent critics, such as Andrew Perchuk, have read the ideas embodied in Pollock's work as 'attributable to many factors, among them the paintings' ability to satisfy, at least within the picture plane, some of the tensions and anxieties that were creating a masculinity crisis in the immediate postwar period'.[120]

As Michael Kimmel has argued, 'In the 1960s the "masculine mystique" – that impossible synthesis of sober, responsible breadwinner, imperviously stoic master of his fate, and swashbuckling hero – was finally exposed as a fraud.'[121] Since then many artists have interrogated, even if only within the privacy of the studio, the conceptualization of avant-garde masculinity that sometimes also alludes to the discourses of amateur needlecrafts. Ed Rossbach, one of the most influential makers and teachers of fiber arts in late twentieth-century America, for instance, stated, 'I have felt uncomfortable doing anything like sewing, darning, applique-ing, embroidering. I avoid it in my own work as somehow not appropriate activity for a man. Knitting also. Any of the textile techniques my sisters did.'[122] Yet he made work with 'macramé, braiding, looping, knotted netting, twining, coiling, and plaiting' and 'explored the techniques of needle and bobbin laces'.[123] In the series of works depicting kitschy icons from popular culture, such as his *Mickey Mouse Lace* (1971) (Figure 4.12), Rossbach references both the language used to dismiss feminine crafts (even if taught by a man), and also as an infantilizing image (of a cartoon character) it returns men's needlework to the maternal. In the 1960s and 1970s in an age of great social upheaval and cultural fragmentation embroidery became for men, Rozsika Parker has speculated, a sort of counter-cultural gesture, if for women it perpetuated the interlocking systems of femininity, fertility and fecundity: 'For men, long hair and embroidered clothing constituted a rebellious gesture against a hierarchical, puritanical, masculine establishment. However, this was less a subversion of sex roles than a longing for the freedom of an idealized image of childhood – mother-loved, anarchic and untouched by daddy's world.'[124] Not all men panicked at the feminine or maternal associations of needlework. Robert Rauschenberg is known for outsourcing his sewing to women, but he is also recorded as stitching himself, especially early on in his career. In the early 1950s his then wife, Susan Weil, has recalled he even made maternity dresses for her. It is also well known that one of the decisive influences on Rauschenberg was his childhood memories of watching his mother dressmaking on a domestic sewing machine. Sewing became critical in his later work and although acknowledged it is never analysed as something of significance in itself.

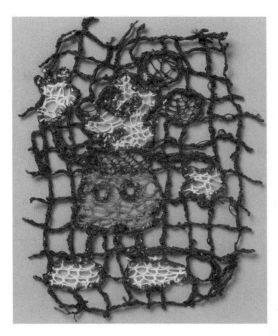

**Figure 4.12** Ed Rossbach, *Mickey Mouse Lace*, cotton and rayon needlepoint lace, 1971, 3½ x 3 in. (8.9 x 7.6 cm) © The Estate of Ed Rossbach, Photo. © The Museum of Fine Arts, Boston, The Daphne Farago Collection (2004–2111).

If since the Second World War, needlework was marked as middlebrow and meretricious, and stigmatized as emasculating and feminizing, it is easy to see why many men felt prohibited in taking it up or conflicted when they did so. Yet many men, like George Platt Lynes and those in his circle, seem attracted to it for this very reason, subversively loading it with queer signification. In the 1980s Andy Warhol's serial photographs, stitched together by Brigid Berlin on a sewing machine, continued this subversion of both medium and message. William Ganis has suggested Warhol's *recherché* use of black-and-white film allowed him to 'perform modernism' by visually connecting him to a canon of early twentieth-century male photographers with their emphatic masculinity and compulsory heterosexuality.[125] The subversive act of sewing the prints together into a grid (in groups of four and up to twelve) was as provocative as the use of male nudes, what Warhol called his 'porno pics' (Figure 4.13).[126] Indeed, one of the superstars of Warhol's Factory, the poet and photographer Gerard Malanga, recalled, 'Those dangling threads have an eroticism and sexual nuance about them,

**Figure 4.13** Andy Warhol, *Male Nude*, 1987, four photographs, silver gelatin print on paper and thread, 28 x 22 in. (71.1 x 55.9 cm) © Tate, London 2018 © The Andy Warhol Foundation for the Visual Arts, Inc/Licensed by DACS, London and ARS, New York, 2018.

as if they were symbolic pubic hairs.'[127] Warhol's fascination with 'the male body' was one of the ways that disclosed his 'queerness'.[128] A review of the 1987 exhibition of Warhol's sewn photographs linked them to Warhol's early hand-painted artwork from the early mid-1960s, which was drawn from images associated with popular culture, the domestic realm and childhood.[129] Warhol's queerness was fully apparent even in the 1960s, a decade when homophobia was so pervasive than *Time* magazine felt able to publish the bizarrely de-contextualized comment by the English writer Somerset Maugham that homosexuals were mostly 'failed artists', but they possess 'a wonderful gift for embroidery'.[130] The choice to return to the domestic act of sewing in his photographs was, for Warhol, affirmation of needlework's potential as a queer signifier that had evolved out of the disavowal of the feminine in the modern avant-garde.

5

# Masculinity and 'the politics of cloth': From the 'bad boys' of postmodern art to the 'boys that sew club' of the new millennium

Throughout the late twentieth century Rozsika Parker mapped the intersection of domestic craft techniques and feminist art practices on the pages of *Spare Rib* (1973–93). When assembling her archive into a book, in collaboration with Griselda Pollock that would confirm the central role art had played in the history of the Women's Liberation Movement, Parker was largely dependent on the ephemeral traces of exhibitions as institutional and critical engagement with much of the art she and Pollock documented was often negligible.[1] In a similar way men's engagement with craft practices such as needlework in the late twentieth and early twenty-first centuries can only be surveyed (in terms of presence as well as absence) through the temporality of exhibitions as such work has largely fallen outside the purview of collectors and critics. Following the publication of Parker's *Subversive Stitch* in 1984, two exhibitions held in Manchester's Whitworth Art Gallery and the Cornerhouse brought together much of the work discussed in the book. Both 'Embroidery in Women's Lives 1300–1900', curated by Jennifer Harris, and 'Women and Textiles Today', curated by Pennina Barnett, sought to explore Parker's contention that embroidery's reputation as 'homogeneously feminine rather than as the hugely diverse enterprise it is' helped relegate women to the margins of the art world where craft was often located.[2] Almost no reference was made of men in the historical or contemporary overviews of embroidery in either of these exhibitions aside from fleeting mention of the contemporary knitters Richard Rutt and Kaffe Fassett in the accompanying publication.[3]

Although the effacement of men and the collapsing of women into a single category were little commented on at the time (or since), these shows inspired several other less well-known exhibitions of needlework that would include work by men. For example, *Out of Time: Contemporary and Historical Embroidery and Stitch* at the Crafts Council Gallery in London (1992), *Under Construction: Exploring Process in Contemporary Textiles* at the same venue (1996) and *Craft* at the Richard Salmon Gallery in London (1997) all included needlework by men. Pamela Johnson curiously traced the impulses of contemporary experiments in textiles (by both men and women) back through a lineage of male postmodernists: Robert Rauschenberg's quilted bed, Claes Oldenburg's flaccid sculptures, Robert Morris's cut and draped fabrics, Michelangelo Pistoletto's rag piles and Joseph Beuys's handmade felt suit.[4] Similarly, Pennina Barnett thought the work in *Out of Time* was unconcerned with embroidery's history and reflected, if anything, the preoccupations of the modern avant-garde.[5]

In 1991, two subsequent exhibitions entitled *The Subversive Stitch*, organized independently in Australia and America, showed not just the reach of Parker's ideas but also an increasing gender variability. In Melbourne, at an exhibition at Monash University's Gallery, emphasis was placed on textiles that were, the curator Natalie King suggested, 'out-manoeuvring the closures and reductions of modernism', and included the work of at least one man.[6] In New York at Simon Watson's Gallery artists, such as Félix González-Torres, Jimmie Durham and Fred Wilson, were seen to be following the lead of feminist artists, such as Elaine Reichek and Faith Ringgold (who both also featured in this show), in focusing on the 'social meaning' as much as the 'aesthetic merit' of craft techniques such as sewing or knitting.[7] Two further major North American exhibitions inspired by Parker's book showed a much greater range of work by men. The large *Division of Labor: 'Women's Work' in Contemporary Art* exhibition at the Bronx Museum of the Arts, New York, in 1995 suggested that 'the very notion of fixed gender categories can no longer be assumed' as male artists such as Charles LeDray, Oliver Herring, Jim Isermann, Robert Kushner and Nicolas Moufarrege (all included in the show) were exploring the idea of masculinity through materials and practices traditionally associated with feminism.[8] Also taking her cue from *The Subversive Stitch*, the curator Marcia Tucker, in her survey of the current prevalence of craft in contemporary art, entitled *A Labor of Love*, organized for New York's New Museum of Contemporary Art the following year, noted a discernible rise in men, such as Jim Isermann and Mike Kelley (included in the show), 'who quilt, embroider, knit, crochet, sew, bead and do appliqué or needlepoint' and who (like many the women before them) desire to recoup 'traditional skills and materials and used them to newly trenchant and generative ends, indicating just how saturated with meaning they remain'.[9] Yet men also faced disapproval in their use of techniques so associated with constructions of the feminine. One art critic was compelled to comment about such work:

> Surely the irony has not escaped notice that when male artists appropriate domestic objects such as pots and pans (Haim Steinbach), slipcovers or a wedding dress (Robert Gober), tapestries (Meyer Vaisman), or crocheted blankets (Mike Kelley), they are accredited with engaging in the discourse of commodification, whereas the same artifacts have been essentially off-limits to female artists seeking to develop an authoritative voice.[10]

A man's use of amateur needleskills remained troubling in that it could be not only transgressive, in its play with gender non-conformity, but also conservative, in its validation of an essentialized 'avant-garde' masculine ideal through the authority and agency accorded to transgression. In many instances men's needlework became absorbed into the discussion of a 'bad boy' stereotype. For the artist and critic Laura Cottingham the term 'bad boys' referred not just to male artists, who consciously played with a lineage stretching back to modernism's male avant-garde but those who also consciously co-opted aspects of feminism's radicalism. She saw it as originating in recent discussions of 'the white boy as abstraction', and from Adrian Piper's description of 'artists engaged with various kinds of masculine assertion and the essentialization of a "male identity"' as 'bad little boys'.[11] These discussions took place against the backdrop of a series of exhibitions in the 1990s that sought to map the rise of 'bad girls' in the art world. Such exhibitions also provided some scope to reflect on why men also continued to work in ways traditionally associated with the feminine. Critics, such as Cottingham, remained anxious, however, about the lack of distinction between men's recent work and the paradigm-shifting feminist interventions of the 1970s and after, stingingly suggesting there should be a corresponding 'exhibition of Mike Kelley, Jeff Koons and Richard

Prince to be titled "Stupid Idiots".[12] The use of domestic crafts by the artist Mike Kelley in particular as 'signifiers of the "pathetic", "abject", or "failed"' was seen as reifying 'his bad boy masculinity' and rather than undermining the masculine subject it reasserted the primacy of male privilege.[13]

Many of the concerns about men's appropriation of women's needlecrafts found an echo in emerging debates about a new 'crisis of masculinity' that demonstrated, critics contended, the process by which 'male power can be consolidated through cycles of crisis and resolution, enabling men to deal with the threat of female power by absorbing and assimilating it'.[14] Mira Schor argued that Kelley's *More Love Hours than Can Ever Be Repaid* (1987) (Figure 5.1) was a literal plagiarism of Miriam Schapiro's *Wonderland* (1983).[15] And Faith Wilding added that such work by male artists amounted to 'a mere reversal of gender signifiers (while often funny and consciousness raising) does not seem

**Figure 5.1** Mike Kelley, *More Love Hours than Can Ever Be Repaid and the Wages of Sin*, 1987, stuffed fabric toys and afghans on canvas with dried corn; wax candles on wood and metal base, 120¾ × 151¾ × 31¾ in. (306.7 × 385.4 × 80.6 cm), Whitney Museum of American Art, New York; purchase with funds from the Painting and Sculpture Committee 89.13a-d. © Mike Kelley Foundation for the Arts. All Rights Reserved/VAGA at ARS, New York and DACS, London 2018.

to be enough to get rid of gender roles and stereotypes'.[16] The artist Robert Kushner who learnt to sew as a boy, and like Schapiro became associated with the anti-minimalist, pro-feminist Pattern and Decoration movement in the 1970s, was similarly reproached. Yet the curator Temma Balducci has argued:

> Two hundred years from now, if Schapiro's *Barcelona Fan* were discovered along with Kushner's *Aurora's Chador*, art historians of the future would find it difficult to understand why one might have been considered feminist and the other not. Their use of materials, their size, the ways they draw attention to methods of production associated with the domestic are strikingly familiar. It should go without saying that there is no feminist aesthetic that inheres in the work of Schapiro based on her gender or sex, no aesthetic accessible to only one half of the human race, and Kushner is not off the hook because he has a penis.[17]

In her analysis of how gender was being explored through new forms of 'transgression and subversion' in contemporary art, Marcia Tucker rejected criticism of her decision to include the work of men in the 'bad girls' exhibition she curated as it seemed 'counterproductive to turn away willing soldiers because of their gender, much less their age, race or class'.[18] While Meyer Vaisman's hybrid fusion of historic tapestry and kitschy popular imagery, Robert Gober's handsewn *Wedding Gown* (1989) (Figure 5.2) or the needlework of Joel Otterson was unfairly yoked to the banalities of 'bad boy logic', the critic James Lewis suggested such experiments with amateur and domestic crafts were actually of some significance for the subject.[19] Lewis suggested it was 'precisely the estrangement of men from sewing' in everyday life that gave such work its charge.[20] He argued that men's interest in domestic textile crafts

> is a little less prone to cliché than some of its apparent models; there are no homespun pities here, no paeans to the Ur-Woman, no truck given to the claim that domesticity is a woman's thing, and you wouldn't understand. Instead, as befits and honors the medium, work sewn by men has been everything from consoling to disturbing, and [has] proved – again, from another angle, toward another end – that 'women's work' is powerful and expressive enough to serve as the grounds for an esthetic practice equal to any, and that home life acts out its own complex account of the world.[21]

**Figure 5.2** Robert Gober, *Wedding Gown*, 1989, silk satin, muslin, linen, tulle, welded steel, 54¼ x 57 x 38½ in. (137.2 x 144.8 x 96.5 cm), © Robert Gober, Courtesy Matthew Marks Gallery.

The increasing range of needlecrafts produced by men from Mike Kelley's use of children's soft toy and soiled rugs and Charles LeDray's handsewn miniature clothes to Grayson Perry's transvestite alter-ego, Claire, dressed in baby-doll dresses, was rarely analysed in any depth, or in relation to feminist practice, and often collapsed into a sort of 'maternal fetishism'.[22] There was some truth in that characterization that such work reflected a 'return to the maternal', as Parker herself had termed it. But Kelley, LeDray and Perry were also actively engaged in modes of interrogation of their own gendered and sexual identities. Kelley's saccharine charity shop aesthetic disturbs rather than reinforces inscriptions of gender. He taught himself to sew as a teenager in order to antagonize and challenge his father's authority. LeDray was taught to sew as a young boy by his mother and his desire to 'make' continually returns him to that moment, hence his child-sized fabrications, which often upend the heroics and swagger of the masculine archetype as mediated, and fetishized, through uniforms, for example his *Army, Navy, Air Force, Marines* (1993) unstitches the power dynamics inherent in manly stereotypes by diminishing their scale (Plate 8).[23] Equally, Perry has stated his 'little girl dresses', such as the one he wore to receive the Turner Prize in 2003, stem from the suppression of feelings of 'sensitivity and vulnerability' in his boyhood (Plate 9).[24] Cary Levine has recently argued that the use of needlework to conflate 'canonical modernism and homespun knickknacks', in Kelley's work, needs to be read as 'in dialogue with' rather than in opposition to feminism.[25]

Postmodern masculinity, often defined in relation to changes in men's labour practices, has been also interpreted as shaped by feminist discourses.[26] At this historical juncture masculinity became a critical issue for feminists and for many men feminism became the liberating means to interrogate their own subjectivity as socially and culturally constructed.[27] The deconstruction of the masculine, through an exploration of the feminine, in the work of artists such as Kelley, or LeDray and Perry, directly paralleled the development of queer theory and its de-binarizing strategies in the 1990s and after. Men's interest in needlework may reflect in the words of Lynne Segal, 'the fashionably "postmodern" attention to surface, style and performance in re-staging and de-centring the gendered basis of power', but it further 'serves to emphasise the conceptual mutability of gender categories, exposing their survival as highly regulated performances'.[28] The rest of this final chapter brings together a range of case studies, from the postmodern to the post-millennial, that consider men's needlework (which I contend has been unfairly overlooked) made in the context of the AIDS epidemic; as modes of resistance to the assimilation of queerness into heteronormative modes of feeling in terms of private domesticity and public sex; and finally, in relation to contemporary debates about the politics inherent in making by hand.

## Men's needlework in the aftermath of AIDS: Sewing against silence

In *Love! Valour! Compassion!* (1998) a film version of Terence McNally's hit Broadway play, a group of eight gay male friends ponder life and love over a series of weekend breaks spanning three summers.[29] Of all the men, loosely grouped around the protagonist, Gregory, a Broadway choreographer, there are two who are HIV-positive: Buzz, a costume designer, who falls in love with James, a sweet, effeminate Englishman. As Gregory plans to put on a charity ballet, an all-male drag version of *Swan Lake*, it falls to Buzz and James to sew the dresses. However, as James's health begins to deteriorate, and we learn he is going to die of AIDS, his increasing physical fragility, his slipping into silence, is resisted in the unexpected image of him embroidering onto a tambour frame while sitting convivially amongst friends.[30] The act of sewing has a long history of association with sickness but also with subversion and it is in this historical moment that the latter seems to supplant the former. Originating in European sexological and psychiatric discourses of the late nineteenth century the collapsing of effeminacy and embroidery into one another was, by the late twentieth century, certainly a well-worn cliché, but during the 1980s and 1990s it was to take on a new melancholic resonance in the context of the AIDS epidemic.

In 1985 on a march to commemorate the murder of the San Francisco gay rights activist and city supervisor, Harvey Milk, and Mayor George Moscone, the young activist, Cleve Jones, encouraged people to bring signs with the names of those who had died of AIDS. When these were taped together onto the façade of a federal building, Jones recalls, it occurred to him that they looked like a patchwork quilt. Thinking of well-known examples of the quotidian textile being transformed into a 'homely, [yet] powerfully moving statement', like Judy Chicago's *Dinner Party*, Jones formulated the idea of the quilt as a memorial. He later recalled: 'That it was a woman who did the sewing was an important element. At the time, HIV was seen as a by-product of aggressive gay male sexuality; and it seemed that the homey image and familial associations of a warm quilt would counter that.'[31] The NAMES Project Memorial AIDS Quilt was formally inaugurated two years later and since then has become one of the largest and best-known memorials in the world finding continued resonance as according to the World Health Organization an estimated 70 million people have contracted the HIV virus since it was first detected and today there are 36.9 million people living with it.[32] Each individual panel, measuring 0.91 m x 1.8 m (the size of an average grave), commemorates someone who died of AIDS and was made by lovers, families and friends. It brought much attention to amateur sewing, as stitchers were drawn from all corners of America, and it not only encouraged and inspired gay men to learn how to sew but it further gave visibility to gay men who already had an interest in needlework. There were 'sewing bees in gay bars' and a revival of some of the small commercial producers of gay-interest needlepoint kits, such as 'Gary's Sew Gay Needlecrafts' (based in east Los Angeles), a survivor of the queer subcultural strand of the 'needlepoint boom' in the 1970s whose camp craft aesthetics fed into many panels of the AIDS Quilt.[33]

In an age touched by a renewed 'crisis of masculinity', there was also something of a 'panic' around straight men sewing for the AIDS Quilt, as Marita Sturken, Lena Williams and Peter Hawkins have all pointed out.[34] Many gay men, however, including those who had learnt to sew as boys, many of whom were documented in the literature surrounding the epidemic, such as Rod Schelbutt or John Miller, quickly put their skills to good use sewing against the silence that death by AIDS initially entailed in its stigmatization by organizations from the cultural and religious to the medical and legislative.[35] One of the most reproduced panels from the Quilt is that made by a young Texan as a memorial to himself. It reads: 'My name is Duane Kearns Puryear. I was born on December 20, 1964. I was diagnosed with AIDS on September 7, 1984 at 4:45 pm. I was 22 years old. Sometimes, it makes me very sad. I made this panel myself. If you are reading it, I am dead' (Figure 5.3). The panel was made by Puryear at a quiltmaking workshop at the Dallas Resource Center. In

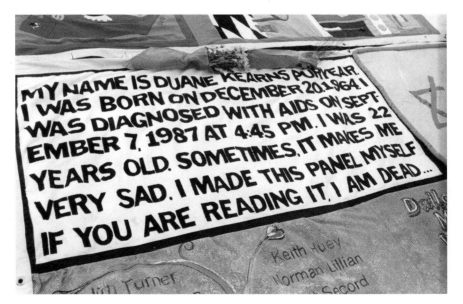

**Figure 5.3** 'My Name Is Duane Kearns Puryear...' NAMES Project Memorial Quilt, 1992, Courtesy the NAMES Project, Photo. Fred W. McDarrah, © Premium Archive/Getty Images.

October 1988 Puryear brought the panel to Washington for the second national display of the AIDS Quilt but lost it on the return flight home to Dallas. After he died his mother recreated the panel from a photograph that was taken of her son holding it in Washington.[36] The panel, in a way, returns us to Cleve Jones's original comment about the appeal of the AIDS Quilt to the wider public through the analogy between sewing and the domestic, the feminine and the maternal. But in Puryears's panel something new emerges in the affect generated by the layers of mother and son stitching against sorrow and silence. Like the image of James embroidering in *Love! Valour! Compassion!* (itself, perhaps, a well-placed, and conscious, nod to contemporary AIDS stitchers), or that of the artist David Wojnarowicz sewing his lips shut in his film *Fire in the Belly* (1986–7), sewing against censorship and effacement, making the personal the political, was one of the most affective legacies of the AIDS Quilt. Few other textiles of the twentieth century dissolve and render obsolete the mechanisms of binary gender. Contemporaneous with the publication of Parker's *The Subversive Stitch* the AIDS Quilt is, quite literally, the realization of her hope that embroidery could be a 'revolutionary art'.[37]

Ironically, needlework by gay men who lived with HIV or who died of AIDS is little documented, outside that associated with the Quilt. As a result, the work of several significant artists is often overlooked – in relation not only to the cultural impact of the AIDS crisis but also to the cultural history of needlework. The artist Nicolas Moufarrege, part of the legendary East Village art scene in early 1980s New York, made embroideries that drew on high art (eighteenth-century painting and modernist abstraction), vernacular and popular cultures (from Egyptian hieroglyphics to comic books and Disney cartoons) and queer subculture (in homoerotic imagery).[38] Although picking and mixing motifs from immediately recognizable artworks by a pantheon of male masters, from Pierre-Auguste Renoir, Edvard Munch and Pablo Picasso to Yves Klein, Katsushika Hokusai and the anonymous craftsmen of Islamic art, the kitschiness of the juxtapositions, often with images of Spiderman, the Silver Surfer, Donald Duck, and their fabrication with needle and thread destabilize the masculine authority inherent in modern art. Furthermore, the layering of cultural references moves the work beyond commentary on commoditization, through its frequent referencing of the artist's multiculturalism (born in Egypt, raised in Beirut, trained in Paris, living in New York), which has been called his 'special brand of Orientalism'.[39] Indeed, as the curator Dean Daderko has aptly commented, Moufarrege's embroideries possess a particular relevance to our age of 'queer issues of transnational migration'.[40] Like other artists before him Moufarrege explored the abject nature of amateur craft, and its relational pull to the culture of high art, through the use of commercially available pre-prepared needlepoint kits. One example, arranged in a diptych format, has on the left a double needlepoint canvas, unstitched, of *Le Chiffres d'amour d'après Fragonard*, and on the right adjoined to it is a needlepoint copy of Roy Lichtenstein's *Spray* (Plate 10).[41] The woman's hand with the aerosol spray in the Lichtenstein image almost seems to be spraying graffiti onto the Fragonard, onto which Moufarrege has stitched his name, in thick letters, in deep, sparkling, disco blues and reds. These are subtle references both to black, urban subculture, in graffiti and to queer subculture in the reference to disco, which as Douglas Crimp has pointed out 'mirrored the ethos of gay liberation' in its 'expansion of affectional possibility'.[42] Needlework here becomes imbricated in a process of 'disidentification', of transgression as transformation, in its subversion of dominant and counter-cultures to forge new visual strategies for the artist. As José Esteban Muñoz has commented, 'Like melancholia, disidentification is an ambivalent structure of feeling that works to retain the problematic object and tap into the energies that are produced by contradictions and ambivalences.'[43]

For the artist José Leonilson, like Moufarrege, sewing also became a central motif in his work. He had been inspired early on by the fantastical embroideries of Arthur Bisop Rosário, and the proto-feminist work of Lygia Clark in his native Brazil, where he had learnt to sew as a boy. After he was diagnosed HIV-positive in 1991 Leonilson worked intensely in embroidery often referencing the traditional format of quilts or samplers.[44] In *O Penélope* Leonilson stitched together ten small panels of diaphanous fabrics (Figure 5.4). Gauze, netting and voile are patchworked together to form a structure that references both the quilt and the shroud. The title is in reference to Penelope, wife of Odysseus in Homer's *Odyssey*, who fearing her husband's death in the Trojan War refuses her predatory new suitors by making a shroud to mourn her loss. Each day she weaves and each night she unpicks the thread so it is never finished and she is never free. Referencing ideas of making and unmaking are layered here,

**Figure 5.4** José Leonilson, *O Penélope*, 1993, thread on voile, 90.1 x 31.4 in. (229 x 80 cm), © Tate, London 2018 © Projeto Leonsilson.

for Leonilson, as he uses in his Portuguese title the masculine article and feminine noun to disrupt the inevitability of gender.

José Leonilson died from an AIDS-related illness in 1993; Nicolas Moufarrege had died from the virus in 1985. The 'focus on loss and mortality in the era of AIDS' in their needlework finds an extension in the knitted objects and performances of the German-born, New York-based, artist Oliver Herring in the early 1990s.[45] Herring's knitted work began in response to the death of the drag queen, actor and writer, Ethyl Eichelberger, who committed suicide in 1990 after becoming unable to tolerate the then only available medication used to treat HIV-related conditions. As a body of work, it is a deeply personal gesture of mourning and memorializing and akin to the elegiac portraits of Eichelberger by Peter Hujar and Nan Goldin. Using the unfamiliar material of transparent Mylar tape (employed for its light-absorbing and reflective properties) Herring constructed a large flower (beauty used to mask grief) and then a series of 'knit sculptures', often coats and blankets. Janet Koplos suggested such objects became 'surrogates' for the artist.[46] However, it was not so much the finished artwork that becomes the 'transitional object', but rather the reparative process of making itself.[47] Made as offerings, like gifts, Herring has said that the passage of time inherent in handmaking became consoling in the moment of loss.[48] Needlework, in this instance, becomes a means to deal with 'feelings and thoughts', a form of what Eve Kosofsky Sedgwick has called 'reparative reading'.[49] Rather than suspiciously viewing men's needlework as simply a reworking of the feminist reclamation of women's history, Sedgwick's concept of the 'reparative', over the 'paranoid', offers a much richer way to index, appreciate and remember instances of queering 'the subversive stitch'.

## Sewing away shame: From queer domesticity to gay pornography

Surveying work by contemporary male artists the American critic and curator Stefano Catalani recently suggested that as feminists in the 1970s had 'reclaimed traditional techniques such as sewing, hooking, quilting and embroidery', today male artists are investing in 'feminine fiber materials, processes, and traditions to question and disenfranchise stereotypes at work in their lives as a result of societal codes of conduct'.[50] These artists, Catalani suggests, employ needlework not just to unsettle the inscription of the domestic as essentially and exclusively feminine but further they point to the queer resignification of the domestic as erotic. Nathan Vincent's life-size crocheted *Locker Room* (2011), the site of many gay boy's humiliation and homoerotic fantasy, like Ben Cuevas's knitted *Jockstrap* (2014), disrupts and disturbs masculinist and elitist modes of installation and performance not just through their 'homely' stitching but by returning to the moment of queer awakening, the first time many gay men perceive, and begin to question, their sexuality and gender identity (in the overtly homosocial context of sport). Craft, these examples suggest, can be deployed to expose masculinity as a myth that is both constructed and contested. But Vincent and Cuevas are interested in how identity is shaped through the cultural stigmatization of effeminacy, inherent in the image of the male needleworker, which in their work becomes eroticized for the viewer.

Vincent's crocheting takes place out of sight but Cuevas's performance is dependent on the spectacle of his (naked) body making and modelling the jockstrap. Not only the erotic investment in the effeminate embroiderer but further the use of homoerotic imagery as a source for men's needlework have been pronounced in recent years.

The very recent acceptance of gay men and women into heteronormative narratives of domestic life, monogamous union and the nuclear family and the eliding of existing (and historic) strategies of resistance through queer desire and kinship has been criticized as the co-option and depoliticization of everything queer by prevailing neoliberal politics in Western countries.[51] The process of assimilation has drawn much commentary by queer artists often working in collaborative ways (like earlier feminists) and who use craft not just to investigate the social value of labour as a means to ameliorate the inherent market logic of contemporary art but further to harness domesticity as a tool to interrogate the construction of masculine identities.[52] Many contemporary male artists, as couples/lovers/domestic partners, have used needlecrafts to explore how masculinity is shaped through domesticity.[53] The domestic life of

**Figure 5.5** Dutes Miller and Stan Shellabarger, *Untitled (Pink Tube)*, 2003–present, performance view, Museum of Contemporary Art, Chicago, 2013, Photo. Courtesy of Nathan Keay, © Dutes Miller and Stan Shellabarger and Museum of Contemporary Art, Chicago.

the Chicago-based artists Dutes Miller and Stan Shellabarger, who have been life partners for over twenty years, provides the conceptual and ideological basis for a series of collaborative projects in which everyday needlework, from crocheting to sewing, takes central focus. In *Untitled Performance (Pink Tube)* both men sit opposite each other crocheting acrylic pink yarn (Figure 5.5). Over the past fifteen years, in various instalments of this ongoing performance, this flaccid, tumescent pink tube has become more and more engorged. Following a recent performance of this at the Museum of Contemporary Art in Chicago, same-sex marriage was legalized in the state, prompting one reviewer to ask if the tube was a symbol of 'a gold wedding band or other markers of normative marriage' denied to gay couples.[54] Other viewers have interpreted it as a phallus, as an umbilical cord and as a classic soft 'transitional object', but, in fact, the voluptuous length of fabric is not supposed to make sense while the couple are alive. In a way it is a shroud, a kind of mourning, as when one of them dies, the other will begin to unravel the tube.

Similarly, the Buenos Aires-based artists Leo Chiachio and Danny Giannone, 'partners in art, love and domesticity', learnt to sew as boys and today make intricate embroideries together.[55] Their unique domestic space is often the focus of their work – images of 'exotic parrots hyacinths, Latin American saints' are juxtaposed with eroticized images of the male body as sexualized fantasy: 'firemen, policemen, All American cowboys'.[56] They often include a double self-portrait in their work in reference to the traditional family photograph. It is this powerful, often imperceptible, almost ubiquitous image defining the very essence of family, affirming and authorizing normative sexual and social identities, that Chiachio and Giannone seek to expose and subvert. Their stitched queer self-portraits suggest that the idea of the normative family is 'always phantasmagoric, fictional, narrative'.[57] It is often in the context of family that queer children learn to feel shame.[58] Before prohibition and before repression queer childhood is defined by rejection. Shame as a feeling, Eve Kosofsky Sedgwick suggests, then, precedes performativity. Dressing up is a key part of Chiachio and Giannone's sensual domestic space. Their *Marineritos* (2005), for example, shows the couple dressed as sailors and evokes a queer archive of celebrated homoerotic images of sailors from the work of gay writers, film-makers, composers, fashion

**Figure 5.6** Leo Chiachio and Daniel Giannone, *Marineritos*, 2005, hand embroidery with cotton thread, graphite and stone appliqué on fabric, 31.5 x 41 in. (80 x 105 cm), © Leo Chiachio and Danny Giannone.

designers and photographers and, in the delicate stitches, the needlework of nineteenth-century sailors themselves (Figure 5.6).

Like queer domesticity homoeroticism itself, often drawing on gay pornography (images whose primary purpose is sexual arousal and release), as a conceptual as much as a visual source in men's needlework is increasingly discernible. Typing the words 'gay porn' into any internet search engine returns almost a billion results, in less than a second, such is its pervasiveness in contemporary life. Virtual pornography invites surveillance to such a degree that it renders a perceived private experience a public act. There are a multitude of contemporary artists making work that references gay pornography through needlecrafts. They appear drawn to craft for its incongruity and ironic commentary, but as the Canadian artist Peter Hobbs has perceptively suggested the attraction might be more psychological, perhaps even unconscious. 'The sewing needle is both prick and hole, it penetrates and is penetrated.'[59] The use of pornography, in general, as a source in contemporary art is far from uncommon. Artists such as Berend Strik are known for making, on occasion, pornographic needlework. The focus on the female body as a site of both pleasure and subordination, as in Strik's work, has been challenged and subverted in the needlework of artists such as Tracey Emin and Ghada Amer, through their exploration of women's bodies, desires and sexual identities.[60] However, less well known is the increasing use of gay pornography as source material by men and some women, such as Maria E. Piñeres. Unlike heterosexual pornography, which has been widely criticized for its reproduction of gendered systems of inequality, dominance and submission, that produced for and by gay men has been interpreted differently. Michael Bronski has argued that in gay pornography 'identification exists simultaneously with objectification', offering forms of validation beyond sexual release.[61] Richard Dyer has, further, suggested 'tenderness [and] emotional feeling' can be found in gay pornography even though a great deal of what is on offer reinforces 'the worst aspects of the social construction of masculinity that men learn to experience [with] their bodies'.[62]

Kang Seung Lee, a South Korean artist based in Los Angeles, has collated an index or archive of images that capture the homoerotic and the queer as part of a project that explores the visual representation of masculinity in Western culture from the canonical history of art to gay pornography. The project, which he developed partly in collaboration with the writer and former gay porn star Conner Habib, was resolved in a series of small needlepoints. Included was one after George Plank's decadent illustration of Aunt Georgie from E.F. Benson's *The Freaks of Mayfair* (1916) (Figure 3.5), an image of the archetypal 'effeminate embroiderer'. In a process of self-identification with the past, Seung Lee, then, photographed himself as Benson's character in *Untitled (Me as Aunt Georgie)* (2013) (Figure 5.7). The English artist, Nigel Hurlstone, has used needlework in a similar way, to return to the queer past, by exploring the personal experience of sexual awakening. Remembering his love of classic Hollywood melodramas, that he was drawn to and avidly watched as a boy, Hurlstone attempted to recapture the romantic grainy black-and-white quality of classic movies by machine embroidering large versions of several well-known homoerotic photographs of working-class youths, by early twentieth-century amateur photographer Montague Glover, and projecting them onto the gallery wall – fusing memory with fantasy (Figure 5.8). Although these are more suggestively erotic than explicitly sexual, Hurlstone nonetheless maintains he has 'made queer porn for the gallery wall'.[63] The American artist Aaron

136  Queering the Subversive Stitch

**Figure 5.7** Kang Seung Lee, *Untitled (Me as Aunt Georgie)*, 2013, C-Print, 16 x 24 in. (40.6 x 60.9 cm), © Kang Seung Lee.

**Figure 5.8** Nigel Hurlstone, *What Pleasure*, 2013, cotton, organdie, cotton and burmilana thread, digital print, couching, 85.8 x 37 in. (218 x 94 cm), © Nigel Hurlstone.

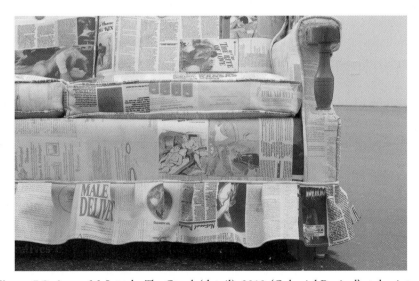

**Figure 5.9** Aaron McIntosh, *The Couch* (detail), 2010, 'Colonial Revival'-style vintage couch, digital prints (from romance novels, gay pornography and gay erotica) on cotton canvas, batting, thread, 35 x 72 x 36 in. (89 x 183 x 91 cm), Photo. Terry Brown, © Aaron McIntosh.

McIntosh has also made work about burgeoning gay desire but that references the tactile language of quilting from the region, in East Tennessee, where he grew up. In *The Couch* (2010) (Figure 5.9) McIntosh takes a ubiquitous homely object ('mom's or grandma's old couch') as the site of queer self-identification through the private consumption of romantic pulp fiction, queer magazines and gay porn. Images drawn from these are patchworked together and placed, like the projected film of memory, onto the surface of the couch. McIntosh suggests that the queer experience of growing up in a world of compulsory heterosexuality where gay children and teenagers, at those crucial junctions of sexual development, realize that the very core of their existence is denied and despised, can find consolation and comfort in the domestic and the maternal: 'As gay men, despite forays into virtual fantasies of man-on-man action, we are often still surrounded by the products of our domesticity, the cherished accoutrements given to us by our mothers.'[64] The work of Lee, Hurlstone and McIntosh, in different contexts and in different ways, reimagines homoerotic desire not as a site of shame but as part of a process of self-knowing and self-healing, as a way to explore intimate and tender feelings.

As a private act steeped in pleasure and self-satisfaction the gratification created by merging needlework as a visual medium (pleasurable to make) with explicit sexual imagery (pleasurable to view) has proliferated over the last few years in the millennial DIY handicrafts boom. As a solitary act, a kind of 'autoeroticism', sewing like other forms of intimacy, such as viewing porn, can perhaps be understood through the mechanisms of shame and secrecy that have defined the history of gay men's lives. Eve Kosofsky Sedgwick has suggested the idea of self-pleasure atrophied in the creation of homosexual and heterosexual identities since the nineteenth century.[65] Sewing like masturbation has been a source of moral panic that has been widely and actively discouraged in boys. Largely, but not exclusively, the work of amateur self-taught men who often sell their work through internet sites from Etsy to Instagram, the new wave of gay porn-inspired needlecrafts is not necessarily always drawn from pornography, in terms of specifics, but rather finds analogies in its cinematic language and spectatorial structure of the gaze.

'Kinky Needles' (aka Juan Diego) depicts men in various stages of undress and in the throes of sexual ecstasy, the design often left in embroidery hoops stressing the tension between their 'soft' material and 'hard' imagery.[66] Artists such as Max Colby, Scott Ramsay Kyle and FullMano (aka José Teixeira) have all sewn subversively onto vintage male physique magazines or gay pornography; John Thomas Paradiso and James Hunting have aestheticized erotic gay imagery through floral fabrics; Paul Yore and Ton of Holland have deployed needlecrafts to depict aspects of queer sexual subcultures; the list is every-growing. Greg Climer's *Pornography Quilts* uses digital printing and the traditional 'sewing bee' to domesticate explicit homoerotic imagery.[67] The installation *XXX: A Brief History of Gay Porn Films 1971–2016* by 'Beefcake Craft Arcade' (aka Matthew Monthei), first shown at the Shown at Hive Gallery, Los Angeles, comprised handstitched titles of eighty-two famous gay porn films, 'from the Pre-Condom early years through Golden Age to the Current Digital Age', on a ribbon 35 metres in length, spooled onto the gallery floor from a vintage gay porn VHS tape.[68] Humour is central to this phenomenon as much as self-interrogation. Zach Nutman, an artist who 'sews dirty queer needlepoints in New York City', jokes his work is 'just like Grandma's'.[69] In spite of the ubiquity and accessibly of gay pornography today the work it inspires is ignored in the wider culture of needlework. The young men who make it are not advocating the uncritical normalization of pornography but rather they seek to interrogate the construction of the sexual self in, and through, ideas such as pleasure, acceptance and even shame.[70] It possesses a serious questioning of both masculine images and archetypes, especially the distorted images of the commoditized male body produced under capitalism, and the amateur work reflects popular social and cultural concerns often ignored by the professionalized art and craft worlds. Gay male 'needleporn', as Nutman wittily puts it, is a subject that to date has been largely marginalized.

## The Subversive Stitch Revisited: *Masculinity, politics and cloth*

In a new 'Introduction' to the final re-issue of *The Subversive Stitch* (2010), penned twenty-five years after the book was originally published, Rozsika Parker commented on how third-wave feminism of the new millennium had re-engaged with the gendered discourses of needlework in a context that had many correspondences with that of the earlier Women's Liberation Movement (global economic recession, pervasive gender inequality, mass commercialization of needlecrafts as a popular pastime). The millennial revival of interest in needlecrafts Parker also acknowledged was fuelled, to some degree, by young men. Often described rather effusively (and frequently without irony) in the press as a 'male knitting revolution', it was most evident in the deluge of 'how-to' books for men.[71] These range from Mark del Vecchio's *Knitting with Balls* (2006) and Kristin Spurkland's *The Knitting Man(ual)* (2007) to Debbie Stoller's *Son of Stitch'n Bitch* (2007), which recalled something of the books by men that formed part of the 1970s 'needlepoint boom'. Emphasis on inclusivity, especially of everything that was deemed queer in post-millennial publishing, however, often sounded more like marketing rhetoric than effective political change.[72] There was, nonetheless, much engaged discussion about teaching boys to sew and knit in school, of the acceptance of men's place in professional needlework circles as a legitimate marker of gender equality ('men can make kickass fiber art too', as one zine put it) and of men who embraced the artisanal as a tool for social activism.[73] One of the earliest, and high-profile, examples of needlecrafts being used as a form of radical politics was Grant Neufeld's founding of the Revolutionary Knitting

**Figure 5.10** Grant Neufeld (second left) and the Revolutionary Knitting Circle (RKC) knitting protest at the G8 Summit, Calgary, Alberta Canada, 26 June 2002, Photo. Don MacKinnon © Getty Images.

Circle in Calgary, Canada, by staging a 'Global Knit-In' protest outside the G8 Summit in June 2002 (Figure 5.10).[74] Similar knitting circles seemed to spring up all over the world. There have been all-male sewing bees, knitting groups and quilting parties set up everywhere from North America to Europe to Australasia. Emanating from North America documentaries, such as Wendy Eidson's *Real Men Knit* (2005) and Faythe Levine's *Handmade Nation* (2009), as well as Kelly Shindler's analysis of the phenomenon published by *BUST* magazine (2005–6) under the title 'Lords of the Strings', sought to chronicle and contextualize the movement.[75] Julie Morstad's illustration for 'Lords of the Strings' showing boys knitting revealed this to be widely understood as a sort of contemporary youth movement and one that seemed to loop back to the infantilizing rhetoric used to describe the needle-wielding 'bad boys' (Figure 5.11). Shindler also drew comparisons in her text to 1970s craft books such as Rosey Grier's *Needlepoint for Men* (1973).

**Figure 5.11** Julie Morstad, illustration for 'Lords of the Strings.' *BUST* (136) (December 2005/January 2006): 82 © Julie Morstad, Courtesy of *BUST* magazine.

The political register of cloth is nowhere more evident than in the production of flags and banners – a historic industry in which men have retained proximity to making processes. Although processional flags and banners are today largely machine produced the resonance of resistance in the fabricating of such textiles by hand has been widely deployed by contemporary artists. In the 1990s George Tutill Ltd, one of the oldest manufacturers of flags and trade union banners in Britain, made a series of large flags for an installation by the artist Jonathan Parsons, for instance, and Ed Hall, a well-known trade union banner maker, has worked with the artist Jeremy Deller since 2000 in the fabrication of banners for several installations and performances.[76] However, for many contemporary male artists 'handmaking' forms the 'critical' component of their practice. The English artist Michael Brennand-Wood has long been interested in the political symbolism and formal aesthetics of textiles such as flags in his multi-faceted, and multi-media, exploration of embroidery.[77] His visualizations of pattern in three dimensions are often used to explore contemporary politics. His *Flower Head–Narcissistic Butterfly* (2005) (Figure 5.12), for example, takes as its base a mirror (to arrest the spectator's gaze) onto which individual digitally embroidered flowers are projected, on piano wire, at various lengths, each has at its centre a photograph of a human face, 'a motley crew of modern political leaders and figures'.[78] Brennand-Wood has employed textile patterns and processes as a means to interrogate issues as diverse as the social inscription of class, racial oppression, the machismo of militarism and the marginalization of textiles in the formation of cultural canons. Similarly, the American artist Nick Cave has investigated the semiotics of pattern in a series of performative artworks known as *Soundsuits*. These are full-body bodysuits (or headpieces) fashioned from a glittering assortment of everyday objects that are found, crafted or recycled, the 'detritus of both nature and culture'.[79] Referencing African ceremonial costumes, shamanistic ritual, contemporary fashion and the history of American popular culture, they also incorporate knitted, crocheted and appliquéd fabrics. In Cave's *Soundsuit #5* (2010) handmade flowers engulf the wearer's head, but they are not meant to mask the body but rather protect it by becoming a sort of soft armour (Plate 11). Cave suggests that 'wearing' art serves to deactivate and neutralize reactions based on gender, race and other identity signifiers

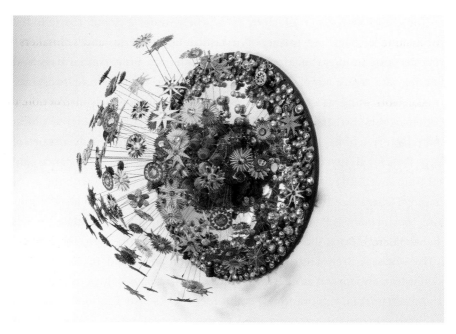

**Figure 5.12** Michael Brennand-Wood, *Flower Head – Narcissistic Butterfly*, 2005, machine-embroidered blooms, mirror, wire, photographs, beads, fabric, thread and acrylic paint on a wood base, 23.6 x 23.6 x 15.7 in. (60 x 60 x 40 cm), collection of the artist, Photo. Peter Mennim, © Michael Brennand-Wood.

that mark social interaction.[80] Cave's first *Soundsuit* was made in response to the brutal beating of Rodney King by Los Angeles police officers in 1991 in the hope of creating an art form that would encourage dialogue about constructions of identity.

In her new 'Introduction', Parker did note the increased presence of men in contemporary needlework exhibitions citing three particular examples: the *New Embroidery: Not Your Grandma's Doily* exhibition at the Contemporary Craft Museum, Portland, Oregon (2006); *Radical Lace and Subversive Knitting* (2006) at Museum of Arts and Design (MAD), New York; and *Pricked: Extreme Embroidery* (2007), the follow-up show at MAD. David Revere McFadden, the curator of the last two shows, suggested that men had 'embraced these stereotypically feminine techniques as ways of exploring issues of their own identity'.[81] Other reviewers suggested that the work in these exhibitions could overturn 'embroidery as a niche feminist medium' and could 'do much to amend the perception that needlework – despite the existence of male tailors, leatherworkers, ecclesiastical embroideries and sailmakers – belongs exclusively to women'.[82] It was, however, an earlier exhibition, *Loose Threads* at the Serpentine Gallery in London (1998), that first suggested men's needlework was an important site of exploring masculinity as a construction. In acknowledging her debt to Parker's book, the curator, Lisa Corrin, contended:

> Male artists, picking up the thread of feminist practice, have engaged the material in a similar spirit. Three past examples come readily to mind: David Medalla's *Stitch in Time* (initiated in 1968, with succeeding, context-specific, versions), in which the audience was invited to participate in a sewing-dialogue that resulted in an organic pattern of collective memories; Alighiero e Boetti's collaborative, language-based embroideries exploring the convergence of different cultural traditions and knowledge systems; [and] Mike Kelley's use of crocheted blankets and soft toys to address loss and dysfunctionality.[83]

Corrin was interested in how the men included in the show used specific types of needleskills to scrutinize the construction of the sexual self. This provoked some reaction in the press. One reviewer opined:

> It is always a bad sign when an exhibition categorises artists in terms of their gender or sexual orientation. Rory Donaldson exhibits shrouds he has embroidered with scenes of gay couplings (how fatuous), Jochen Flinzer shows a textile hanging embroidered with the names and initials of 53 men with whom he had sex in the past year (how sad).[84]

It is hard not to read the shaming of Flinzer's *53 Wochen Glück (53 Weeks of Happiness)* (1994–5), a long turquoise strip of Japanese silk onto which Flinzer handstitched the names of his male lovers between January and December 1994, as anything but homophobia (Plate 12; Figure 5.13).[85] Inspired, in part, by Renaud Camus's novel *Tricks: 33 récits* (1979), a sexual odyssey drawn from the author's own life, the intense descriptions of each sexual encounter Roland Barthes compared to 'haiku', Flinzer's embroidery fuses language and biography in an exploration of the sensual nature of craft.[86] Such opprobrium was, however, unusual as more often than not explicit queer references or subtexts, as in the case of Yinka Shonibare's gloriously dandified *Big Boy* (2002), were simply ignored (Figure 5.14).

**Figure 5.13** Jochen Flinzer, *53 Wochen Glück (53 Weeks of Happiness)*, 1994–1995, embroidery thread on silk, 169 x 12.7 in. (430 x 32.5 cm), installation view, Photo © MMK Museum für Moderne Kunst Frankfurt am Main, Photo. Axel Schneider, © Jochen Flinzer, Courtesy Thomas Rehbein Galerie, Köln.

**Figure 5.14** Yinka Shonibare MBE, *Big Boy*, 2002, Dutch wax-printed cotton fabric, fibreglass figure, 84 x 66 x 55 in. (215 x 170 x 12 cm), plinth 86 in. (220 cm) diameter, Gift of Susan and Lewis Manilow (2004.759), Chicago (IL), Art Institute of Chicago. © 2019, The Art Institute of Chicago/Art Resource, NY/Scala, Florence.

Michael Raedecker, who was also included in the *Loose Threads* exhibition, was often the focus of censure for the use of embroidery thread in his paintings.[87] Raedecker's conscious play on needlework's historic gendered associations seemed to have been accepted so long as his work could be read as painting and not embroidery.[88] Occasionally compared to samplers his paintings have increasingly moved away from a conventional use of landscape and urban imagery to a preoccupation with domestic motifs. A more recent work by Raedecker, such as *material* (2009), takes as its focus an embroidered tablecloth and pushes painting further into textiles to a point where they become indistinguishable (Figure 5.15). Is this a painting of an embroidery or an embroidery of a painting? The artist and writer, Janis Jefferies, responded to criticism of Raedecker, at the time of the *Loose Threads* exhibition, stating that his use of embroidery thread 'opened up a space for hybrid interrogations'

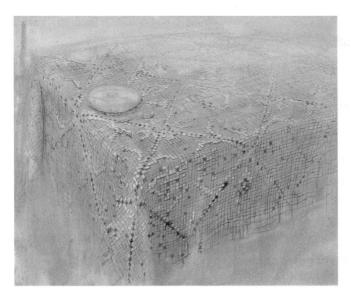

**Figure 5.15** Michael Raedecker, *material*, 2009, acrylic and thread on canvas, 40 1/8 x 46 ½ in. (102 x 118 cm), Private Collection, Photo. Courtesy of the Artist and the Grimm Gallery, Amsterdam and New York, © Michael Raedecker.

of the masculine as much as the feminine, destabilizing both.[89] This prompted Jefferies to think through the issue of men's needlework as a subject worth exploring in itself:

> But as anyone may have noticed over the last few years, 'female-associated' craft-like processes, and most notably textiles, have had something of a resurgence in work made by men, in what I call 'the boys that sew club', and there has been an unprecedented amount of material fabrication and stitch manipulation in the 1990s. One of the ways, it could be argued, in which textile-based work made by men gets its charge is role play; it participates in a critique of an essential masculinity (and femininity) that began to be articulated after the 1970s ... I would argue that Oliver Herring's transparent knitted eulogies to Ethyl Eichelberger, Michael Raedecker's and Roy Voss's deceptively 'nostalgic' threads of domestic solitude, Yinka Shonibare's 'mimicry' of Victorian crinoline dresses, Neil MacInnis's celebration of gay culture through computer-generated rococo silks, and Meyer Vaisman's parody of tapestry in Disneyesque prints all have their antecedents in early feminist art of the 1970s – witness the obsession with domestic interrogations, the phenomenon of empty garments, a labour-intensive

aesthetic, and the assumptions that the personal and the political can be meaningfully bound together. Such work may not demonstrate the 'authentic' agitation of a 'Sisterhood is powerful' slogan, nor subscribe to a consciousness-raising collective, but paradoxically it might just conform to a feminist model of rendering the personal within the political; a site where traditional, gendered biographies and identities are loosened by fragments of cloth and fragile bits of sewing.[90]

In an attempt to disentangle, and differentiate, what she designated 'the boys that sew club' from the 'bad boys' of postmodern art, Jefferies curated an exhibition, entitled *Boys Who Sew* at the Crafts Council, Gallery, London (2004), that included work exclusively by men. Thinking through ideas of gendered and sexual identity, of conformity and transgression, of men's bodies, of experiences, desires and feelings from fear to shame, evocatively demonstrated in Brett Alexander's *Playing with Dolls* (Figure 5.16), the show attempted to unpick the complex tensions between masculinity and needlework.[91] *Boys Who Sew* was, however, only one of a series of exhibitions that took place before and after the millennium, that sought to chart the

**Figure 5.16** Brett Alexander, *Playing with Dolls*, 2003–6, dimensions variable, © Brett Alexander.

contemporary practice and hidden history of men's needlework. In the vast exhibition entitled *Il racconto del filo: Ricamo e cucito nell–arte contemporanea/ The Tale of Thread: Embroidery and Sewing in Contemporary Art*, at the Museo di Arte Moderna e Contemporanea di Trento e Rovereto, Italy (2003), a larger and more diverse range of male artists engaged in various ways with needlework were surveyed and contextualized with better-known work by women. This exhibition also placed significant stress on the modernist origins of contemporary art's appropriation of needlework by inclusion of a selection of male artists from the European avant-garde movements, following the First World War, who designed or made needlework.[92]

These exhibitions and numerous others were often framed as a response to 'a tidal wave of "women artists" exhibitions' of the late twentieth century but were unusual in that they actively encouraged male artists to 'openly acknowledge and explore the emotional aspects of their psyche' as well as a lineage in feminist art.[93] The *Guys Who Sew* exhibition at the University Art Museum, University of California, Santa Barbara (1994), for instance, included a selection of men who openly acknowledged their feminist forbears. The curators saw contemporary work as related, somehow, to the little documented histories of needlework by men ranging from nineteenth-century sailors to popular figures like Rosey Grier in the 1970s.[94] Other exhibitions, such as *Boy Oh Boy* at the Newmark Center Gallery in Seattle (1997), addressed masculinity's relation to constructs of the queer while others, such as *Men of the Cloth: Contemporary Fiber Art* at Loveland Museum/ Gallery, Loveland, Colorado (1999), curated by the embroiderer Stephen Beal, attempted to obviate discussion of 'the issue of gender' completely in a broad survey of over thirty male textile artists.[95] There are numerous other examples such as *Men Who Sew* at the Elsa Mott Ives Gallery, YMCA, New York (2000); *Thread Baring: A Portrait of Masculinity One Stitch at a Time* at the Union Art Gallery, Milwaukee (2009); and the series of six exhibitions of textile art by men, curated by Ludmila Egorova, that took place in Kherson, the Ukraine, between 2011 and 2017, under the title *Fibremen International*. Egorova originated the idea of the exhibition from the 16th Conference of the European Textile Network in Kaunas in Lithuania but also from her reading of William Pollock's *Real Boys* (1998), which was one of several books that appeared towards the end of the century on the subject of 'masculinity in crisis', the

**Figure 5.17** Gavin Fry, *Orlando*, nine panels, dimensions variable, hand embroidery on second-hand, mass-produced sewing kits and Berlin woolwork, 2010, dimensions variable, © Gavin Fry.

remedy for which Pollack argued was the reform of 'boyhood'.[96] The work in these exhibitions was often seen as intending to 'expand the way viewers think about sewing', as it 'turns cross stitching and knitting into political pieces'.[97]

Several more recent exhibitions delved deeper into the unknown history of men's needlework. The English artist Gavin Fry's *Orlando* (Figure 5.17), made for the *Men of Cloth* exhibition at the Lauriston Gallery, Waterside Art Centre, Sale, Manchester (2010), referenced not just the Bloomsbury group's play on gender identity in literature in terms of its subject-matter but further their exploration of the links between painting and Berlin woolwork reflected in Fry's use of pre-made embroidery kits. The *Man-Made Quilts: Civil War to the Present* at the Shelburne Museum, Vermont (2012–13), curated by Jean M. Burks and Joe Cunningham, provided the first-ever survey and analysis of surviving quilts known to have been made by men. In this Cunningham, who has been quilting since the 1970s carefully traced the existence of male quilters even if, he realized, most people choose to believe the 'the DNA of American quilts was encoded as "female"'.[98] The ideas underpinning this exhibition were further explored by the *Man-Made: Contemporary Male Quilters* show at the

Craft & Folk Art Museum, Los Angeles (2015), which included contemporary quilts by seven male artists for whom 'the process of constructing a quilt mirrors the construction of identity and self'.[99]

Whilst Parker would have recognized the political agency of such historical recuperation and was conscious that men contributed, past and the present, to the creation of a wider culture and history of needlework she remained totally silent on the work of gay men, in both her original 1984 publication and her new 2010 introduction.[100] However, there have been several important exhibitions that endeavoured to map the 'queering' of needlework. For example, HOMO*craft* at the Crafts Council of New South Wales's Craftspace in Sydney (1995) explored the idea that the handmade was, for queer men, a means to comment on constructions of normative identity through the deliberate choice of craft media: 'The path which identifies craft with femininity, and poses them in smooth opposition to art and masculinity, is no longer smooth – it never was that simple for artists working in the craft media anyway.'[101] Other exhibitions focused on the intersection of homosexuality and handwork, such as *Material Boys–un[Zipped]* at Object Galleries, Sydney (2000), of which Peter McNeil commented: 'These Material Boys appropriate the tactics of irony and subversion usefully deployed by early feminist practitioners, here also "queering" or recoding conventional notions of sexuality and masculinity.'[102] Of *Nancy Boy*, an exhibition at the Richmond Art Center in California (2005), one reviewer stated: 'Boys being boys, their interpretation of feminine materials and aesthetics naturally extends to include numerous references to phallic imagery,' yet 'one might consider this work in the context of say, Judy Chicago's "Dinner Party," a relationship to feminism might thus emerge'.[103] The *Boys with Needles* at Museum London, Ontario, and Textile Museum of Canada, Toronto (2002–3), suggested that the historic association of textiles with femininity was being deployed by queer artists to contest narrow and prescriptive concepts of the masculine. The curator Anne-Marie Larsen commented, 'As I prepared this exhibition I was repeatedly reminded that, while homosexuality can be viewed as somehow opposite to masculinity, it is also richly *contested* within masculinity.'[104] Most recently *Queer Threads: Crafting Identity & Community* at the Leslie-Lohman Museum of Gay and Lesbian Art, New York (2014), curated by John Chaich, surveyed work by thirty men and women who used needlecrafts to explore the construction of gendered and sexual identities as well as the relationality of 'craft facture' and 'queer experience'.[105] In an age when toxic masculinity seems to have returned with such force Chaich added 'queer quilting bees and sewing circles are acts of activism by just existing'.[106]

From the proliferation of exhibitions that have charted and explored the meaning of men's needlework there has been a discernible interest in understanding such work as a form of affective history. In the late 1990s a short survey by the British society magazine, *Country Life*, of embroidery by four upper-middle-class 'gentlemen' (a manager of a famous hotel, a former chairman of a well-known bank, a celebrated gardener, and a bishop) tentatively mapping the presence of men's needlework and revealing that the model of the eccentric and effeminate male embroiderer of the early mid-twentieth century, as embodied by men such as the Duke of Windsor or Ernest Thesiger, with their proclivity for historical models and inherent good taste, was alive and well (Figure 5.18).[107] Although these men had connections to organizations such as the Embroiderers' Guild and the Royal School of Needlework, they remained amateurs in the most literal sense – they were largely self-taught (though, most received some instruction from

**Figure 5.18** 'Gentlemen of the Needle.' *Country Life* CXVI(6) (February 1997): 28–9, © Country Life Picture Library.

their mothers, other female family members or female friends) and were dedicated to embroidery as a hobby for the pleasure and satisfaction it offered. About the same time the Embroiderers' Guild of America featured an article in their journal that charted men's needlework in the twentieth-century including before the Guild's formation in 1958 (Figure 5.19).[108] One of the interviewees revealed he had been taught to embroider by a Red Cross nurse while convalescing from injuries in an English naval hospital during the Second World War, only to return to it in the 1960s as a hobby, purely as a source of the gratification in itself.

A history of men's needlework has never been written but makers themselves have often turned to what Ann Cvetkovich has called 'archives of feeling' in terms of practice.[109] Unpicking the seams of needlework's queer history, in particular, has revealed an unexpected sense of communion

**Figure 5.19** Cover of *Needle Arts*, XXIX(2) (June 1998), Courtesy of *Needle Arts*, Courtesy of the Embroiderers' Guild of America.

between the present and the past for many men. The Italian artist Francesco Vezzoli, for example, is best known for works such as his *Crying Divas from the Screenplay of an Embroiderer II* (1999), thirty laser printed portraits of famous women onto which Vezzoli stitched tears with metallic thread (Plate 13), and his embroideries of female celebrities, actors and writers, such as Virginia Woolf who were known to embroider (Figure 5.20).[110] However, a scene in his film *An Embroidered Trilogy* (1997–9) shows Vezzoli sitting embroidering in Rome's Museo Mario Praz, the former home of the celebrated aesthete, anglophile and man of letters, who recorded in his memoirs details of his own needlework, examples of which survive in the museum.[111] Vezzoli sits on the sofa embroidered by Praz, embroidery hoop in hand stitching a portrait of the writer. Another example of this affective archiving emerges from the American artist Josh Faught's *Longtime Companion* exhibition at the Lisa Cooley Gallery, New York (2012), in his *It Takes a Lifetime to Get Exactly Where You Are*, a vast woven and handsewn collage that includes a replica of a section of the NAMES Project Memorial AIDS Quilt as well as other references to the 1970s 'needlepoint boom' (Figure 5.21). At *The Subversive Stitch Revisited* symposium, held in honour of Rozsika Parker, who passed away in 2010, at the Victoria and Albert Museum in 2013, the English artist Matt Smith discussed the 'highlander costume' that he made after an original Oliver Messel, the celebrated theatre designer, had created for a C.B. Cochran revue in 1930.[112] Entitled *Piccadilly 1830* (after the title of a skit in the revue) Smith's recreation comprises a jacket handstitched with 'thousands

**Figure 5.20** Francesco Vezzoli, *Who's Afraid of Virginia Woolf (Double Portrait after Man Ray)*, 2011, inkjet print on canvas with metallic embroidery, 11.8 x 11.8 in. (30 x 30 cm), Private Collection, Photo. © Christie's Images/Bridgeman Art Library, © Francesco Vezzoli.

*The Politics of Cloth* 153

**Figure 5.21** Josh Faught, *It Takes a Lifetime to Get Exactly Where You Are*, 2012, handwoven sequin trim, handwoven hemp, cedar blocks, cotton, polyester, wool, cochineal (made from ground-up bugs), straw hat with lace, toilet paper, paper towels, Jacquard woven reproduction of panel from the AIDS quilt, silk handkerchief, indigo, political pins, disaster blanket, gourd, gold leaf, plaster cat, cedar blocks and nail polish, 96 x 240 in./8 x 20 ft. (243 x 610 cm), Photo. Courtesy of the Artist and Lisa Cooley, New York, © Josh Faught.

**Figure 5.22** Matt Smith, *Piccadilly 1830*, 2012, turkey and ostrich feathers, ceramic, metal cage, wool, linen, mirror-backed beads, approx. 90.5 x 23.6 x 11.8 in. (230 x 60 x 30 cm), © Unravelled Arts, Photo. Sussie Ahlberg.

of individual mirror-backed glass bugle beads' and an exaggerated feather bonnet made of ostrich plumes (Figure 5.22). This reimaging was reclamation not just of Messel's sewing but also of Messel's hidden homosexuality as such military dress has long operated a queer sign. Smith's work was installed at Nymans, the Messel family home in Sussex now owned by the National Trust, which prompted Smith to further think of the domestic life of Messel and his partner Vagn Riis-Hansen. There was little trace of the Riis-Hansen at Nymans but following the display of Smith's work, and the conversations it prompted, his name was added to the official family tree.[113] Other examples of this excavating the past have upended more difficult or problematic histories. In the Tokyo-based artist Satoru Aoyama's *Division of Labour* exhibition, at London's White Rainbow Gallery (2016), for example, Aoyama not only stitched onto historic photographs of male embroiderers that are rarely ever seen but, further he re-made (by hand) the large embroideries (*arazzi*) that Alighiero Boetti designed and commissioned anonymous craftswomen in Afghanistan to make. Aoyama's *Embroiderers (dedicated to unknown Embroiderers)* series (2015) (Figure 5.23) explores how the geopolitical map of labour exploitation traps men as well as women.

Nikki Sullivan has argued that such acts can be interpreted as 'queering' forms of popular culture (such as needlework) in that they 'expose and problematise the means by which sexuality is textually constituted in relation to dominant notions of gender'.[114] Alexander Doty has further characterized these as 'queer moments' of 'narrative disruption' akin, in some way, to Parker's conceptualization of the 'subversive stitch' where cultural subjugation is transformed by subverting a symbol of oppression (sewing) into a means of emancipatory expression.[115] Sullivan and Doty are referring, however, to specific forms of cultural production, such as cinema, and like Parker their understanding of 'resistance' implies some sort of agency through awareness or action often in collective terms. The male needleworker in his symbolic renunciation of the licence masculinity entails, on the other hand, is always neutralized by being atomized. Much needlework by men, then, is undermined by its apparent isolation but, as we have seen, it can find connection and cohesion in the archiving of its own past and through its expression of 'structures of feeling'. Often nothing unifies men's needlework beyond its transgressive ability to denaturalize, or queer, normative gender codes. Think

**Figure 5.23** Satoru Aoyama, *Embroiderers (Dedicated to Unknown Embroiderers) #10*, 2015, embroidery on inkjet print, 7 x 10 in. (18 x 26 cm), Photo. Kei Miyajima, © Satoru Aoyama, Courtesy of Mizuma Art Gallery, Tokyo.

of the examination of racial and sexual history: in Chan-Hyo Bae's *Existing in Costume* (2006), in which he is photographed in women's historical dress rich in embroidered detail (Plate 14); the temporal beauty of natural motifs in James Merry's intricately embroidered masks such as *Moth* worn by the musician Björk in her multi-media performances (Plate 15); or Nicholas Hlobo's meditation on the contradictions of contemporary masculinity in South Africa through his of use of ribbon, rubber, latex and fabric to puncture paper with shapes that recall phalluses, testicles, orifices, in large zipper-like baseball stitches in works such as *Macaleni iintozomlambo* (2010) (Plate 16).[116] Rozsika Parker's overarching argument in *The Subversive Stitch* could be easily applied to any of these examples – they have 'sewn a subversive stitch' and 'managed to make meanings of their own in the very medium intended to inculcate self-effacement'.[117] Queering the subversive stitch has revealed the masculine to be just another category of socially constituted subjectivity. Studies of masculinity, then, have much to contribute to the politics of cloth as a discourse of the present as much as the past.

6

# Conclusion: 'Men who Embroider'

'Has the pen or pencil dipped so deep in the blood of the human race as the needle?', so asked Olive Schreiner in *From Man to Man*, a novel she began in 1873 but was eventually published posthumously in 1926. It is an image that has haunted the history of needlework ever since – even appearing as the first line in Rozsika Parker's *The Subversive Stitch*.[1] Yet there are numerous other images of needlework in Schreiner's novels and some are equally, if not more, striking. Take, for instance, Schreiner's enormously popular *The Story of an African Farm* (1883) in which the protagonist Lyndall pictures Gregory, a farm-hand, as a 'man-woman': 'How happy would he be sewing frills into his little girl's frocks, and how pretty he would look in the parlour, with a rough man making love to him!'[2] The earlier quote appears in nearly every book about the culture of needlework; the latter is hardly known and would be seen, I expect, of little relevance to needlework's history.[3] Why is sewing by men often portrayed, as here, as feminizing and, somehow, queer? Is it really so aberrant that it can only exist in the imagination? And what of the connection between female impersonation, needlework and sexuality? These are some of the questions that this book set out to examine.

I began my research in thinking through Schreiner's novels and their immediate late Victorian and early modern context. This revealed that Lyndall's fantasy of Gregory's pleasure in plain sewing and sexual passivity was for the author far from an eccentric twist in the plot. Schreiner, I discovered, had a friendship (and later a relationship) with the influential sexologist Havelock Ellis and her characterization of Gregory drew much from his popularization of the theory of 'inversion', in which a man's taste for 'simpler forms of needlework' may have masked a desire for receptive anal pleasure. Not only did Schreiner and Ellis discuss the characters in *The Story of an African Farm*, of which Ellis wrote a sympathetic review, but their correspondence contains some exchange on the subject of 'inversion'.[4] The visualization of a man plain sewing and a man as sexually passive has rarely been presented together in a single image but since the nineteenth century the former has operated as a sign of the latter.

Ernest Thesiger is perhaps the best-known male embroiderer who was a contemporary of Havelock Ellis and Olive Schreiner. They mixed in similar social circles and shared at least one friend, the writer Radclyffe Hall. Like Schreiner, Thesiger shared Ellis's interest in 'male femininity' as expressed through needlework. Yet today Thesiger's embroidery is largely forgotten. Even though few would connect him to the image of Gregory plain sewing and being buggered in Schreiner's story, the shocking and subversive power of such an image echoes the counternarrative offered by much of his own needlework. Thesiger may have coded his various adventures in embroidery in the interwar semiotics of amusement, but he was widely acknowledged in his day as a leading expert in needlework. Towards the end of his life when repairing some antique embroidered chair covers, for Temple Newsam museum in Leeds, he was interviewed for an article about men who had taken up needlework as a hobby. The interviewer speculated that 'the bedevilled needle, the ludicrously long and tangled thread, the pricked finger, the physical contortions – might [still] raise a laugh', if it was a man doing the sewing (Figure 6.1).[5] Yet in the course of the interview Thesiger made it clear that he had been offered the commission over the Royal School of Needlework, such was his reputation, and he had taken it on purely for personal gratification: 'Mr. Thesiger is doing it for his own pleasure.'[6] What remains marked about Thesiger's comments here is his expression of 'pleasure' in the work as such feelings by men have often gone unrecorded in the historical record. For the most part needlework, I learnt in the course of researching this book, has been couched in a rhetoric of pride in women's work that emphasizes (intentionally or not) an essential femininity. Men are largely excluded, effaced or elided in this story of needlework as 'women's history', to use Parker's memorable phrase. Nearly every book and study of needlework I could find, whether written by women or men, seemed to confirm this as a universal conviction. Yet I remained perplexed as there was evidence to suggest that men (sometimes well-known men like Thesiger) had engaged with a wide range of needlework

**Figure 6.1** 'Men who Embroider.' unattributed magazine cutting (early-mid 1950s), EFT/000066/13, Ernest Thesiger Archive, © The University of Bristol Theatre Collection/ArenaPAL.

in the past and continued to do so in contemporary contexts. Thesiger is one of the few men who are often name-checked in histories of needlework but there has not been a single study of his work since his death in 1961.

I was intrigued by the silence that surrounded the many images and objects that I uncovered. For instance, in Gail Carolyn Sirna's *In Praise of Needlewomen* (2006), needlework is defined as uniquely part of women's experience on par with 'childbirth and childrearing'.[7] Whilst Sirna provides a stimulating historical survey of 'needlewomen' the image of a 'needleman', the first illustration in her book (of which she says nothing), lingered in my mind. Even though, from early on in my research, it seemed possible to locate men in the broad narratives of needlework there seemed to be little interrogation of their work, scant evaluation beyond acknowledgement of its existence. I found nothing to suggest men's needlework was something worth studying in itself. Everything seemed to emphatically insist needlework, as a practice, a history, a form of popular consumption, as a form of exploitation or remunerative labour or even as an increasing presence in contemporary art, spoke only to female experience. Authoritative studies on the history of sewing elide men so completely that Michael Zaki, in a review of an edited volume of essays on the culture of domestic sewing published in 1999, felt compelled to comment that men's absence, and men's desire to sew or not to, urgently 'deserves a companion volume'.[8] No such volume has appeared in the intervening two decades.

This is believed to be the first book ever written about the cultural history of needlework by men. In realizing this daunting task, I have, in the end, opted for a somewhat compact version of this history for space as much as sanity's sake. The full history of men as embroiderers, needlepointers, cross-stitchers, knitters, quilters, lacemakers, dressmakers and rug makers still needs to be fully written. The examples and case studies I have selected reflect, on one level, 'transitional moments' for gender in modern history, in which some form of 'masculinity crisis' was played out. On another level, the broad sweep of such an overview has revealed how needlework intersects with forms of subordinated masculinity (in terms of sexual, racial and class identities) that contest (intentionally or not) dominating forms of hegemonic masculinity. This has afforded new opportunities to locate and understand men's needlework in terms of wider 'structures of feeling'. By returning men to their pasts, often to their actual childhoods, as so many men have proffered stories of learning sewing skills as boys directly from mothers, grandmothers or other caregivers, and to feelings such as pleasure and shame, is not to infantilize or pathologize them but to give a voice to the often unheard private, personal and temporal experiences. Intimate feelings have been key to unlocking the reasons why men have turned to needlework and although there is often little recourse to the historical record (as much regarding men's needlework goes undocumented) the examples I have included offer some insight into the affective relations between men (in terms of kinship, domesticity and sex). In this I have been much influenced by the writings of Raymond Williams, Eve Kosofsky Sedgwick and Ann Cvetkovich. I am also greatly indebted to the new ways of thinking that have emerged from the recent pioneering work on the intersection of the ever-elusive conceptualizations of 'queer' and 'craft' by feminist and queer activists who have placed special emphasis on lesbian history.[9]

Studies of women's needlework as a form of women-only history continue undiminished, however. To be clear though, I am not offering any criticism of this and I am certainly not suggesting a shift of focus to needlework by men, but I do think that what men produce can only really be measured or understood within this broader context. But before we get there it is necessary to excavate something of what motivates men to take up needlework and the meanings they find in it. Needlework as 'meaning-making, identity formation and commemoration' for women, as explored in the recent volume of essays on 'the material culture of needlework & textiles' by Maureen Daly Goggin and Beth Fowkes Tobin, offers a set of conceptual approaches that could equally be applied to the study of men's work.[10] Most recently Clare Hunter's *Threads of Life* has explored the history of needlework through a surfeit of emotions and feelings (emanating from power, fragility, captivity, identity, connection, protest, loss, community and work) that she has tentatively linked to just a few well-known male examples (John Craske, Major Alexis Casdagli and Fine Cell Work) but, I feel, there is much more scope for their use in discussions of work by a wider range of men.[11]

The omission of men from the culture of needlework as a field of art historical enquiry is often covertly underscored by the coding of textiles as somehow heteronormative. If men who embroider are universally *queered*, by *queering* embroidery (by disrupting and destabilizing its narratives) we lay bare those mechanisms through which masculinity has been (and continues to be) constituted. Rather than seeing this study as a form of recuperative history, of the male needleworker through the ages, it has been a problematizing of normatively fixed readings of needlework. The prevailing understanding of needlework as feminine and something to be prohibited or repressed in relation to the masculine must be seen as nothing more than an extension of homophobic violence; and a real and present danger. Consider the use of such rhetoric in the still widespread practice of conversion therapy in which women are encouraged to sew to realign their sexuality and men are discouraged in the hope their sexual desire for other men will atrophy.[12]

My reasons for speaking so directly to the ideas generated by Rozsika Parker in *The Subversive Stitch* have been twofold. Firstly, it is the touchstone for all studies of needlework, and I could easily have been oblique in my referencing of Parker's book, but I thought it better to show how central its provocations are to all discussions of needlework. Secondly, no other book has made me think so deeply about the implicit gendering of hierarchical systems of cultural production and their social, economic and political implications past and present. If for women, as Parker shows, embroidery became the tool of subversion, for men, I add, it became the apparatus of surveillance – silently policing their gendered and sexual identities. But if women found resistance in such confines, men too found space for transgression and transformation that has offered surprising and unanticipated possibilities. Needlework in the modern age has played a complex and a critical role in the making of the masculine. Reflecting on *The Subversive Stitch* exhibitions of the late 1980s, inspired by Parker's book, Pennina Barnett suggested that Parker had opened up rather than closed the subject.[13] This has always reminded me of the generosity inherent in the work of Eve Kosofsky Sedgwick who said of her own writing: 'Part of the motivation behind my work … has been a fantasy that readers or hearers would be variously – in anger, identification, pleasure, envy, "permission," exclusion – stimulated to write accounts "like" this one (whatever that means) of their own, and share those.'[14] I hope both Parker and Sedgwick would have agreed that men and the culture of needlework is a stimulating subject of study and one worth sharing.

# Notes

## Preface

1 Virginia Woolf, *A Room of One's Own* (London: The Hogarth Press, 1929), p. 84.

## Chapter 1

1 Rozsika Parker, *The Subversive Stitch: Embroidery and the Making of the Feminine* (London: The Women's Press, 1984), p. vi.
2 John Ezard, 'Victorian Touch to Credit Cold Britain'. *The Guardian* (6 December 1979): 2; quoted in Parker, *The Subversive Stitch*, p. 1. This information was drawn from a Social Trends report published by the Office of National Statistics.
3 Parker quoted in Anne Caborn, 'Needles Out Men! Who Says Embroidery Has Always Been Strictly for the Girls?' *Liverpool Echo* (17 November 1984): 9. In place of Parker's term 'sissies' Caborn substituted the more antiquated, Victorian-inflected, spelling of 'cissies', used in late nineteenth- and early twentieth-century Britain.
4 The fruits of Parker's research into needlework's role in the construction of femininity were first published in Rosie Parker, 'The Word for Embroidery Was Work'. *Spare Rib* 37 (July 1975): 41–5; and subsequently in Rozsika Parker and Griselda Pollock, *Old Mistresses: Women, Art and Ideology* (London: Pandora Press, 1981), pp. 50–81. Parker and Pollock adapted the concept of 'old mistresses' from an exhibition, *Old Mistresses: Women Artists of the Past*, held at the Walters Art Gallery in Baltimore in 1972. This was one of several exhibitions in North America in the early 1970s that reconsidered the work of women and their place, inside and outside canonical formations of Western art history. For an overview of these see Rosie Parker, 'Old Mistresses'. *Spare Rib* 10 (April 1973): 11–13.
5 Parker knew the earliest writing arising from the American feminist rediscovery of needlework's history such as Patricia Mainardi, 'Quilts: The Great American Art'. *The Feminist Art Journal* 2(1) (Winter, 1973): 18–23; Rachel Maines,

'Fancywork: An Archaeology of Lives'. *The Feminist Art Journal* 3(4) (Winter, 1974–5); and Toni Flores Fratto, 'Samplers: One of the Lesser American Arts'. *The Feminist Art Journal* 5(4) (Winter, 1976–7): 11–15. She read Lippard's 'Making Something from Nothing (towards a Definition of Women's "Hobby Art")'. *Heresies* 4 (Winter 1978): 62–5, upon its publication, and was one of the first British feminists to pen a review of Judy Chicago's *Dinner Party*, see 'Heresies'. *Spare Rib* 75 (October 1978): 23, and 'Judy Chicago's Dinner Party'. *Spare Rib* 104 (March 1981): 46.

6  Parker, 'The Word for Embroidery Was Work', 41.
7  Joan M. Jensen, 'Needlework as Art, Craft, and Livelihood before 1900'. In Joan M. Jensen and Sue Davidson (eds), *A Needle, a Bobbin, a Strike: Women Needleworkers in America* (Philadelphia, PA: Temple University Press, 1984), p. 3.
8  Janet Wolff, 'The Culture of Separate Spheres: The Role of Culture in Nineteenth-Century Public and Private Life'. In *Feminine Sentences: Essays on Women and Culture* (London: Polity Press, 1990), pp. 12–33.
9  Parker, *The Subversive Stitch*, p. 17.
10 Ann Bermingham has defined 'amateurs' as 'artists by avocation and, while they may have received training by professional artists and may even have shown their work in professional exhibitions, they remained amateurs if they did not rely on their art as a source of income', see Ann Bermingham, *Learning to Draw: Studies in the Cultural History of a Polite and Useful Art* (New Haven & London: Yale University Press, 2000), p. 130 and p. 146 for needlework. For a discussion of the social construction of the 'amateur', particularly in relation to modern conceptualizations of craft, see Stephen Knott, *Amateur Craft: History and Theory* (London: Bloomsbury, 2015).
11 Rosie Parker, 'Art of Course Has No Sex. But Artists Do'. *Spare Rib* 25 (July 1974): 34–5.
12 Parker, *The Subversive Stitch*, pp. 6 and 11.
13 Stephen M. Whitehead, *Men and Masculinities: Key Themes and New Directions* (Cambridge: Polity Press, 2002), p. 17.
14 This reading of the historical construction of gender follows that in Michel Foucault, *The History of Sexuality: Volume 1: The Will to Knowledge* (Trans. Richard Hurley) (London: Penguin, 1998 [1976]), p. 5.
15 Whitehead, *Men and Masculinities*, p. 14. For masculinity as a modern 'invention' in social and political (even linguistic) terms, see George L. Mosse, *The Image of Man: The Creation of Modern Masculinity* (Oxford and New York: Oxford University Press, 1996). The relation of debates about the social construction of masculinity (as well as homosexuality) and craft is much overlooked but there

are many parallels in historiography and approach – see David F. Greenberg, *The Invention of Homosexuality* (Chicago: University of Chicago Press, 1988); Jonathan Ned Katz, *The Invention of Heterosexuality* (London: E.P. Dutton, 1995); and Glenn Adamson, *The Invention of Craft* (London: Bloomsbury, 2013).

16 Parker, *The Subversive Stitch*, p. 81.

17 My use of the term 'queer' derives from three propositions – from Teresa de Lauretis's suggestion that queer 'may be understood and imaged as forms of resistance to cultural homogenization'; from Eve Kosofsky Sedgwick's definition of queer as an 'open mesh of possibilities, gaps, overlaps, dissonances and resonances, lapses and excesses of meaning when the constituent elements of anyone's gender, of anyone's sexuality aren't made (or *can't be* made) to signify monolithically'; and David Halperin's proposition that queer 'is *whatever* is at odds with the normal, the legitimate, the dominant. *There is nothing in particular to which it necessarily refers*' (all italics in the originals); see Teresa de Lauretis, 'Queer Theory: Lesbian and Gay Sexualities. An Introduction'. *differences: A Journal of Feminist Cultural Studies* 3(2) (Summer 1991): iii; Eve Kosofsky Sedgwick, *Tendencies* (Durham: Duke University Press, 1993), p. 8; and David M. Halperin, *Saint Foucault: Towards a Gay Hagiography* (Oxford and New York: Oxford University Press, 1995), p. 62. In addition, throughout this book, I deploy the term 'queer' as 'less an identity than a *critique* of identity', as a form of 'resistance to regimes of the normal' and one that exposes the 'intellectual and moral bankruptcy of binary identity categories'; see Annamarie Jagose, *Queer Theory: An Introduction* (New York: New York University Press, 1996), p. 131; Michael Warner (ed.), *Fear of a Queer Planet: Queer Politics and Social Theory* (Minneapolis and London: University of Minnesota Press, 1993), p. xxvi; and William B. Turner, *A Genealogy of Queer Theory* (Philadelphia: Temple University Press, 2000), p. 34.

18 Parker and Pollock, *Old Mistresses*, pp. 60–1.

19 Jensen, 'Needlework as Art, Craft, and Livelihood before 1900', p. 3.

20 Ibid.

21 Parker, *The Subversive Stitch*, p. 133.

22 Mary C. Beaudry, *Findings: The Material Culture of Needlework and Sewing* (New Haven and London: Yale University Press, 2006), p. 175.

23 Bridget Crowley, 'Unlikely Art of Jolly Jack Tar'. *Country Life* CLXXXVI(46) (12 November 1992): 46. Crowley gives the dates as 1845–90, whereas Janet West suggests 1850–75/80, but West adds 'it continued as a pastime until the First World War'; see Janet West, 'Sailor Wool Pictures'. *The Mariner's Mirror* 85(1) (1999): 90–1.

24  Crowley, 'Unlikely Art of Jolly Jack Tar', 46.
25  Parker, *The Subversive Stitch*, p. 10.
26  Crowley, 'Unlikely Art of Jolly Jack Tar', p. 47.
27  Ibid; Janet West, 'Nautical Woolwork Pictures'. *Antique Collecting* 22 (1988): 35.
28  'Needlework of *Jesus Blessing the Children*'. From archive papers relating to Arey in the collection of the Museum of Old Newbury, Newburyport, Massachusetts.
29  Hegemony can be defined as the social position that legitimizes patriarchy through the production of a dominant masculine ideal and a masculine stereotype deployed in the subordination of women and other men. The concept of 'hegemonic masculinity' was formulated by R.W. Connell in 1987 and 1995; see R.W. Connell, *Gender and Power: Society, the Person and Sexual Politics* (Cambridge: Polity Press, 1987), pp. 183–90; and R.W. Connell, *Masculinities* (Cambridge: Polity Press, 1995), pp. 76–8.
30  Bill Arning, 'Elaine Reichek's Rewoven Histories'. *Art in America* (March 1999): 94.
31  Reichek's unpicking of the seams of needlework's history has a close affinity to Parker's project. For a comparison of Parker's and Reichek's work, see Lynne Cooke, 'Elaine Reichek: Memos for the New Millennium'. In David Frankel (ed.), *Elaine Reichek: At Home & in the World* [exhibition catalogue] (Brussels: Palais des Beaux-Arts de Bruxelles, 2000), p. 9; Paula Birnbaum, 'Elaine Reichek: Pixels, Bytes, and Stitches'. *Art Journal* 67(2) (2008): 19; and Glenn Adamson, 'Marginalia'. In Robert Cozzolino (ed.), *The Female Gaze: Women Artists Making Their World* [exhibition catalogue] (Philadelphia: Pennsylvania Academy of Fine Arts, 2012), p. 231.
32  Harry Brod 'Introduction: Themes and Theses of Men's Studies'. In Harry Brod (ed.), *The Making of Masculinities: The New Men's Studies* (Boston, MA, and London: Allen & Unwin, 1987), p. 17; and Whitehead, *Men and Masculinities*, pp. 33–4. Also see Jeff Hearn and David H.J. Morgan, 'Men, Masculinities and Social Theory'. In Jeff Hearn and David Morgan (eds), *Men, Masculinities & Social Theory* (London: Unwin Hyman, 1990), pp. 8–9; and C.J. Pascoe and Tristan Bridges, 'Introduction: (Re)Theorizing Masculinities: History, Hegemony, Reproduction, and Dislocation'. In C.J. Pascoe and Tristan Bridges (eds), *Exploring Masculinities: Identity, Inequality, Continuity, and Change* (New York and Oxford: Oxford University Press, 2015), pp. 1–34.
33  R.W. Connell, 'Masculinities, Relations Among'. In Michael Kimmel and Amy Aronson (eds), *Men & Masculinities: A Social, Cultural, and Historical Encyclopedia*, Vol. 2 (Santa Barbara, CA: ABC-CLIO, 2004), p. 509.
34  A full account of the historiography of women's needlework post-1970 is too vast to recount, however, key works (aside from the works already cited in notes 4

and 5) include, Rachel Maines, 'American Needlework in Transition, 1880-1930'. *University of Michigan Papers in Women's Studies* (May 1978): 57–84, 'Reassessing the Heritage of Art Needlework'. *WAN: Women Artists News* ['Needlework' Special Issue] 6(6–7) (December 1980–January 1981): 4–6, 'Tools of the Workbasket: Needlework Technology in the Industrial Era'. In Jeanette Lasansky (ed.), *Bits and Pieces: Textile Traditions* (Pennsylvania: Oral Traditions Project, 1991), pp. 110–19, and *Hedonizing Technologies: Paths to Pleasure in Hobbies and Leisure* (Baltimore, MD: Johns Hopkins University Press, 2009); Anthea Callen, *Angel in the Studio: Women in the Arts and Crafts Movement, 1870–1914* (London: Astragal, London, 1979); Daryl M. Hafter, 'Toward a Social History of Needlework Artists'. *Women's Art Journal* 2(2)(Autumn 1981–Winter 1982): 25–9; Lisa Tickner, *The Spectacle of Women: Imagery and the Suffrage Campaign, 1907–14* (London: Chatto & Windus, 1987); Anne L. Macdonald, *No Idle Hands: The Social History of American Knitting* (New York: Ballantine Books, 1988); and Maureen Daly Goggin and Beth Fowkes Tobin (eds), *Women and the Material Culture of Needlework & Textiles, 1750–1950* (Farnham, Surrey, and Burlington, VT: Ashgate, 2009).

35   References to men's needlework, if included at all, are often in passing and always brief; see Thomasina Beck, *The Embroiderer's Story: Needlework from the Renaissance to the Present Day* (Newton Abbott, Devon: David & Charles, 1995), pp. 135–40; Elissa Auther, *String, Felt and Thread: The Hierarchy of Art and Craft in American Art* (Minneapolis: University of Minnesota Press, 2010), pp. 160–2 and 166–7; Susan Frye, *Pens and Needles: Women's Textualities in Early Modern England* (Philadelphia and Oxford: University of Pennsylvania Press, 2010), pp. 21–3; and Vivienne Richmond, 'Men's Needlework'. In *Clothing the Poor in Nineteenth-Century England* (Cambridge: Cambridge University Press, 2013), pp. 117–20. Sometimes the making of needlework by men is obscured by discussion of consumption, see Joanne Turney, 'Patterns of Masculinity: Knitting Makes the Man?' In *The Culture of Knitting* (Oxford and New York: Berg, 2009), pp. 29–32. Aside from the work of sailors, embroideries and quilts by soldiers are the only examples of men's needlework to stimulate any serious study but this tends to emanate from specialist fields (from military history to quilt studies or their intersection). See, for example, Dagmar Neuland-Kitzerow, Salwa Joram and Erika Karasek (eds), *Inlaid Patchwork in Europe from 1500 to the Present/ Tuchinstarsien in Europa von 1500 bid heute* [exhibition catalogue] (Regensburg and Berlin: Schnell & Steiner GMBH/Museum Europäischer Kulturen, Staatliche Mussen zu Berlin, 2009); Christopher Breward, 'Sewing soldiers'. In Sue Prichard (ed.), *Quilts 1700–2010: Hidden Histories, Untold Stories* [exhibition catalogue]

(London: V&A Publishing, 2010), pp. 84–7; Sue Prichard, 'Precision Patchwork: Nineteenth Century Military Quilts'. *Textile History* 41(1) (Supplement) (2010): 214–26; Holly Furneaux and Sue Prichard, 'Contested Objects: Curating Soldier Art'. *Museum & Society* 13(4) (2015): 447–61; Annette Gero, *Wartime Quilts: Appliqué and Geometric Masterpieces from Military Fabrics* (Roseville, NSW: The Beagle Press, 2015); Holly Furneaux, *Military Men of Feeling: Emotion, Touch and Masculinity in the Crimean War* (Oxford: Oxford University Press, 2016); Nick Mansfield, *Soldiers as Workers: Class, Employment, Conflict and the Nineteenth-Century Military* (Liverpool: Liverpool University Press, 2016); and Holly Furneaux, *Created in Conflict: British Soldier Art from the Crimean War to Today* [exhibition catalogue] (Compton Verney, Warwickshire: Compton Verney Art Gallery & Park, 2018). The most significant analysis of men's needlework to date is that offered in Matilda Felix's *Nadelstiche. Sticken in der Kunst der Gegenwart* (Bielefeld: transcript Verlag, 2010), but Felix considers both women's and men's work and focuses only on contemporary examples.

36  Natalie Zemon Davis, '"Women's History" in Transition: The European Case'. *Feminist Studies* 3(3–4)(Spring–Summer 1976): 90; Billie Melman, 'Gender, History and Memory: The Invention of Women's Past in the Nineteenth and Twentieth Centuries'. *History and Memory* 5(1) (Spring–Summer, 1993): 10.

37  Feminist enquiry often began with the examination of women's own subjective position, for a comparative male example of this, see David Morgan, 'Men, Masculinity and the Process of Sociological Enquiry'. In Helen Roberts (ed.), *Doing Feminist Research* (London and New York: Routledge, 1981), p. 84.

38  R.W. Connell, *Masculinities*. p. 68. Lynne Segal has further stated: 'a "pure" masculinity cannot be asserted *except* in relation to what is defined as its opposite. It depends upon perpetual renunciation of "femininity,"' see Lynne Segal, 'Introduction'. In *Slow Motion: Changing Masculinities, Changing Men* (London: Virago, 1990), p. 114. I follow Connell's definition of 'masculinity' (pp. 67–71) as a position and a process rather than a stable subjectivity; and for Segal's notion that masculinity is always 'culturally contingent', see Lynne Segal, 'Introduction to the Third Edition–Men after Feminism: What's Left to Say?' In *Slow Motion: Changing Masculinities, Changing Men* (Houndmills, Basingstoke: Palgrave Macmillan, 2007 [Third, revised edition]), p. xxv.

39  Although 'female masculinity' has been widely discussed in recent years there is little on 'male femininity' aside from a short discussion in David M. Halperin's *How to be Gay* (Cambridge, MA: The Belknap Press of Harvard University Press, 2012), pp. 301–21. For the political agency of 'male femininity' as a form of

'*receptive* desire', see Leo Bersani, 'Is the Rectum a Grave?' *October* 43 (Winter 1987) ('AIDS: Cultural Analysis, Cultural Criticism'): 197–222; and Brian Pronger, 'On Your Knees: Carnal Knowledge, Masculine Dissolution, Doing Feminism'. In Tom Digby (ed.), *Men Doing Feminism* (New York and London: Routledge, 1998), pp. 69–80.

40 These statistics were compiled by the Men's Health Forum (2016–17) drawing on those provided by the Office of National Statistics, https://www.menshealthforum.org.uk/key-data-mental-health (accessed 1 June 2018).

41 I follow Sally Hesketh's differentiation between the different types of needlework: 'In the nineteenth century the term "needlework" could be divided into two broad categories –"decorative" needlework, also known as "ornamental" or "fancy" work; and "plain" needlework. "Decorative" needlework was one of the accomplishments' of a refined education, and was therefore the preserve of the gentlewoman. Its branches included embroidery, netting (using special needles or shuttles to produce a fine mesh), and pictorial embroidery using fine silks and wools. "Plain" sewing included hemming, darning, marking, knitting and lace-making, and was frequently regarded as the province of the lower classes.' See Sally Hesketh, "Needlework in the Lives and Novels of the Brontë sisters." *Brontë Studies* 1 (June 1997): 72.

42 A. Mary Murphy, 'The Theory and Practice of Counting Stitches as Stories: Material Evidences of Autobiography in Needlework'. *Women's Studies* 32(5) (2003): 643.

# Chapter 2

1 When it was published in 1984 *The Subversive Stitch* was received as a pathbreaking intervention in the history of art, as 'profound, well-researched, passionately argued'; its impact and continued relevance are testified by its reprinting in 1986 and re-issue in 1989, 1996 and 2010; see Hannah O'Shea, '*The Subversive Stitch* by Rozsika Parker'. *Spare Rib* 158 (September 1985): 40. Reprints and re-issues were by The Women's Press except that in 2010, which was by I.B. Tauris.

2 Rozsika Parker, 'Introduction'. In *The Subversive Stitch: Embroidery and the Making of the Feminine* (London and New York: I.B. Tauris, 2010), p. xiii.

3 Gay men, in particular, have often been seen as dangerous to domesticity (and the nuclear family). For example, in Alan Hollinghurst's novel *The Line of Beauty*,

set in Thatcher's Britain, the gay protagonist gets his comeuppance at the end of the novel by being told 'You can't have a real family, so you attach yourself to someone else's', *The Line of Beauty* (London: Picador, 2004), p. 481.
4 'Stitch in Time'. *The Times* (25 January 1996): 10.
5 Zoe Wood, 'A Stitch in Time – New Era for Home Sewing'. *The Guardian* (28 February 2017): 13.
6 Stuart Hillard, *Sew Fabulous: Inspiring Ideas to Bring the Joy of Sewing to Your Home* (London: Weidenfeld & Nicolson, 2013).
7 Paul Kendall, 'Sewing for Men: Believe Me, Chaps, Sew and Ye Shall Reap', *Telegraph* online, (7 April 2013), http://www.telegraph.co.uk/lifestyle/9975958/Sewing-for-men-Believe-me-chaps-sew-and-ye-shall-reap.html (accessed 9 July 2015); and John-Paul Flintoff, *Through the Eye of a Needle* (East Meon, Hampshire: Permanent Publications/The Sustainability Centre), 2009 – this was republished in a slightly revised form as *Sew Your Own* (London: Profile, 2010).
8 For example, in 2012 the English footballer Michael Ball was fined £6,000 by Britain's Football Association for a homophobic tweet about the actor Anthony Cotton in which Ball wrote: 'That fucking queer, get back to your sewing machine in Corrie, you moaning bastard.' Quoted in 'Racism and Homophobia in Football, Written Evidence Submitted by Stonewall'. House of Commons Select Committee (February 2012), https://publications.parliament.uk/pa/cm201213/cmselect/cmcumeds/89/89vw04.htm (accessed 17 November 2013).
9 Damien Barr, 'Why is Cooking Cool but Sewing is Cissy?' *The Times* (29 August 2002): 19.
10 Jane Gallop, *The Daughter's Seduction: Feminism and Psychoanalysis* (Ithaca, NY: Cornell University Press, 1982), p. 36.
11 Ibid., p. 37.
12 Parker, *The Subversive Stitch*, p. 45.
13 W.R. Lethaby, 'Notes on Some Mediaeval Embroiderers'. *Proceedings of the Society of Antiquarians* Second Series (12) (1907): 86.
14 A.J.B. Wace, 'Foreword'. In Mary Symonds and Louisa Pesel, *Needlework through the Ages: A Short Survey of Its Development in Decorative Art, with Particular Regard to Its Inspirational Relationship with Other Methods of Craftsmanship* (London: Hodder & Stoughton, 1928), p. vii.
15 I follow Parker's use of the term 'female heroines', *The Subversive Stitch*, p. 97.
16 Harrison is one of the very few historical male embroiderers to be documented, see Patricia Wardle, 'The King's Embroiderer: Edmund Harrison (1590–1667): I The Man and His Milieu'. *Textile History* 25(1) (1994): 29–59; and 'The King's

Embroiderer: Edmund Harrison (1590–1667): II His Work'. *Textile History* 26(2) (1995): 139–84.

17 Sigmund Freud, *An Infantile Neurosis and Other Works* (*The Standard Edition of the Complete Psychological Works of Sigmund Freud*: Vol. XVII) [Trans. James Strachey] (London: The Hogarth Press, 1964 [1918]).

18 Elaine Showalter, 'Piecing and Writing'. In Nancy K. Miller (ed.), *The Poetics of Gender* (New York: Columbia University Press, 1986), p. 223.

19 Sandra M. Gilbert and Susan Gubar, *The Madwoman in the Attic: The Woman Writer and the Nineteenth-Century Literary Imagination* (New Haven and London: Yale University Press, 1979), p. 6.

20 Cardinal describes this process as: 'La fille pareille que la mère, et la grand-mère, et l'arrière grand-mère, nous donnant naissance les unes aux autres', see Marie Cardinal, *Le Passé empiété* (Paris: Editions Grasset & Fasquelle, 1983), p. 31. Cardinal's title can be translated as 'the past re-appropriated' or 'the backstitch' – for a comparison of Cardinal's and Parker's titles and books, see Carolyn A. Durham, 'The Subversive Stitch: Female Craft, Culture, and Écriture'. *Women's Studies* 17(3&4) (January 1990): 341–59.

21 Rozsika Parker (and Amanda Sebestyen) 'A Literature of Our Own [an interview with Elaine Showalter]'. *Spare Rib* 78 (January 1979): 27.

22 Rozsika Parker, 'Images of Men'. *Spare Rib* 99 (October 1980): 8.

23 Eve Kosofsky Sedgwick, *Between Men: English Literature and Male Homosocial Desire* (New York: Columbia University Press, 1985), pp. 174–5.

24 Parker, 'A Literature of Our Own'. 27.

25 Richard Rutt, *A History of Hand Knitting* (London: B.T. Batsford, 1987), p. 151.

26 She also called him the 'Christian Dior of knitting', see Marjorie Proops, 'Foreword'. In *Knit with Norbury* (London: Odhams Press, 1952), p. 6.

27 Kaffe Fassett, *Glorious Inspiration: Kaffe Fassett's Needlepoint Source Book* (London: Ebury Press, 1991).

28 Grayson Perry, *The Descent of Man* (London: Allen Lane, 2016), p. 4.

29 Sue Taylor, 'Mark Newport's Meta-Heroes: Unravelling Myths of Masculinity'. In Gregory Wittkopp and Emily Zilber (eds), *Mark Newport: Superheroes in Action* (Cranbrook, MI: Cranbrook Art Museum, 2009), p. 16.

30 Wendell Brown, 'Tracing the Stitches'. *International Review of African-American Art* 15(4) (1998): 37.

31 Kellie Jones, 'To the Max: Energy and Experimentation'. In *Energy/Experimentation: Black Artists and Abstraction, 1964–1980* [exhibition catalogue] (New York: Studio Museum in Harlem, 2006) p. 15.

32 Norman Willis, 'How I Got Stitched Up …'. *Cross Stitcher* 72 (August 1998): 74.
33 Roger Hutchinson, *The Silent Weaver: The Extraordinary Life and Art of Angus McPhee* (Edinburgh: Birlinn, 2011); William Lazaro et al., *Arthur Bispo do Rosário* [exhibition catalogue] (Rio de Janeiro and London: Réptil Editora for the Fudação Nacional de Artes, Funarte and the Victoria and Albert Museum, 2012); and Thérèse Lebrun et al., *Jules Leclercq, 1894–1966* [exhibition catalogue] (Lille: Musée d'art modern Lille Métropole, 2006).
34 Amy Nutt, 'A Stitch in Time'. *Sports Illustrated* (16 October 1994): 17, 19; Amy Fusselman, 'Through the Needle: The Art of Ray Materson'. *Raw Vision* 17 (Winter, 1996/1997): 46–9; and Ray Materson and Melanie Materson, *Sins and Needles: A Story of Spiritual Mending* (Chapel Hill, NC: Algonquin Books, 2002).
35 Mark Godfrey, 'Boetti and Afghanistan'. In Lynne Cooke, Mark Godfrey and Christian Rattemeyer (eds), *Alighiero Boetti: Game Plan* [exhibition catalogue] (London: Tate, 2012), pp. 163–75. The women who made Boetti's embroideries were first brought to light in Randi Malkin, *Boetti by Afghan People: Peshawar, Pakistan, 1990* (Santa Monica, CA: RAM Publications, 2011).
36 Adrian Searle, 'Alighiero Boetti: Signor Lazybones'. *The Guardian* (27 February 2012), http://www.guardian.co.uk/artanddesign/2012/feb/27/alighiero-boetti-tate-modern/print (accessed 17 September 2016).
37 Clyde Olliver, 'Forget-Me-Not: British Servicemen's Embroidery'. *Embroidery* 54 (January 2003): 38–9; Paddy Hartley, 'The Forgotten Fighters'. *Embroidery* 69 (January/February 2018): 36–7; and Gavin Fry, 'Male Textile Artist Motivations in 1980s Britain: A Practice-Based Enquiry'. Unpublished PhD dissertation, University of Brighton, 2018. Gavin Fry has also conducted research on the history of men as teachers of needlework in occupational therapy. I am deeply grateful to him for talking to me about his work and for many suggestions and references over many years.
38 Mark Newport, 'The Masculine in Fiber Art'. *Surface Design Journal* 22(3) (Spring 1998): 29.
39 Stephen Beal, *The Very Stuff: Poems on Color, Thread and the Habits of Women* (Loveland, CO: Interweave Press, 1995).
40 J.W. Mackail, *The Life of William Morris*, Vol. I (London: Longmans, Green & Co., 1899), p. 129.
41 Burden later recorded that her husband 'taught me the first principles of laying stitches together so as to cover the ground smoothly and radiating them properly afterwards. We studied old pieces and by unpicking &, we learnt much but it was uphill work fascinating but only carried through by his enormous energy and perseverance', British Library Manuscript Department BL Add. Mss. 45341.

42  Mackail, *The Life of William Morris*, Vol. I, p. 129.
43  Frederick Kirchhoff, *William Morris: The Construction of a Male Self, 1856–1872* (Athens: Ohio University Press, 1990), p. 39.
44  Ibid., pp. 51–2.
45  Nancy Chodorow, *The Reproduction of Mothering: Psychoanalysis and the Sociology of Gender* (Berkeley: University of California Press, 1978), p. 9.
46  Charlotte Abrahams, 'A Stitch in Time'. *Selected Journal* 2 (Spring–Summer 2015): 24–8; and Katy Emck, 'A Stitch in Time'. *Selvedge* 70 (May 2016): 36–9.
47  D.W. Winnicott, 'Mirror-Role of Mother in Family Life and Child Development'. [1967] In *Playing and Reality* (London: Tavistock Publications, 1971), pp. 111–18.
48  'Prison Stories: Karl'. http://www.finecellwork.co.uk/ourstory and 'Prison Stories: Rehabilitation'. http://www.finecellwork.co.uk/ourstory (accessed 6 December 2010).
49  Cheryl Conway-Hughes, *The Making of the Wandsworth Prison Quilt* (Privately Published, 2010) [copy in V&A National Art Library Special Collections VA.2013.0018].
50  Claire Smith, 'Doing Time: Patchwork as a Tool of Social Rehabilitation in British Prisons'. *V&A Online Journal* 1 (Autumn 2010), http://www.vam.ac.uk/content/journals/research-journal/issue-01/doing-time-patchwork-as-a-tool-of-social-rehabilitiation-in-british-prisons/ (accessed 1 December 2011).
51  Jenny Hart, 'Man-broidery', http://whipup.net/2009/02/6/man-broidery (accessed 12 March 2013).
52  'Manbroidery: An Interview with Johnny Murder'. In Leanne Prain, *Hoopla: The Art of Unexpected Embroidery* (Vancouver: Arsenal Pulp Press, 2011), pp. 45–9.
53  Parker, 'Introduction', p. xiii.
54  'Subverting the Traditional: An Interview with Rosa Martyn'. *Hoopla*, p. 381.
55  Parker, 'Introduction'. p. xiii.
56  Paul Callan, 'Rock, a Soul in Torment'. *Mirror* (3 October 1985), quoted in Simon Watney, *Policing Desire: Pornography, AIDS and the Media* (London: Cassell, 1987), p. 88; and Baz Bamigboye and Peter McKay, 'The Last Days of Rock Hudson'. *Daily Mail* (3 October 1985), quoted in Neil Bartlett, *Who Was That Man? A Present for Mr. Oscar Wilde* (London: Serpent's Tail, 1988), p. 63.
57  ' … Stitch One'. *The Financial Times* (29 January 1977): 7; John Slim, 'Hanging a Bright Image by Tapestry'. *The Birmingham Post* (12 January 1979): 6. Also see Richard and Elizabeth Adler, *Needlepoint: A New Look* (London: Sidgwick & Jackson, 1981).
58  Bill Jones, *Alone: The Triumph and Tragedy of John Curry* (London: Bloomsbury, 2014), p. 329.

59 'By Way of Recreation, Everett Enjoyed Needlework', *Telegraph* online, (5 April 1995), http://www.telegraph.co.uk/news/obituaries/culture-obituaries/tv-radio-obituaries/5060997/Kenny-Everett.html (26 June 2015).
60 Anne Caborn, 'Needles Out Men! Who Says Embroidery Has Always Been Strictly for the Girls?' *Liverpool Echo* (17 November 1984): 9.
61 Parker, *The Subversive Stitch*, p. 17.
62 Sigmund Freud, *Jokes and Their Relation to the Unconscious* (*The Standard Edition of the Complete Psychological Works of Sigmund Freud*: Vol. II) [Trans. James Strachey] (London: The Hogarth Press, 1960 [1905]).
63 Mahrukh Tarapor, 'John Lockwood Kipling and British Art Education in India'. *Victorian Studies* 24(1) (Autumn, 1980): 53–81.
64 Anna Hickey-Moody and Timothy Laurie, 'Masculinity and Ridicule'. In Bettina Papenburg (ed.), *Gender: Laughter* (Farrington Hills, MI: Macmillan Reference, 2017), pp. 215–28.
65 Alexander Doty, *Flaming Classics: Queering the Film Canon* (New York and London: Routledge, 2000), p. 182.
66 *Home Improvement*, 'A Sew, Sew Evening', season 3, episode 4; *Friends*, 'The One With Ross's Teeth', season 6, episode 8; *30 Rock*, 'Corporate Crush', season 1, episode 19; *The Big Bang Theory*, 'The Champagne Reflection', season 8, episode 10.
67 *Family Guy*, 'North by North Quahog', season 4, episode 1.
68 *Curb Your Enthusiasm*, 'I Think He Might Be Gay … ', season 8, episode 10.
69 *Are You Being Served?* 'Do You Take This Man?', season 6, episode 3; and 'Gambling Fever', season 10, episode 4.
70 *Will & Grace*, 'Whoa, Nelly', season 4, episode 13; 'All about Christmas Eve', season 5, episode 11; 'Field of Queens', season 5, episode 12; 'Fagmalion 3: Bye Bye Beardy', season 5, episode 17; 'East Side Story', season 6, episode 17; 'Queen's for a Day', season 7, episode 10; and 'Kiss and Tell'. season 7, episode 24.
71 *Will & Grace*, 'Looking for Mr Good Enough', season 6, episode 14.
72 Judith Rossner, *Looking for Mr. Goodbar* (New York: Simon & Schulster, 1975), p. 335.
73 Michel Foucault, *The History of Sexuality: Volume 1: The Will to Knowledge* (Trans. Richard Hurley) (London: Penguin, 1998 [1976]), p. 43.
74 See Kaja Silverman's 'A Woman's Soul Enclosed in a Man's Body: Femininity in Male Homosexuality'. In *Male Subjectivity at the Margins* (New York and London: Routledge, 1992), pp. 339–88.
75 Carl O. Westphal, 'Die konträre Sexualempfindung: Symptom eines neuropathischen (psychopathischen) Zustandes'. *Archiv für Psychiatrie und*

*Nervenkrankheiten* (2) (1869–70): 73–108, reprinted as 'Contrary Sexual Feeling: Symptom and a Neuropathic (Psychopathic) Condition'. In Michael A. Lombardi-Nash (ed. and trans.), *Sodomites and Urnings: Homosexual Representations in Classic German Journals* (New York: Harrington Park Press, 2006), pp. 87–120.

76  David M. Halperin, 'How to Do the History of Homosexuality'. *GLQ: A Journal of Lesbian and Gay Studies* 6(1) (2000): 109.

77  Foucault, *The History of Sexuality: Volume 1*, p. 101.

78  Caroline Evans, 'Dreams That Only Money Can Buy … or, the Shy Tribe in Flight from Discourse'. *Fashion Theory* 1(2) (1997): 170.

79  Letter from Truman Capote to Donald Cullivan, 20 June 1960, quoted in Gerald Clarke (ed.), *Too Brief a Treat: The Letters of Truman Capote* (New York: Vintage, 2004), p. 286.

80  Edmund White, *A Boy's Own Story* (Boston: E.P. Dutton, 1982), pp. 152–3; *The Beautiful Room Is Empty* (New York: Alfred P. Knopf, 1988), pp. 108, 204; and Edmund *The Farewell Symphony* (London: Chatto & Windus, 1997), pp. 162 and 290.

81  Alan Hollinghurst, *The Swimming-Pool Library* (London: Chatto & Windus, 1988), p. 89; and *The Stranger's Child* (London: Picador, 2011), p. 70.

82  R.W. Burchfield (ed.) *A Supplement to the Oxford English Dictionary*, Vol. III (Oxford: Clarendon Press, 1982), p. 541. Auden's review of Ackerley's book appeared in the *New York Review of Books* but Burchfield's citation of '[popularized by W.H. Auden (see 1980)]' refers to a comment by John Lenton (in 'W.H. Auden'. *The Times Literary Supplement* (21 March 1980): 324) which states 'I suspect "Plain-Sewing" to be Auden's own invention, but its meaning is fairly clear, as it involves a pun on "sowing" (seed or semen) and a reference to the two-and-fro [*sic*] action of the hand in sewing'.

83  For women's experiences of the use of this phrase, see Pamela Johnson, 'Art and Women's Work? News from the "Knitting Circle"'. *Oral History* ('The Crafts' Special Issue) 18(2) (Autumn 1990): 50–3.

84  Nicholas Owen, 'Men and the 1970s British Women's Liberation Movement'. *The Historical Journal* 56(3) (September 2013): 801–26.

85  Ian Townson, 'The Brixton Fairies and the South London Gay Community Centre, Brixton 1974–6' (14 February 2012), http://www.urban75.org/blog/the-brixton-fairies-and-the-south-london-gay-community-centre-brixton-1974-6/ (accessed 1 August 2015); and Peter Cross, 'Revolting Queers: A Memory of South London Gay Liberation'. In Astrid Proll (ed.), *Goodbye to London: Radical Art & Politics in the 70's* (Berlin: Hatje Cantz Verlag for neue Gesellschaft für bildende Kunst, 2010), p. 77.

86 There are numerous references to the activities of gay organizations in *Spare Rib*, even though they are conspicuously absent from Rozsika Parker and Griselda Pollock (eds), *Framing Feminism: Art and the Women's Movement 1970–85* (London: Pandora, 1987).

87 Parker makes no direct reference to this image in her text ([illus. no.] 3) but the source is given as *Gay Left*. It was originally published in Alison Hennegen, 'Lesbians in Literature'. *Gay Left: A Gay Socialist Journal* 9 (Winter 1979): 22.

88 Simon Watney, 'The Ideology of the GLF'. In Gay Left Collective, *Homosexuality: Power and Politics* (London: Verso, 1980), p. 74.

89 David Medalla, 'A Stitch in Time'. *South Hill Park Bulletin* (July/August 1982), quoted in Guy Brett, *Exploding Galaxies: The Art of David Medalla* (London: Kala Press, 1995), pp. 95–7.

90 Ibid., p. 194 [no. 13].

91 John A. Walker, *Left Shift: Radical Art in 1970s Britain* (London and New York: I.B. Tauris, 2002), p. 47.

92 José Esteban Muñoz, 'Just Like Heaven: Queer Utopian Art and the Aesthetic Dimension'. In *I Remember Heaven: Jim Hodges and Andy Warhol* (St. Louis, MO: Contemporary Art Museum St. Louis, 2007), pp. 18–33.

93 See Olga M. Viso, 'Beauty and Its Dilemmas'. In *Regarding Beauty: A View of the Late Twentieth Century* (Washington, DC: Hirshhorn Museum and Sculpture Garden, Smithsonian Institution, 1999), p. 210, for a photograph of Hodges's mother sewing.

94 Olga Viso, 'The Eros of Everyday Life'. In *Jim Hodges: Give More than You Take* [exhibition catalogue] (Dallas and Minneapolis: Dallas Museum of Art and Walker Art Center, 2014), p. 113.

95 Ibid.

96 Holland Cotter, 'Art Review: Messages Woven, Sewn or Floating in the Art'. *New York Times* (25 September 1998): E37.

97 See, for example, Maria Tamboukou, *Sewing, Fighting and Writing: Radical Practices in Work, Politics and Culture* (London and New York: Rowan & Littlefield, 2016); and Rachel P. Maines, *The Technology of Orgasm: 'Hysteria', the Vibrator, and Women's Sexual Satisfaction* (Baltimore and London: The Johns Hopkins University Press, 1998).

98 Nanette Salomon, 'The Art Historical Canon: Sins of Omission'. In Joan E. Hartman and Ellen Messer-Davidow (eds), *(En)gendering Knowledge: Feminists in Academe* (Knoxville: University of Tennessee Press, 1991), p. 222.

99 Elaine Showalter, 'Pen Men'. *London Review of Books* (20 March 1986): 8

100 See my, 'The 1904 Feis na nGleann: Craftwork, Folk Life and National Identity'. *Folk Life: Journal of Ethnological Studies* 45(1) (2006): 24–39.
101 These ideas are explored more fully in my, 'From Parnell's Suit to Casement's Closet: Masculinity, Homosexuality and the Fashioning of the Irish Nation'. In Fintan Cullen (ed.) *The Visual Culture of Ireland and Empire* (Bern and Oxford: Peter Lang, forthcoming).
102 This term was first coined in J.C. Flugel, *The Psychology of Clothes* (London: The Hogarth Press, 1930), pp. 110–11.
103 Christopher Breward, 'Renouncing Consumption: Men, Fashion and Luxury, 1870–1914'. In Amy de la Haye and Elizabeth Wilson (eds), *Defining Dress: Dress as Object, Meaning and Identity* (Manchester and New York: Manchester University Press, 1999), pp. 48–62; and idem, *The Hidden Consumer: Masculinities, Fashion and City Life 1860–1914* (Manchester and New York: Manchester University Press, 1999).
104 Donald E. Hall, *Queer Theories* (Basingstoke: Palgrave Macmillan, 2003), p. 7.
105 For an overview of this see Gail Bederman, 'Why Study "Masculinity," Anyway? Perspectives from the Old Days'. *Culture, Society & Masculinities* 3(1) (2011): 13–25.
106 Paul Smith, 'Men in Feminism: Men and Feminist Theory'. In Alice Jardine and Paul Smith (eds), *Men in Feminism* (New York and London: Routledge, 1987), p. 34; Stephen Heath, 'Male Feminism'. In, *Men in Feminism*, p. 4.
107 Margaret R. Higennot, 'Fictions of Feminine Voice: Antiphony and Silence in Hardy's *Tess of the d'Urbervilles*'. In Laura Claridge and Elizabeth Langland (eds), *Out of Bounds: Male Writers and Gender(ed) Criticism* (Amherst: University of Massachusetts, 1990), pp. 197–8.
108 Elaine Showalter, 'Critical Cross-Dressing; Male Feminists and Woman of the Year'. In Jardine and Smith (eds), *Men in Feminism*, p. 12.
109 Constance Penley and Sharon Willis (eds), *Male Trouble* (Minneapolis: University of Minnesota Press, 1993), xvii.
110 Judith Butler, *Gender Trouble: Feminism and the Subversion of Identity* (New York and London: Routledge, 1990), p. 30.
111 Judith Butler, 'Imitation and Gender Subordination'. In Diana Fuss (ed.), *Inside/Out: Lesbian Theories, Gay Theories* (New York and London: Routledge, 1991), p. 22.
112 Butler has stated 'performativity is neither free play nor theatrical self-presentation; nor can it be simply equated with performance', see Judith Butler, *Bodies That Matter: On the Discursive Limits of 'Sex'* (New York & London: Routledge, 1993), p. 95.

113  R.W. Connell, 'A Very Straight Gay: Masculinity, Homosexual Experience, and the Dynamics of Gender'. *American Sociological Review* 57(6) (December 1992): 742.

114  Darryl B. Hall, '"Feminine" Heterosexual Men: Subverting Heteropatriarchal Sexual Scripts?' *The Journal of Men's Studies* 14(2) (Spring 2006): 145–59.

115  Parker, *The Subversive Stitch*, pp. 26, 58, 89, 139 and 214.

116  Ann Cvetkovich, 'Public Feelings'. *South Atlantic Quarterly* 103 (3) (Summer 2007): 453.

117  Raymond Williams, 'Structures of Feeling'. In *Marxism and Literature* (Oxford and New York: Oxford University Press, 1977), pp. 128–35 [p. 133].

118  Eve Kosofsky Sedgwick, 'Queer Performativity: Henry James's *The Art of the Novel*'. *GLQ: A Journal of Lesbian and Gay Studies* 1(1) (1993): 5.

119  Cvetkovich, 'Public Feelings': 462.

120  For these points see Susan Frye, *Pens and Needles: Women's Textualities in Early Modern England* (Philadelphia and Oxford: University of Pennsylvania Press, 2010), p. 26; Cheryl Buckley, 'From the Margins: Theorizing the History and Significance of Making and Designing Clothes at Home'. *Journal of Design History* 11(2) (June 1998): 171; Rosemary Mitchell, 'A Stitch in Time?: Women, Needlework, and the Making of History in Victorian Britain'. *Journal of Victorian Culture* 1(2) (1996): 185–202; Rohan Amanda Maitzen, 'Stitches in Time: Needlework and Victorian Historiography'. In *Gender, Genre, and Victorian Historical Writing* (New York and London: Garland, 1998), pp. 61–102; Linda Pershing, 'Review: *The Subversive Stitch: Embroidery and the Making of the Feminine* by Rozsika Parker …' *Signs* 14(2) (Winter 1989): 508; and Lisa Vinebaum, 'Carole Frances Lung's Sewing Rebellion: Resisting the Global Apparel Industry, One Stitch at a Time'. Paper delivered at 'The Subversive Stitch Revisited: The Politics of Cloth', Victoria and Albert Museum, London, 30 November 2013, https://soundcloud.com/goldsmithsuol/subversive-stitch-vinebaum?in=goldsmithsuol/sets/the-subversive-stitch (accessed 1 July 2014).

121  For conceptualizations of the various twentieth-century and twenty-first-century 'crises of masculinity', see Michael S. Kimmel, 'The Contemporary "Crisis" of Masculinity in Historical Perspective'. In Harry Brod (ed.), *The Making of Masculinities: The New Men's Studies* (Boston, MA, and London: Allen & Unwin, 1987), pp. 121–53; Roger Horrocks, *Masculinities in Crisis: Myths, Fantasies, and Realities* (Houndmills, Basingstoke: Palgrave Macmillan, 1994); Abigail Solomon-Godeau, *Male Trouble: A Crisis in Representation* (London and New York: Thames and Hudson, 1997); Sally Robinson, *Marked Men:*

*White Masculinity in Crisis* (New York: Columbia University Press, 2000); John MacInnes, 'The Crisis of Masculinity and the Politics of Identity'. In Stephen M. Whitehead and Frank J. Barrett (eds), *The Masculinities Reader* (Cambridge: Polity Press, 2001), pp. 311–29; and John Benyon 'Masculinities and the Notion of Crisis'. In John Benyon (ed.) *Masculinities and Culture* (Philadelphia: Open University Press, 2002), pp. 75–97.

122 John Tosh, 'The Making of Masculinities: The Middle Class in Late Nineteenth-Century Britain'. In Angela V. John and Claire Eustance (eds), *The Men's Share?: Masculinities, Male Support and Women's Suffrage in Britain, 1890–1920* (London and New York: Routledge, 1997), p. 39.

123 Robert J. Corber, *Homosexuality in Cold War America: Resistance and the Crisis of Masculinity* (Durham & London: Duke University Press, 1997).

124 Anthony Clare, *On Men: Masculinity in Crisis* (London: Chatto & Windus, 2000); for a more recent overview, see Pankaj Mishra, 'Masculinity in Crisis: Man Trouble'. *The Guardian* [Review Supplement] 9 (17 March 2018): 6–11.

125 John MacInnes, *The End of Masculinity: The Confusion of Sexual Genesis and Sexual Difference in Modern Society* (Buckingham: Open University Press, 1998), p. 11.

126 Susan Faludi, *Stiffed: The Betrayal of the Modern Man* (London: Chatto & Windus, 1999), p. 6.

127 Rozsika Parker and Griselda Pollock, *Old Mistresses: Women, Art and Ideology* (London: Pandora, 1981), p. 58.

128 Images sissifying sewing for boys have been relatively commonplace in the history of children's literature. Recently the tide has started to turn. Examples include, the teenage boy, Ben Fletcher, who becomes the winner of an All-UK Knitting Competition in T.S. Easton's *Boys Don't Knit* (London: Hot Key Books, 2014) and *An English Boy in New York* (London: Hot Key Books, 2014); or Aya Kanno's *Otomen* manga series (2007–13) in which the lead character, Asuka Masamune, a sporty schoolboy secretly 'loves girly things – sewing, knitting, making cute animals and reading shojo comics'. Such books explore how a boy's interest and aptitude in needlework can be accepted even if it goes against prevailing social codes. The quote is Grayson Perry's from 'Martin Parr: Made in Britain'. *The Observer Magazine* (24 February 2019): 34.

129 Sandra Alfoldy has imaginatively speculated that Minecraft, as well as several games for the Sony PlayStation and Nintendo DS, employ textiles not just as visual markers but also in terms of haptic play and affect. See Sandra Alfoldy, 'Cyber Comfort: Textiles as Markers of Care in Video Games'. *Textile: Cloth and Culture* 16(1) (February 2018): 24–33.

## Chapter 3

1. Frankland, Noble, *Prince Henry: Duke of Gloucester* (London: Weidenfeld and Nicolson, 1980), p. 27.
2. Ibid., p. 36.
3. Duke of Windsor, *A King's Story: The Memoirs of H.R.H. The Duke of Windsor* (London: Cassell, 1951), p. 34.
4. Christopher Warwick, *Abdication* (London: Sidgwick & Jackson, 1986), pp. 73–4.
5. 'James Wilson–Boy Sampler Stitcher'. http://needleprint.blogspot.com/2010/08/james-wilson-boy-sampler-stitcher-1828.html (accessed 2 December 2012).
6. Marcus B. Huish, *Samplers & Tapestry Embroideries* (London: Longmans, Green & Co., 1913), p. 84.
7. Parker makes no reference to this sampler in her text but makes this comment below the illustration. The illustrations to her text are unpaginated. See Parker, *The Subversive Stitch*, illustration no. 105.
8. I am following Parker in her reading of Chodorow's *The Reproduction of Mothering*. Parker drew on Chodorow to explore needlework in the mother-daughter relationship, but Chodorow's actual ideas, especially with regard to 'mirroring,' were also meant to be applied to boys, see Parker, pp. 128–30. Parker did later begin to apply her ideas to boys (but not directly to boy's needlework) see Rozsika Parker, *Torn in Two: The Experience of Maternal Ambivalence* (London: Virago, 1995), pp. 262–302.
9. For Parker's comments on how young girls aired their 'misery, rebellion and frustration' in samplers, see Parker, 'The Word for Embroidery Was Work', 44; and *The Subversive Stitch*, p. 132.
10. This is in a private collection.
11. Julie Grant, 'A "Real Boy" and Not a Sissy: Gender, Childhood, and Masculinity, 1890–1940'. *Journal of Social History* 37(4) (Summer, 2004): 829–51.
12. Maureen Daly Goggin, 'An "Essamplaire Essai" on the Rhetoricity of Needlework Sampler-Making: A Contribution to Theorizing and Historicizing Rhetorical Praxis'. *Rhetoric Review* 21(4) (2002): 332.
13. Josef Breuer and Sigmund Freud, *Studies on Hysteria* (*The Standard Edition of the Complete Psychological Works of Sigmund Freud*: Vol. II) [Trans. James Strachey] (London: The Hogarth Press, 1955 [1895]), p. 13.
14. Kathleen Bailey, '"Pain and Nothing Fancy": Her Majesty's Inspectors and School Needlework in the 1870s'. *Journal of Educational Administration and History* 18(1) (1986): 34–45.

15 'Metropolitan Pauper Schools'. *The Illustrated London News* LX (4 May 1872): 441
16 'Needlework for Boys'. *Women's Penny Paper* (26 October 1889): 53.
17 Parker, *The Subversive Stitch*, p. 8. The 'Angel in the House' concept was devised by a man, Coventry Patmore, in his narrative poem (1854), and popularized by leading Victorians from Alfred Tennyson to John Ruskin.
18 Elizabeth Langland, *Nobody's Angels: Middle-Class Women and Domestic Ideology in Victorian Culture* (Ithaca and London: Cornell University Press, 1995), p. 8.
19 Elaine Showalter, 'Killing the Angel in the House: The Autonomy of Women Writers'. *The Antioch Review* 32(3) (Fall 1972): 339.
20 Parker, *The Subversive Stitch*, p. 165.
21 Clare M. Tylee, '"A Better World for Both": Men, Cultural Transformation and the Suffragettes'. In Maroula Joannou and June Purvis (eds), *The Women's Suffrage Movement: New Feminist Perspectives* (Manchester and New York: Manchester University Press, 1998), p. 152. For a more recent attempt to address this see my 'The Spectacle of Masculinity: Men and the Visual Culture of the Suffrage Campaign'. In Miranda Garret and Zoë Thomas (eds), *Suffrage and the Arts: Visual Culture, Politics and Enterprise* (London: Bloomsbury, 2018), pp. 205–29.
22 Rozsika Parker, '"Killing the Angel in the House": Creativity, Femininity and Aggression'. *International Journal of Psychoanalysis* 79(4) (1998): 770 and 758.
23 J.A. Mangan and James Walvin (eds), *Manliness and Morality: Middle-Class Masculinity in Britain and America, 1800–1940* (Manchester: Manchester University Press, 1987), pp. 1 and 6.
24 Donald E. Hall, *Fixing Patriarchy: Feminism and Mid-Victorian Male Novelists* (New York: New York University Press, 1996), pp. 3–4.
25 Carol Christ, 'Victorian Masculinity and the Angel in the House'. In Martha Vicinus (ed.), *A Widening Sphere: Changing Roles of Victorian Women* (Bloomington & London: Indiana University Press, 1977), p. 160.
26 James Eli Adams, *Dandies and Desert Saints: Styles of Victorian Manhood* (Ithaca and London: Cornell University Press, 1995), pp. 1–20; and Christopher Lloyd, *The Burdens of Intimacy: Psychoanalysis and Victorian Masculinity* (Chicago & London: Chicago University Press, 1999), pp. xi–xxi.
27 Virginia Woolf, *Killing the Angel in the House: Seven Essays* (London: Penguin, 1995 [1931]), p. 5. The term 'Angel in the House' was first deployed by Woolf in her 'Professions for Women,' paper delivered to The Women's Service League on 21 January 1931. This paper was published posthumously in *The Death of the Moth and Other Essays* (London: The Hogarth Press, 1942), pp. 149–54. And see *Catalogue of the Exhibition of English Needlework (Past and Present) in Aid of the*

*Artists' General Benevolent Institution* [exhibition catalogue] (London: Printed Privately for The Lord & Lady Maud Carnegie, 1934). For increasing interest in men's needlework, see the Pathé News film of this exhibition that gives over much of the discussion to the Duke of Windsor (then the Prince of Wales) who 'heads a list of distinguished man who choose needlework as an interesting and useful hobby'; it also shows Duncan Grant in the process of drawing a design for an embroidery. Pathé News, *Needlework De Luxe*, 15 March 1934 [Film ID 1626. 13], https://www.britishpathe.com/video/needlework-de-luxe/query/VIII (accessed 30 June 2014).

28  Letter from Henry James to Alice James, 10 March 1869, in Percy Lubbock (ed.), *The Letters of Henry James*, Vol. I (London: Macmillan and Co., 1920), p. 17.
29  Miranda Seymour, *A Ring of Conspirators: Henry James and His Literary Circle, 1895–1915* (London: Hodder and Stoughton, 1988), p. 117.
30  George Santayana, *The Middle Span* (London: Constable, 1947 [1945]), p. 128.
31  Edith Wharton, *A Backward Glance* (New York and London: D. Appleton-Century Co., 1934), p. 227.
32  A.C. Benson, *Memories and Friends* (London: John Murray, 1924), p. 261.
33  Edmund White, 'Introduction'. In Howard Sturgis, *Belchamber* (New York: NYRB, 2008 [1904]), p. vii.
34  Wharton, *A Backward Glance*, p. 225; Percy Lubbock, *Mary Cholmondeley: A Sketch from Memory* (London: Jonathan Cape, 1928), pp. 58–9.
35  Benson, *Memories and Friends*, pp. 271–2.
36  Santayana, *The Middle Span*, pp. 126–7.
37  Letter from Henry James to Edith Wharton, 29 October 1909, quoted in Hermione Lee, *Edith Wharton* (London: Pimlico, 2013 [2007]), p. 245.
38  Susan E. Gunter and Steven H. Jobe, 'Introduction'. In Susan E. Gunter and Steven H. Jobe (eds), *Dearly Beloved Friends: Henry James's Letters to Younger Men* (Ann Arbor: University of Michigan Press, 2004), p. 115.
39  Letter from Henry James to Howard Sturgis, 10 April 1900, in ibid., pp. 126–7.
40  H.O. Sturgis, *Belchamber* (London: Archibald Constable & Co., 1904), p. 19.
41  Letter from Henry James to Howard Sturgis, 18 November 1913, in Susan E. Gunter and Steven H. Jobe (eds), *Dearly Beloved Friends*, p. 133.
42  Wharton, *A Backward Glance*, p. 235.
43  E.M. Forster, 'Howard Overing Sturgis [1935]'. In *Abinger Harvest* (Penguin, 1967 [1936]), p. 137. Not a single piece of embroidery by Sturgis seems to have survived. I am grateful to Matthew Sturgis, Miranda Seymour and Henry Porter for their help locating information about Sturgis's needlework.

44 Benson's mother had asked James to read it, see E.F. Benson, *Final Edition: Informal Autobiography* (London: That Hogarth Press, 1988 [1940]), pp. 1–2.
45 E.F. Benson, *Paul* (London: Heinemann, 1906), pp. 68, 75 and 106.
46 E.F. Benson, *The Countess of Lowndes Square and Other Stories* (London: Cassell & Co., 1920), pp. 269 and 271.
47 E.F. Benson, *Dodo the Second* (London: Hodder and Stoughton, 1914), pp. 121–2.
48 Mosse, *The Image of Man*, p. 82.
49 Benson, *Dodo the Second*, p. 21.
50 The queer image of Aunt Georgie recalls not only Parker's description of the female embroider but also Eve Kosofsky Sedgwick's description of shame as 'eyes down, head averted'; see Parker, *The Subversive Stitch*, p. 10, and Sedgwick, 'Queer Performativity', 5.
51 E.F. Benson, *The Freaks of Mayfair* (London: T.N. Foulis, 1916), pp. 33–47.
52 E.F. Benson, *Queen Lucia* (London: Hutchinson & Co., 1920), p. 40. The sexual subtext of Georgie's embroidery was clearly an 'open secret'. Nancy Mitford later recalled: 'No writer nowadays would allow Georgie to do his embroidery and dye his hair and wear his little cape and sit for hours chatting with Lucia and playing celestial Mozartino, without hinting at Boys in the background.' See, Nancy Mitford, 'Garden of Delights: *Lucia's Progress* and *Mapp and Lucia* by E.F. Benson'. *The Sunday Times* (23 April 1967): 50.
53 John Tosh, 'Domesticity and Manliness in the Victorian Middle Class: The Family of Edward White Benson'. In Michael Roper and John Tosh (eds), *Manful Assertions: Masculinities in Britain since 1800* (London and New York: Routledge, 1991), pp. 45 and 66.
54 John Tosh, *A Man's Place: Masculinity and the Middle-Class Home in Victorian England* (New Haven and London: Yale University Press, 1999), p. 191.
55 E.F. Benson, *Mother* (London: Hodder and Stoughton, 1930), p. 246; Geoffrey Palmer and Noel Lloyd, *E.F. Benson: As He Was* (London: Lennard, 1988), p. 87.
56 Brian Masters, *The Life of E.F. Benson* (London: Chatto & Windus, 1991), p. 10.
57 See, for instance, David Williams, *Genesis and Exodus: A Portrait of the Benson Family* (London: Hamish Hamilton, 1979), p. 210. Simon Goldhill in *A Very Queer Family Indeed: Sex, Religion, and the Bensons in Victorian Britain* (Chicago and London: University of Chicago Press, 2016) suggests the Bensons were all 'queer' to some degree but 'also a family whose sexual history takes place in and through the invention of modern sexuality', p.15.
58 Arthur Christopher Benson, *Hugh: Memoirs of a Brother* (London: Smith, Elder & Co., 1915), p. 12; and E.F. Benson, *Mother*, p. 246.

59 Reginald J.J. Watt, *Robert Hugh Benson: Captain in God's Army* (London: Burns & Oates, 1918), p. 9.
60 Richard Howden, 'Anecdotes of Hugh Benson'. In *Memorials of Robert Hugh Benson* (New York: P.J. Kennedy & Sons, n.d. [1915]), p. 76.
61 Letter from R.H. Benson to Frederick Rolfe, 10 May 1906, quoted in A.J.A. Symons, *The Quest for Corvo: An Experiment in Biography* (London: Cassell & Co., 1934), p. 172.
62 Watt, *Robert Hugh Benson*, p. 30; Donald Weeks, *Corvo* (London: Michael Joseph, 1971), p. 387.
63 'About the Penance of Paisalettrio'. In Frederick Baron Corvo, *In His Own Image* (London: John Lane, The Bodley Head, 1901), pp. 252–72. The original stories were published as: 'Stories Toto Told Me'. I and II. *The Yellow Book* 7 (October 1895): 209–24; 'Stories Toto Told Me'. III and IV. *The Yellow Book* 9 (April 1896): 86–101; and 'Stories Toto Told Me'. V and VI. *The Yellow Book* 11 (October 1896): 143–62. These were collected and published as *Stories Toto told Me* (London: John Lane, The Bodley Head, 1898) and then expanded for *In His Own Image*.
64 They are no longer at Hare Street House but survive in the Archives of the Archdiocese of Westminster. I am very grateful to Fr. Nicholas Schofield for information about Benson's embroideries.
65 Although often referred to as 'stitched tapestries' they are 'appliqué work', see Benson, *Hugh: Memoirs of a Brother*, p. 160; and C.C. Martindale, *The Life of Monsignor Robert Hugh Benson*, Vol. II (London: Longmans, Green & Co., 1916), p. 146.
66 Donald Weeks, *Corvo*, p. 65; and see reference to 'arras of sized linen', in Miriam J. Benkovitz, *Frederick Rolfe: Baron Corvo: A Biography* (London: Hamish Hamilton, 1977), p. 49. Benkovitz further records, 'To his paintings Rolfe added embroidery, *paillettes*, and other ornamentation surprisingly appropriate to his fixed, almost stylised figures.' One critic has compared Corvo, 'as a gifted amateur', to Howard Sturgis; see Elmer Borklund, 'Howard Sturgis, Henry James and 'Belchamber''. *Modern Philology* 58 (4) (May 1961): 269.
67 Quoted in Weeks, *Corvo*, p. 65.
68 E.F. Benson, *Our Family Affairs 1867–1896* (London: Cassell and Co., 1920), p. 154.
69 David Newsome, *On the Edge of Paradise: A.C. Benson: The Diarist* (London: John Murray, 1980), p. 261.
70 Ross Posnock, *The Trail of Curiosity: Henry James, William James, and the Challenge of Modernity* (Oxford: Oxford University Press, 1991), p. 195.

71 'The Beast in the Jungle'. In Henry James, *The Better Sort* (London: Methuen & Co., 1903), p. 206.
72 Ibid., p. 244.
73 Eve Kosofsky Sedgwick, 'The Beast in the Closet: James and the Writing of Homosexual Panic'. In Ruth Bernard Yeazell (ed.), *Sex, Politics, and Science in the Nineteenth-Century Novel* (Baltimore and London: Johns Hopkins University Press, 1986), p. 174.
74 E.M. Forster, 'Howard Overing Sturgis [1935]'. p. 137.
75 Talia Schaffer, 'Berlin Wool'. *Victorian Review* 34(1) (Spring 2008): 39 and 42.
76 Bloomsbury was a loosely grouped set of artists, writers and intellectuals, in early the twentieth century working in London and then Sussex, who rejected prevailing Victorian modes of thinking and being and sought modern social and sexual liberation through their work. For more detail on the history and meaning of needlework in Bloomsbury see my '"Knitting is the saving of life; Adrian has taken it up too": Needlework, Gender, and the Bloomsbury Group'. In Johanna Amos and Lisa Binkley (eds), *Stitching the Self: Identity and the Needle Arts* (London: Bloomsbury, 2020), pp. 67–79, 187–93.
77 Robert Ross, 'The Post-Impressionists at the Grafton: The Twilight of the Idols'. *Morning Post* (7 November 1910): 3.
78 'The New English Arts Club'. *Pall Mall Gazette* (23 May 1911): 5.
79 'Berlin Wool Embroideries'. *Pall Mall Gazette* (28 December 1911): 3. Berlin woolwork was very much in the public eye leading up to the First World War. It was much debated in the press especially as its name suggested it was 'foreign' and there was much anxiety in the drapery and textile trades in deflecting its obvious German origins. There were moves by manufacturers to change its name and reinvent it as a sort of domestic tapestry due to anti-German sentiment (the Royal family, of course, changed their name during the war from Saxe-Coburg-Gotha to Windsor for the same reason).
80 *Daily Express* (18 March 1913): 5; and *Pall Mall Gazette* (27 March 1913): 7.
81 M.M.B., 'Post-Impressionist Furniture'. *Daily News and Leader* (7 August 1913): 10.
82 Frances Spalding, *Duncan Grant* (London: Chatto & Windus, 1997), p. 136.
83 This comparison, and phrasing, is Alan Hollinghurst's from his 'Don't Ask Henry'. *London Review of Books* 30(19) (9 October 2008); http://www.lrb.co.uk/v30/n19/alan-hollinghurst/dont-ask-henry (accessed 1 December 2011).
84 E.F. Benson, *Paul*, p. 67.
85 'Art Exhibition: Mr. Duncan Grant'. *The Times* (22 April 1927): 10.
86 Roger Fry 'The Ottoman and the Whatnot'. *Athenaeum* 4652 (27 June 1919): 529.

87  Virginia Gardner Troy, *The Modernist Textile: Europe and America, 1890–1940* (London: Lund Humphries, 2006). Also see Neil Baldwin, *May Ray: American Artist* (New York: Da Capo Press, 2000 [1988]), p. 16; Virginia Gardner Troy, 'Stitching Modernity: The Textile Work of Fortunato Depero'. *Journal of Modern Italian Studies* 20(1) (2015): 24–33; Gérard Denizeau, *Jean Lurçat* (Lausanne: Actaos, 1998), p. xxxiv; Nicolette Misler, 'Il ricamo suprematista'. In Giorgio Verzotti et al., *Il racconto del filo: Ricamo e cucito nell-arte contemporanea* [exhibition catalogue] (Milan: Skira for Museo di Arte Moderna e Contemporanea di Trento e Rovereto, 2003), pp. 28–36; Bibiana K. Obler, 'Taeuber, Arp, and the Politics of Cross-Stitch'. *The Art Bulletin* 91(2) (June 2009): 207–29, and idem, *Intimate Collaborations: Kandinsky & Münter, Arp & Taeuber* (New Haven and London: Yale University Press, 2014).

88  Obler, *Intimate Collaborations*, p. 14.

89  Lois Bibbings, 'Images of Manliness: The Portrayal of Soldiers and Conscientious Objectors in the Great War'. *Social & Legal Studies* 12(3) (September 2003), p. 347.

90  Eve Kosofsky Sedgwick, 'The Beast in the Closet'. p. 183

91  Paul Nash, 'Modern English Textiles'. *Artwork* 2(6) (1926): 83; and Paul Nash, *Room and Book* (London: The Sorcino Press, 1932), p. 26.

92  Letter from Virginia Woolf to Jacques Raverat, 26 December 1924, in Nigel Nicolson and Joanna Trautmann (eds), *A Change of Perspective: The Letters of Virginia Woolf, Vol. III, 1923–1928* (London: The Hogarth Press, 1977), p. 150.

93  For Angus Davidson see Christopher Reed, *Bloomsbury Rooms: Modernism, Subculture, and Domesticity* (New Haven and London: Yale University Press, 2004), pp. 234–8.

94  Frances Partridge, 'Bloomsbury Houses'. *Charleston Newsletter* 11 (June 1985): 32.

95  For a reading of Bloomsbury men (like Grant) as agents of patriarchy, see Barbara Caine, 'Bloomsbury Masculinity and Its Victorian Antecedents'. *The Journal of Men's Studies* 15(3) (Fall 2007): 271–81.

96  Simon Watney, *The Art of Duncan Grant* (London: John Murray, 1990), pp. 43–4. Ethel Grant kept a record of all the embroideries she made for her son and other artists: 'Ethel Grant's List of Embroideries'. Duncan Grant Papers, Tate Gallery Archive (hereafter TGA) 20078. I am grateful to Christopher Reed, Frances Spalding and especially the late Henrietta Garnett for their help in locating this list and for further references to Bloomsbury needlework.

97  My use of the term 'feeling' has been deliberate in this chapter as in discussions about men and masculinity it is often excluded or used as a signifier of weakness. Masculinity is generally aligned with concepts of logic, reason,

action as well as aggression and violence. My thinking has been influenced by Raymond Williams's concept of 'structures of feeling', especially in terms of his characterization of 'tolerance' and 'affection' in the Bloomsbury group emanating from both its male and female protagonists; see Raymond Williams, 'The Significance of 'Bloomsbury' as a Social and Cultural Group'. In Derek Crabtree and A.P. Thirlwall (eds), *Keynes and the Bloomsbury Group* (London and Basingstoke: Macmillan, 1980), p. 49.

98  Spalding, *Duncan Grant*, p. 55.
99  Virginia Woolf, *Orlando: A Biography* (London: The Hogarth Press, 1928), p. 104.
100 D.W. Winnicott, 'String'. *Child Psychology and Psychiatry* 1 (January 1960): 52 and 51.
101 Carol Mavor, *Reading Boyishly: Roland Barthes, J.M. Barrie, Jacques Henri Lartigue, Marcel Proust and D.W. Winnicott* (Durham and London: Duke University Press, 2007), p. 72.
102 Isabelle Anscombe, *Omega and After: Bloomsbury and the Decorative Arts* (London: Thames & Hudson, 1981), p. 111.
103 Mary Hogarth, 'Modern Embroidery'. *Vogue* (London) (late October 1923): 67.
104 *The Embroiderers' Guild* [exhibition catalogue] (London: Walker's Galleries, 118 New Bond Street, 1923).
105 *Catalogue, Exhibition of Modern British Embroidery, Victoria and Albert Museum* [exhibition catalogue] (London: British Institute for Industrial Art, 1932).
106 *Catalogue of the Exhibition of English Needlework (Past and Present).*
107 R.R.T., 'Modern Designs in Needlework'. *The Burlington Magazine* 47(271) (October 1925): 208; Clive Bell, 'October Shows in London'. *Vogue* (London) (Early November 1925): 70.
108 *The Arts and Crafts Exhibition Society, Catalogue of the Fifteenth Exhibition, at The Royal Academy, Burlington House, W., 1931* [exhibition catalogue] (London: ACES, 1931), 'No. 352', p. 76.
109 *Catalogue of an Exhibition of 20th Century Needlework* [exhibition catalogue] (London: Ernest Brown & Phillips, n.d. [1935]).
110 Letters from Rosamund Willis to Duncan Grant, 6 and 13 January 1943, about Bloomsbury needlework, Duncan Grant Papers, TGA 20078/1/605. The exhibition was organized by CEMA and toured the country from 1943 to 1945.
111 Margaret H. Bulley, 'Embroideries'. In *Have You Good Taste? A Guide to the Appreciation of the Lesser Arts* (London: Methuen & Co., 1933), p. 35.
112 Julia Cairns, 'The Vogue of Tapestry'. *Weldon's Tapestry. No. 1* (London: Weldons Ltd., Fashion, Pattern and Transfer Publishers, n.d. [*c.*1920]), p. 5.
113 *Weldon's Antique Tapestry. Part 2* (London: Weldons Ltd., Fashion, Pattern and Transfer Publishers, n.d. [*c.*1920]), pp. 10–11.

114 This is, however, rarely acknowledged by historians, see for instance Ross McKibbin, 'Work and Hobbies in Britain, 1880–1950'. In Jay Winter (ed.), *The Working Class in Modern British History: Essays in Honour of Henry Pelling* (Cambridge: Cambridge University Press, 1983), pp. 127–46

115 'Mr. Ralph Lion'. *The Sketch* (19 March 1930): 530.

116 The 1933 exhibition of his work at the Warren Gallery included twenty-six embroideries, see *Sea Pictures by John Craske (Exhibition XXV)* [exhibition catalogue] (London: Warren Gallery, 1933).

117 For Craske see Lesley Miller and Jan Miller, *John Craske: Fisherman Painter in Wools* (Sheringham, Norfolk: Sheringham Museum Trust, 2016), pp. 27–8.

118 Julia Blackburn, *Threads: The Delicate Life of John Craske* (London: Jonathan Cape, 2015), p. 218.

119 Mark Kinkead-Weekes, *D.H. Lawrence: Triumph to Exile 1912–1922: Vol. II* (Cambridge: Cambridge University Press, 1996), p. 844 (note 54). And see *Paintings by D.H. Lawrence (Exhibition XII)* [exhibition catalogue] (London: Warren Gallery, 1929).

120 Letter from Katherine Mansfield to Lady Glenavy (*c*.1920) discussing Lawrence's sewing and hemming in Beatrice Lady Glenavy, *'Today we will only Gossip'* (London: Constable, 1964), p. 94. Incidentally, Mansfield's husband, John Middleton Murry, knitted.

121 Juliette Huxley, *Leaves of the Tulip Tree: Autobiography* (London: John Murray, 1986), p. 117.

122 D.H. Lawrence, *Sons and Lovers* (London: Duckworth & Co., 1913), pp. 202–3.

123 Ernest Thesiger, *Practically True* (London: William Heinemann, 1927), p. 112.

124 Ibid., p. 121. One newspaper report stated 'stitchery' spread like an 'epidemic' in hospitals where men were convalescing, see 'Soldiers and Stitches'. *The Illustrated London News* (24 May 1916): iv.

125 Ernest Thesiger, 'Autobiography'. Incomplete manuscript, undated [*c*.1955], EFT/000065, Ernest Thesiger Archive, Theatre Collection, University of Bristol [hereafter Thesiger Archive].

126 For the history and achievements of the organization see my '"The work of masculine fingers": The Disabled Soldiers' Embroidery Industry, 1918–1955'. *Journal of Design History* 31(1) (February 2018): 1–23 (Advance Access, 21 October 2016; https://doi.org/10.1093/jdh/epw043).

127 'Exhibition of Soldier Broderers' Work'. *The Times* (17 February 1922), Disabled Soldiers' Embroidery Industry, Press Cuttings Books, Private Collection. The chair survives at Lamb House. I am grateful to Susannah Mayor and Claire Reed, of the National Trust, for help in locating information about this commission.

128 G.B.H., 'Embroideries by Disabled Soldiers'. *The Queen* (27 May 1931), Disabled Soldiers' Embroidery Industry, Press Cuttings Books, Private Collection.

129 A.E.L., 'The World of Women'. *The Illustrated London News* (19 April 1924): 710.

130 'Men, Maids and Matters'. *Vogue* (London) (Late April 1924): 94.

131 For more information on Thesiger see my '"Nothing is more terrifying to me than to see Ernest Thesiger sitting under the lamplight doing this embroidery": Ernest Thesiger (1879–1961), "Expert Embroiderer."' *TEXT: Journal for the Study of Textile Art, Design and History* 43 (2015/16): 20–6; and 'Queer Hobbies: Ernest Thesiger and Interwar Embroidery'. *Textile: Cloth and Culture* 15(3) (September 2017): 292–322.

132 'Men who Embroider'. Unattributed and undated magazine clipping, EFT/000066/13, Thesiger Archive.

133 Ernest Thesiger, 'Autobiography', p. 1, EFT/000065, Thesiger Archive.

134 Ibid., pp. 9–10.

135 Daniel Rock, *Textile Fabrics: A Descriptive Catalogue of the Collection of Church-vestments, Dresses, Silk Stuffs, Needlework and Tapestries, Forming That Section of the South Kensington Museum* (London: Chapman and Hall, 1870). See Lady Marian Alford, *Needlework as Art* (London: Sampson Low, Marston, Searle and Rivington, 1886); and A.G.I. Christie, *English Medieval Embroidery: A Brief Survey of English Embroidery Dating from the Beginning of the Tenth Century until the End of the Fourteenth* (Oxford: Clarendon Press, 1938).

136 During the 1920s the sewing circle and queer subculture seem to have temporarily coalesced. The best-known example was that in Hollywood, oscillating around the actor Marlene Dietrich, in which 'sewing' became a well-known euphemism for the homosexuality of female stars, see Alex Madsen, *The Sewing Circle: Hollywood Greatest Secret: Female Stars Who Loved Other Women* (London: Robson Books, 1995); and Diana McLellan, *The Girls: Sappho Goes to Hollywood* (New York: LA Weekly Books for St. Martin's Press, 2000).

137 Beauchamp and his family were the model for the Marichmains in Evelyn Waugh's *Brideshead Revisited: The Sacred and Profane Memories of Captain Charles Ryder* (London: Chapman and Hall, 1945). For Beauchamp see my 'Queer Hobbies', pp. 296, 307, 311 and 314–15.

138 Hugo Williams, 'Mordaunt Shairp and *The Green Bay Tree*'. In *Freelancing: Adventures of a Poet* (London: Faber and Faber, 1995), p. 164. In his published memoir Thesiger recorded he had been described as 'sybaritic', see Thesiger, *Practically True*, p. 4.

139 Mordaunt Shairp, *The Green Bay Tree* (1933). In Michael Wilcox (ed.), *Gay Plays: Vol. I* (London and New York: Methuen, 1985), p. 64.

140 Nancy Mitford, *Love in a Cold Climate* (London: Hamish Hamilton, 1949), p. 84. Mitford clearly drew on Thesiger, Ranken and Beauchamp for the character Boy Dougdale. Their embroideries have many marked similarities to Dougdale's including his miniature needlework designs for Queen Mary's Dolls' House. Thesiger and Ranken were among the original artists commissioned for the Dolls' House and Thesiger and Beauchamp were also donors; see A.C. Benson and Lawrence Weaver (eds), *The Book of the Queen's Dolls' House* (London: Methuen & Co, 1924), pp. 54 and 62.

141 Havelock Ellis, *Studies in the Psychology of Sex: Vol. II: Sexual Inversion* (Philadelphia: F.A. Davis, 1915 [1897] third edition, enlarged and revised), pp. 114 and 226.

142 This 'reference sampler' was entered in an Embroiderers' Guild competition in 1947, in which it won third prize. See D. [Dorothea] Nield, 'Canvas Stitch Sampler Competition'. *Embroidery* IX(2) (June 1947): 22–3.

143 Beverly Nichols, 'Woad! Celebrities in Undress: IX. Ernest Thesiger'. *The Sketch* CXXXIV(1737) (26 May 1926): 284.

144 Ernest Thesiger, 'Needlework as a Hobby'. *The Home Magazine*, XXXIV(119) (March 1926): 27. When Thesiger eventually published a book on needlework he made several references to work by men, which almost all other contemporary books omitted, see Ernest Thesiger, *Adventures in Embroidery* (London and New York: The Studio, 1941).

145 Earl Spencer, 'In Praise of the Needle'. *The Listener* XXIV(863) (26 July 1945): 93. The published version of Spencer's speech was accompanied by an image of a prize-winning quilt by a 'wounded soldier'. Like Thesiger, Earl Spencer had been a prominent male needleworker in the interwar years and had participated in the period's 'masculine needlework' exhibitions; see 'An Earl's Needlework', *The Sunday Times* (18 March 1924): 28.

146 See, for example, Norah Alice Haworth and Elizabeth Mary Macdonald, *Theory of Occupational Therapy for Students and Nurses* (London: Baillière, Tindall & Cox, 1940), p. 140.

147 S.F., 'Occupational Therapy'. *Embroidery* 8(3) (December 1945): 75.

148 Michael Roper, 'Mothering Men'. In *The Secret Battle: Emotional Survival in the Great War* (Manchester and New York: Manchester University Press, 2009), pp. 119–203.

149 Mavor, *Reading Boyishly*, p. 72; the term 'effeminophobia' was formulated in the context of the hysterical homophobia which accompanied the height of the AIDS crisis and is taken from Eve Kosofsky Sedgwick's 'How to Bring Your Kids

Up Gay: The War on Effeminate Boys'. In *Tendencies* (Durham: Duke University Press, 1993), p. 157.
150 Sedgwick, 'Queer Performativity', p. 6.
151 Ibid., pp. 8 and 11. Sedgwick further explores the idea of 'male parturition' in 'Is the Rectum Always Straight? Identification and Identity in *The Wings of the Dove*'. In *Tendencies*, p. 99; 'Shame and Performativity: Henry James's New York Edition Prefaces'. In David McWhirter (ed.), *Henry James's New York Edition: The Construction of Authorship* (Stanford: Stanford University Press, 1995), p. 216; and 'Inside Henry James: Toward a Lexicon for *The Art of the Novel*'. In Monica Dorenkamp and Richard Henke (eds), *Negotiating Lesbian and Gay Subjects* (New York and London: Routledge, 1995), p. 132. In the latter Sedgwick also relates James's discussion of 'anal discomfort' with the coded language of the 'sexual secret'.

# Chapter 4

1 Greenberg made his comments in a review of Herbert Read's *The Grass Roots of Art: Four Lectures on Social Aspects of Art in an Industrial Age* (London: Faber and Faber, 1946), which was the published version of Read's Yale lectures given in the spring of 1946; see Clement Greenberg, 'An Ideal Climate for Art: Review of *The Grass Roots of Art* by Herbert Read'. In John O'Brian (ed.), *Clement Greenberg: The Collected Essays and Criticism: Volume 2: Arrogance and Purpose, 1945–1949* (Chicago and London: University of Chicago Press, 1986) p. 147.
2 Clement Greenberg, 'Modernist Painting'. In John O'Brian (ed.), *Clement Greenberg: The Collected Essays and Criticism: Volume 4: Modernism with a Vengeance, 1957–1969* (Chicago and London: University of Chicago Press, 1993), p. 91.
3 Clement Greenberg, 'Review of Ben Nicholson and Larry Rivers'. In *Clement Greenberg: The Collected Essays and Criticism: Volume 2*, p. 209.
4 Ibid. In *The History of Sexuality* Michel Foucault points out that the development of nineteenth century sexology built on the historic religious association of sexual deviance and sin, see Foucault, *The History of Sexuality*, p. 9.
5 Stephens, Chris, 'Ben Nicholson: Modernism, Craft and the English Vernacular'. In David Peters Corbett, Ysanne Holt and Fiona Russell (eds), *The Geographies of Englishness: Landscape and the National Past 1880–1940* (New Haven and London: Yale University Press, 2002), pp. 225–6.

6 H.R. [Herbert Read], 'Discussions between Realists and Surrealists'. *London Gallery Bulletin* 1 (April 1938): 20.

7 Philip James (ed.), *Henry Moore on Sculpture* (London: Macdonald, 1966), p. 135.

8 See, for example, Herbert J. Hall and Mertice M.C. Buck, *The Work of Our Hands: A Study of Occupations for Invalids* (New York: Moffat, Yard & Company, 1915); Herbert J. Hall and Mertice M.C. Buck, *Handicrafts for the Handicapped* (New York: Moffat, Yard & Company, 1916); and Douglas C. McMurtrie, *The Disabled Soldier* (New York: Macmillan, 1919).

9 Gertrude D. Ross, 'Occupational Therapy: A Post War Service of Art and Crafts'. *Design* 44(4) (1943): 19.

10 See William Rush Dunton, *Occupation Therapy: A Manual for Nurses* (Philadelphia and London: W.B. Saunders, 1915), *Reconstruction Therapy* (Philadelphia and London: W.B. Saunders, 1919) and *Old Quilts* (Cantonsville, MD: William Rush Dunton Jr., 1946). Dutton seemed especially interested in English Arts and Crafts approaches to textile making and was familiar with Luther Hooper's *Hand-Loom Weaving* (London: John Hogg, 1910) and Grace Christie's *Embroidery and Tapestry Weaving* (London: John Hogg, 1912).

11 'Our Fighting Men's Hobbies Go on Display; Best Fancy Needlework Done by a Soldier'. *The New York Times* (26 October 1942): 17.

12 'Crafts in a German P.O.W. Camp'. *Craft Horizons* 5(12) (February 1946): 29.

13 Anne Orr, 'Everybody's Doing Needlework!' *Good Housekeeping* 108(10) (1 January 1939): 60–1.

14 Josephine Christie, 'To 18,000,000 Needleworkers'. *Vogue* (New York) (1 June 1950): 70.

15 'Queen Mary's Rug'. *Life* 28(19) (8 May 1950): 95, 97.

16 'King Gustaf V of Sweden'. *Life* 5(2) (11 June 1938): 37; and 'Europe's Only Free King'. *Life* 13(12) (21 September 1942): 46.

17 Malin Grundberg, *Manligt–ur Gustaf V: s garderob/Manly–From the Wardrobe of King Gustaf V* [text based on exhibition wall panels] (Stockholm: Livrustkammaren/The Royal Armoury, 2011), n.p. I am grateful to Malin Grundberg for providing me with a copy of this text. In Sweden the King's needlework was considered the opposite of 'manly' but understood as part of his wider interest in fashion and dress, as part of his 'closet', in terms of 'modernity and luxury'. For example, his needle and scissors case was specially made by van Cleefs & Arpels, Paris.

18 'British Notables Who Knit for a Hobby'. *The New York Times* (5 February 1933): SM18.

19  Clement Greenberg, 'The Crisis of the Easel Picture'. In *Clement Greenberg: The Collected Essays and Criticism: Volume 2*, p. 225.
20  T.J. Clark, 'Jackson Pollock's Abstraction'. In Serge Guilbaut (ed.), *Reconstructing Modernism: Art in New York, Paris and Montreal, 1945–1964* (Cambridge, MA: MIT Press, 1990), p. 178.
21  E.M. Forster, 'America Journal (1947 and 1949)'. In Philip Gardner (ed.), *The Journals and Diaries of E.M. Forster*, Vol. 3 (London: Pickering & Chatto, 2011), p. 75.
22  Jerry Rosco, *Glenway Wescott Personally: A Biography* (Madison: University of Wisconsin Press, 2010), p. 70. The day-bed is illustrated in David Leddick, *Intimate Companions: A Triography of George Platt Lynes, Paul Cadmus, Lincoln Kirstein, and their Circle* (New York: St. Martin's Press, 2000), p. 95. The man and woman depicted are Jared French and his wife Margaret, see Wendy Moffat, *E.M. Forster: A New Life* (London: Bloomsbury, 2010), p. 267.
23  Martin Duberman, *The Worlds of Lincoln Kirstein* (New York: Alfred A. Knopf, 2007), p. 320.
24  Letter from Katherine Anne Porter to George Platt Lynes, 28 July 1939, in Isabel Bayley (ed.), *Letters of Katherine Anne Porter* (New York: Atlantic Monthly Press, 1990), p. 171.
25  Quotes drawn from entries in George Platt Lynes's unpublished diaries for November and December 1942 and August 1944, in George Platt Lynes Diaries and Memorabilia, Yale Collection of American Literature, Beinecke Rare Book and Manuscript Library, Yale University Library, YCAL MSS 147, Box 1, Folder 4, Series 1 (hereafter George Platt Lynes Papers, Yale).
26  Richard Barrios, *Dangerous Rhythm: Why Movie Musicals Matter* (Oxford and New York: Oxford University Press, 2014), p. 216.
27  Glenn Loney, *Unsung Genius: The Passion of Dancer-Choreographer Jack Cole* (London: Franklin Watts, 1974), p. 304.
28  Ibid., p. 307.
29  Leddick, *Intimate Companions*, p. 254.
30  Forster certainly thought Cadmus's St. Luke's Place studio was rather like Bloomsbury, see Wendy Moffat, 'A New Bloomsbury? Forster, Cadmus and the Frenches in Greenwich Village'. *Archives of American Art Journal* 49(3/4) (Fall 2010): 26–33.
31  Frances Spalding, *Duncan Grant* (London: Chatto & Windus, 1997), p. 249; and Sarah Knights, *Bloomsbury's Outsider: A Life of David Garnett* (London: Bloomsbury, 2015), p. 181.

32  Mina [Kirstein] Curtiss, *Other People's Letters: A Memoir* (Boston: Houghton Mifflin, 1978), p. 24.
33  Letter from Mina Kirstein, 10 December [1924], Duncan Grant Papers, Tate Gallery Archive 20078/1/136. The 'copy of Vogue' sent by David Garnett, Kirstein is more than likely referring to Mary Hogarth, 'Modern Embroidery'. *Vogue* (London) (late October 1923): 66–7, which contained images of two chairs covered in needlework designs by Grant.
34  Weymer Mills, 'London Goes Back to Its Wool-Work'. *Vogue* (New York) (1 February 1925): 65.
35  See, for example, Winifred Wilson, 'Tapestry Embroidery in Vogue: Men Rival Women in Their Enthusiasm to Revive This Antique Craft'. *Arts & Decoration* XXI(4) (August 1924): 28, 29, 61, 63; Dorothy Alston, 'England in Embroidered Maps'. *Vogue* (New York) (15 June 1928): 104, 112, 118. Even commissions such as that from the Prince of Wales for a series replica maps, translated from tapestry to embroidery, by the Disabled Soldiers' Embroidery Industry were reported in the American press, see 'Prince of Wales Studies Old Maps'. *The Brooklyn Daily Eagle* (8 December 1929): 67.
36  Dorothy Adlow, 'An Exhibit of Modern Designs: The Artistic Talent Turns to Needlework'. *Vogue* (New York) (15 December 1925): 118, 122. Images of the exhibition were published in the same issue as 'Modern Designs in Needlework': 77.
37  Joan Cook, 'Men Turning to Knitting and Therein Lies a Yarn'. *The New York Times* (20 August 1959): 28.
38  Ibid.
39  For male winners at the National Exhibition of Amateur Needlework of Today see 'Needlework: An Old and Distinguished Art Enjoys a Modern Revival', *Life* 27(11) (12 September 1949): 68. One man wrote into the magazine after seeing this article stating, 'I hope that more men will take up this fascinating pastime', and recording details of the prize he won for embroidery Palmyra Union Agricultural Fair and the New York State Fair; see 'Letters to the Editor: "Needlers" [H.W. Connell]'. *Life* 27(14) (3 October 1949): 5.
40  'The New American Domesticated Male'. *Life* 36(1) (4 January 1954): 42; and Michael S. Kimmel, *Manhood in America: A Cultural History* (Oxford University Press US, 2006 [1996]), p. 161.
41  K.A. Cuordileone, *Manhood and American Political Culture in the Cold War* (London and New York: Routledge, 2005), pp. 144–52.
42  Even in homosexual circles needlework became emblematic of effeminacy, see, for example, *The Mattachine Review* (August 1958): 13.

43　For this transatlantic exchange see Paul Robinson, *The Modernization of Sex: Havelock Ellis, Alfred Kinsey, William Masters and Virginia Johnston* (Ithaca, New York: Cornell University Press, 1976).

44　Lewis Terman and Catherine Cox Miles, *Sex and Personality: Studies in Masculinity and Femininity* (New York and London: McGaw-Hill, 1936), pp. 314–15.

45　Stephen J. Whitfield, *The Culture of the Cold War* (Baltimore and London: The Johns Hopkins University Press, 1991), p. 43; and Robert J. Corber, *In the Name of National Security: Hitchcock, Homophobia, and the Political Construction of Gender in Postwar America* (Durham and London: Duke University Press, 1993), p. 14.

46　Corber, *Homosexuality in Cold War America*, p. 228.

47　John D'Emilio, 'The Homosexual Menace: The Politics of Sexuality in Cold War America'. In Kathy Peiss and Christina Simmons with Robert A. Padgug (eds), *Passion and Power: Sexuality and History* (Philadelphia: Temple University Press, 1989), pp. 226–40.

48　See Richard Meyer, 'Rock Hudson's Body'. In Diana Fuss (ed.), *Inside/Out: Lesbian Theories, Gay Theories* (New York and London: Routledge, 1991), p. 279.

49　For Lincoln Kirstein's contact with Bloomsbury see Nicholas Jenkins (ed.), *By With To & From: A Lincoln Kirstein Reader* (New York: Farra, Strauss & Giroux, 1991), p. 150; and Duberman, *The Worlds of Lincoln Kirstein*, pp. 24, 42.

50　Bernard Perlin quoted in Leddick, *Intimate Companions*, p. xi. For a recent redress of the centrality of queerness of this group, and its wider critical neglect, see Richard Meyer, 'Threesomes: Lincoln Kirstein's Queer Arithmetic'. In Samantha Friedman and Jodi Hauptman (eds), *Lincoln Kirstein's Modern* [exhibition catalogue] (New York: The Museum of Modern Art, 2019), pp. 98–105.

51　Stephen S. Prokopoff, *George Platt Lynes: Photographic Visions* [exhibition catalogue] (Boston, MA: Institute of Contemporary Art, March 5 to April 29, 1980): n.p.

52　Whilst living in Paris, perhaps encouraged by Gertrude Stein, Lynes read novels by Virginia Woolf and Lytton Strachey and in 1926 he made a trip to London, 'Five Year Diary [1925–1926]'. and 'Year by Year Book [1928–1930]'. YCAL MSS 147, Box 1, Folder 2, Series 1 and YCAL MSS 147, Box 1, Folder 3, Series 1, George Platt Lynes papers, Yale.

53　Allen Ellenzweig, 'The Private Utopia of George Platt Lynes'. In Steven Haas (ed.), *George Platt Lynes: The Male Nudes* (New York: Rizzoli, 2011): n.p.

54  Alfred C. Kinsey, Wardell B. Pomeroy and Clyde E. Martin, *Sexual Behaviour and the Human Male* (Philadelphia and London: W.B. Saunders, 1948), p. 637.
55  James Crump, 'Iconography of Desire: George Platt Lynes and Gay Male Visual Culture in Postwar New York'. In James Crump et al., *George Platt Lynes: Photographs from the Kinsey Institute* (Boston: Bulfinch Press, 1993), p. 151.
56  Monroe Wheeler was involved in the major Paul Klee exhibition at MoMA in 1949. The conflation of the decorative/femininity/homosexuality had also been discussed in relation to the work and the career of Klee; for this see Jenny Anger, *Paul Klee and the Decorative in Modern Art* (Cambridge: Cambridge University Press, 2004).
57  Lynes referred to these as the 'Moon and Stars' pillows.' Lynes's description corresponds with the pair of his needlepoint cushion covers sold at Sotheby's New York on 3 October 2012.
58  Louis J. Gartner Jr., *Needlepoint Design (A House & Garden Book)* (New York: William Morrow & Co., 1970), p. 20.
59  Kirstein, *Paul Cadmus*, p. 68; Leddick, *Intimate Companions*, p. 185.
60  Gartner, *Needlepoint Design*, p. 70.
61  Eve Kosofsky Sedgwick, *Epistemology of the Closet* (Berkeley: University of California Press, 1990), p. 3.
62  Leddick, *Intimate Companions*, p. 16.
63  Russell Lynes, *A Surfeit of Honey* (New York: Harper & Brothers, 1957), p. 56.
64  Leddick, *Intimate Companions*, p. 101.
65  Letter from Amateur Needlework of Today, Inc., November 1957, Russell Lynes Papers, Yale Collection of American Literature, Beinecke Rare Book and Manuscript Library, Yale University Library, YCAL MSS 553 Box 10 (hereafter Russell Lynes Papers, Yale).
66  Russell Lynes, 'Introduction'. In Mary Brooks Picken and Doris White, *Needlepoint for Everyone* (New York: Harper & Row, 1970), n.p.; and 'Men and Needlepoint', pp. 158–66 [p. 159].
67  Letter from Gloria Safier, 11 September 1970, Russell Lynes Papers, Yale.
68  Sylvia Sidney's *Needlepoint Book* (New York: Reinhold, 1968), like Mary Martin's *Needlepoint* (New York: William Morris & Co., 1969), had proved a massive, if unexpected, success.
69  Lynes makes this recollection in a letter to Barbara Wyden, 22 April 1972, Russell Lynes Papers, Yale. The book Lynes was writing was his history of MoMA; see Russell Lynes, *Good Old Modern: An Intimate Portrait of the Museum of Modern Art* (New York: Atheneum, 1973).

70  Sophia Frances Anne Caulfeild and Blanche C. Saward, *The Dictionary of Needlework: An Encyclopaedia of Artistic, Plain, And Fancy Needlework* (London: L. Upcott Gill, 1882). The book was dedicated to HRH Princes Louise, Marchioness of Lorne who was a patron of several needlework charities and who was on the founding committee of the Royal School of Needlework. This had been founded by HRH Princess Christian of Schleswig-Holstein in 1872. Princess Christian and Princess Louise were the third and fourth daughters of Queen Victoria. The facsimile edition was published (unabridged) by the Arno Press in 1972.

71  Lynes's hand-corrected proof of 'The Needlepoint Boom'. Russell Lynes Papers, Yale. This was published as 'The Needlepoint Boom'. *New York Times Magazine* (11 July 1972): 56–8.

72  Ibid.

73  Karal Ann Marling, *As Seen on TV: The Visual Culture of Everyday Life in the 1950s* (Cambridge, MA: Harvard University Press, 1994), p. 51.

74  Clement Greenberg, 'Review of Exhibitions of the American Abstract Artists, Jacques Lipchitz, and Jackson Pollock'. In *Clement Greenberg: The Collected Essays and Criticism: Volume 2*, p. 75.

75  Russell Lynes, 'Highbrow, Lowbrow, Middlebrow'. *Harper's* (February 1949): 19–28; and Clement Greenberg, 'The State of American Writing, 1948: A Symposium'. In *Clement Greenberg: The Collected Essays and Criticism: Volume 2*, pp. 257–8.

76  For a detailed analysis of the context of this exhibition see my 'Needlepoint for Men: Craft and Masculinity in Postwar America'. *The Journal of Modern Craft* 10(3) (2015): 301–31.

77  Russell Lynes, 'The Mesh Canvas'. *Art in America* 56(3) (May/June 1968): 49.

78  Ibid., pp. 29 and 49.

79  'Noted Modern Artists Turn to New Medium, Needlepoint Canvas to be Exhibited at FAR Gallery'. Press Release, FAR Gallery, 746 Madison Ave (65 St.), New York, 6–18 May 1968, Russell Lynes Papers, Yale.

80  The Stella needlepoint kit was recently re-issued to coincide with the major Frank Stella exhibition at the Whitney Museum of American Art (2015–16), again in collaboration with *A.i.A.* It was released as a limited edition at a retail price of $335, see https://shop.whitney.org/the-mesh-canvas-frank-stella.html.

81  Rita Reif, 'Pop Goes the Needlework–Officially'. *The New York Times* (6 May 1968): 54. Castelli's Gallery held a show of Warhol's flower paintings in 1965.

82  Lynes, 'The Mesh Canvas', p. 49.

83 Letter from Audrey Sokoloff to Katherine Gauss Jackson, 30 December 1969; and letter from Russell Lynes to Audrey Sokoloff, 4 January 1970, Russell Lynes Papers, Yale.

84 These are illustrated in Anne Lane Hedlung, *Gloria F. Ross & Modern Tapestry* (New Haven and London: Yale University Press, 2010), p. 8. Lynes also received press clippings about similar research including one about men's needlework in England that referenced Lord Bearsted, who started embroidering during the war, Roland Muir, the Director of Unilever, who started needlework upon his retirement, and Franis Burne of the Hazlitt Gallery who was taught to sew as a boy and who admired Ernest Thesiger's needlework, see Leslie Field, 'Men on the needle … ' *Sunday Times Magazine* (10 December 1972): 42.

85 Letter from Annette Lep, 7 May 1968; letter from Joan H. Koslan Schwartz, 20 May 1968; and letter from Adelaide C. Sohier, undated [May 1968]; all Russell Lynes Papers, Yale.

86 Letter from Mr. Ned J. Phillips, Louisville, 24 October 1968, Russell Lynes Papers, Yale.

87 Russell Lynes, 'Confessions of a Needlepointer'. *House Beautiful* 108(11) (November 1966): 252 and 295.

88 Russell Lynes, 'The Pleasure of Making It'. *House & Garden* 142(1) (July 1972): 82. Lynes also often alluded to the 'Victorian lady' as the female archetypal stereotype of the needlepointer. When asked by Cécile Dreesman if he would give an image for her forthcoming book, *Samplers for Today* (New York: Van Nostrand Reinhold, 1972), she was especially keen on the embroidered *trompe l'oeil* covers for hi-fi speakers he had made, he declined as they were being reproduced in Joan Scobey and Lee Parr McGrath, *Celebrity Needlepoint* (New York: The Dial Press, 1972), adding; 'There is certainly no shortage of needlepoint these days, though I'm not quite sure what is a sampler and what is not. I thought a sampler was something a young woman did in the last century and before as a sort of exercise to demonstrate her proficiency, not something an aging man does to cover up the loud speakers of a hi-fi set', letter to Cécile Dreesman, 18 July 1971, Russell Lynes Papers, Yale.

89 Letter from Sherry Baker, undated (April 1974), Russell Lynes Papers, Yale.

90 Michael S. Kimmel, *Manhood in America*, p. 185; Michael Kimmel, 'Men's Liberation'. In Michael Kimmel and Amy Aronson (eds), *Men & Masculinities: A Social, Cultural and Historical Encyclopedia*, Vol. 2 (Santa Barbara, CA: ABC-CLIO, 2003), pp. 524–6; and Jack Nichols, *Men's Liberation: A New Definition of Masculinity* (New York: Penguin, 1975).

91  See, for example, Joseph H. Pleck and Jack Sawyer (eds), *Men and Masculinity* (New Jersey, NJ: Prentice-Hall, 1974) pp. 12 and 174.

92  Herb Goldberg, *The Hazards of Being Male: Surviving the Myth of Masculine Privilege* (New York: Nash, 1976), p. 65; and Deborah S. David and Robert Brannon, *The Forty-Nine Percent Majority: The Male Sex Role* (Reading, MA: Addison-Wesley, 1976), pp. 13–19 and 49–88. A typical example from this selection of books is one male interviewee, in the David and Bannon volume, who is mocked for his plain needlework by his wife and friends, including his neighbour, who asks; 'Billy, my wife would like you to join the girls at the sewing circle next week', p. 283.

93  Judy Chicago's *Dinner Party*, like Russell Lynes's *Mesh Canvas*, drew attention to the dynamics of female artist/designer and male fabricator as among the group of needleworkers acknowledged for their work on *The Dinner Party* is Peter Fieweger, who was photographed in the process of sewing the 'Millennium runner', see Judy Chicago, with Susan Hill, *Embroidering Our Heritage: The Dinner Party Needlework* (New York: Anchor Press, 1980), p. 281. For an analysis of men's needlework in Carol Shields's novel, see Ellen McWilliams, 'Knitting *Paradise Lost*: Masculinity and Domesticity in the Novels of Carol Shields'. In Sarah S.G. Frantz and Katharina Rennak (eds), *Women Constructing Men: Female Novelists and Their Male Characters, 1750–2000* (Lanham, MD: Lexington Books, 2010), pp. 171–84. And for a useful comparison of Chicago and Shields see Wendy Roy, 'Brenda Bowman at Dinner with Judy Chicago: Feminism and Needlework in Carol Shields's *A Fairly Conventional Woman*'. *Atlantis* 33(1) (2008): 125–36.

94  Nina Mortellito, *Needlepoint for the Whole Family* (New York: Walker and Co., 1973), p. 13.

95  Margalit Fox, 'Erica Wilson Dies; Led a Rebirth of Needleworking'. *The New York Times* (14 December 2011), http://www.nytimes.com/2011/12/14/nyregion/erica-wilson-dies-at-83-led-a-rebirth-of-needleworking.html?_r=0 (accessed 10 January 2012); and Veronica Howell, 'Erica Wilson: Obituary'. *The Guardian* (2 January 2012), http://www.theguardian.com/lifeandstyle/2012/jan/02/erica-wilson (accessed 3 January 2012).

96  Howell, ibid.

97  'Crewel Comeback'. *Life* 54(11) (15 March 1963): 49.

98  Valerie J. Nelson, 'Erica Wilson dies at 83; needlework instructor built embroidery empire'. *Los Angeles Times* (17 December 2011), http://articles.latimes.com/2011/dec/17/local/la-me-erica-wilson-20111218 (accessed 5 January 2012).

99 Florence Petit, 'What's Wrong with the Craft Books Boom!' *Craft Horizons* 35(5) (October 1975): 31 and 48.
100 Maines, 'Reassessing the Heritage of Art Needlework', p. 5.
101 Ibid.
102 'Henry Fonda's Needlework'. *Good Housekeeping* 183(2) (August 1976): 102–3, 133; and Kimmel and Aronson (eds), *Men & Masculinities*, Vol. 2, p. 465.
103 Jonathan Holstein, *Abstract Design in American Quilts* [exhibition catalogue] (New York: Whitney Museum of American Art, 1971) and the critique in Susan E. Bernick, 'A Quilt Is an Art Object When It Stands Up like a Man'. In Cheryl B. Torsney and Judy Elsley (eds), *Quilt Culture: Tracing the Pattern* (Columbia: University of Missouri Press, 1994), pp. 137. And see Patty Mucha, 'Sewing in the Sixties'. *Art in America* 90(11) (November 2002): 79–87.
104 Scobey and McGrath, *Celebrity Needlepoint*, pp. 99–107, 133–6.
105 Lucy R. Lippard, 'Making Something from Nothing (Toward a Definition of Women's "Hobby Art")'. *Heresies* 1(4) (Winter, 1978): 63–4.
106 Parker, *The Subversive Stitch*, p. 291.
107 Rita Reif, 'While Everybody Does It (Men Too) Erica Wilson Sews Up the Business End of Needlework'. *People* 8(4) (12 December 1977): 74.
108 Robert Illes, *Men in Stitches* (New York: Van Nostrand Reinhold, 1975), p. 8.
109 Jeannette Bruce, 'Shopwalk'. *Sports Illustrated*, undated clipping, enclosed in letter from Jeannette Bruce, 12 June 1972, Russell Lynes Papers, Yale.
110 Roosevelt 'Rosey' Grier (with Dennis Baker), *Rosey, An Autobiography: The Gentle Giant* (Tulsa OK: Honor Books, 1986), p. 5.
111 *Rosey Grier's Needlepoint for Men* (New York: Walker and Co., 1973), pp. 127–40.
112 Ibid., p. 17.
113 Grier and Baker, *Rosey*, p. 242.
114 Ibid., p. 243.
115 Grier's needlepoint was profiled everywhere from broadsheets to the sports press, see, for example, Judy Klemesrud, 'Once a Terror on the Gridiron, Rosey Grier now Does Needlepoint for Fun and to Relax'. *The New York Times* (8 October 1973): 45; and Barbara La Fontaine, 'Booktalk: A new look at the needlepoint game, viewed through Rosey-colored glasses'. *Sports Illustrated* (26 November 1973): M1.
116 Sally O'Quin, 'Man That Needle'. *Life* 70(20) (28 May 1971): 80–4.
117 Editor's Note, 'Our Intrepid Men Take Up Needlework'. *Life* 70(20) (28 May 1971): 3.

118 Clement Greenberg, 'Jackson Pollock: Inspiration, Vision, Intuitive Decision'. *The Collected Essays and Criticism: Volume 4*, p. 245.
119 'Jackson Pollock's Abstractions'. *Vogue* (New York) (1 March 1951): 159.
120 Andrew Perchuk, 'Pollock and Postwar Masculinity'. In Andrew Perchuk and Helaine Posner (eds), *The Masculine Masquerade: Masculinity and Representation* (Cambridge, MA: MIT Press, 1995), p. 32.
121 Kimmel, *Manhood in America*, p. 173.
122 Quoted in Jane Fassett Brite and Rebecca Caldwell, 'Ed Rossbach'. In Anne Pollard Rowe and Rebecca T. Stevens (eds), *Ed Rossbach: 40 Years of Exploration and Innovation in Fiber Art* (Asheville, NC: Lark Books for The Textile Museum, Washington DC, 1990), p. 13.
123 Anne Pollard Rowe, 'Textile Explorations'. In *Ed Rossbach*, p. 78.
124 Parker, *The Subversive Stitch*, pp. 204–5.
125 William V. Ganis, 'Straight Photographs and Queer Threads'. In *Andy Warhol's Serial Photography* (Cambridge: Cambridge University Press, 2004), p. 107.
126 Andy Warhol, diary entry, Tuesday, January 27, 1987, quoted in Pat Hackett (ed.), *The Andy Warhol Diaries* (New York: Grand Central, 1991), p. 798.
127 John Perreault, 'Working With Warhol [by Gerard Malanga]'. *The Village Voice* XXXII(18) (5 May 1987): 7.
128 Jennifer Doyle, Jonathan Flatley and José Esteban Muñoz, 'Introduction'. In *Pop Out: Queer Warhol* (Durham and London: Duke University Press, 1996), p. 1.
129 Andy Grundberg, 'Warhol Sews a Subversive Pattern in Black and White'. *The New York Times* (11 January 1987): H33.
130 'The Homosexual in America'. *Time* 87(3) (21 January 1966): 40. Maugham's comment was made in an essay on El Greco but it may well be a coded swipe at Ernest Thesiger, as it sounds like a description of him (Slade-trained but famed for his embroidery in spite of exhibitions of his paintings throughout the 1910s, 1920s and 1930s). Thesiger was known to make fun, especially at parties, of Maugham's stammer. Maugham's comment was originally made in 'El Greco'. In John Beecroft (ed.), *Mr. Maugham Himself* (New York: Doubleday, 1954), p. 246.

# Chapter 5

1 Published as Parker and Pollock (eds), *Framing Feminism*.
2 Rozsika Parker, 'Foreword'. In *The Subversive Stitch* [exhibition catalogue] (Manchester: Whitworth Art Gallery & Cornerhouse, 1988), p. 6.

3 Pennina Barnett, 'Women and Textiles Today'. In *The Subversive Stitch* [exhibition catalogue] (Manchester: Whitworth Art Gallery & Cornerhouse, 1988), pp. 37 and 45. In addition to *The Subversive Stitch* shows other exhibitions, including *Quilting, Patchwork and Appliqué 1700–1982: Sewing as a Woman's Art* (1983) and *Knitting: A Common Art* (1987), both at the Crafts Council Gallery in London, explored similar issues exclusively in terms of women's work.
4 Johnson, Pamela, 'Under Construction: Exploring Process in Contemporary Textiles'. In *Under Construction: Exploring Process in Contemporary Textiles* [exhibition catalogue] (London: Crafts Council, 1996), pp. 6–11.
5 Pennina Barnett, 'A Stitch Out of Time'. *Women's Art Magazine* 51 (March/April 1993): 11–13.
6 Natalie King, 'The Subversive Stitch'. In *The Subversive Stitch* [exhibition catalogue] (Melbourne: Monash University Gallery, 1991), p. 7.
7 Roberta Smith, 'The Subversive Stitch'. *The New York Times* (12 July 1991): C23.
8 Lydia Yee, 'Division of Labor: "Women's Work" in Contemporary Art'. In Lydia Yee and Anastasia Aukeman (eds), *Division of Labor: 'Women's Work' in Contemporary Art* [exhibition catalogue] (New York: The Bronx Museum of the Arts, 1995), p. 9.
9 Marcia Tucker, 'A Labor of Love'. In *A Labor of Love* [exhibition catalogue] (New York: The New Museum of Contemporary Art, 1996), pp. 13 and 55.
10 Jan Avgikos, 'Sue Etkin [Review]'. *Artforum* 29(9) (May 1991): 144.
11 Laura Cottingham, 'The Masculine Imperative: High Modern, Postmodern'. In Joanna Frueh, Cassandra L. Langer and Arlene Raven (eds), *New Feminist Criticism: Identity, Art, Action* (New York: IconEdition/HarperCollins, 1994), p. 150 [no. 12]. And see Tavia M. Fortt and Terry R. Myers, 'White Boys as Abstraction: Do We Really Need Another New York School?' *Arts Magazine* (February 1991): 42–3.
12 Laura Cottingham, 'What's So Bad about 'Em?' In Kate Bush, Emma Dexter and Nicola White, *Bad Girls* [exhibition catalogue] (London and Glasgow: Institute of Contemporary Art and Centre for Contemporary Art, 1993), p. 59 [no. 3].
13 Faith Wilding, 'Monstrous Domesticity'. *M/E/A/N/I/N/G* 18 (November 1995): 8.
14 Tania Modleski, *Feminism without Women: Culture and Criticism in a 'Postfeminist' Age* (New York & London: Routledge, 1991), p. 7.
15 Mira Schor, 'Backlash and Appropriation'. In Norma Broude and Mary D. Garrard (eds), *The Power of Feminist Art: The American Movement of the 1970s, History and Impact* (New York and London: Harry N. Abrams and Thames & Hudson, 1994), p. 251.

16 Wilding, 'Monstrous Domesticity': 8.
17 Temma Balducci, 'The Elephant in the Room: Pattern and Decoration, Feminism, Aesthetics, and Politics'. In Anne Schwarz (ed.), *Pattern and Decoration: An Ideal Vision in American Art, 1975-1985* [exhibition catalogue] (Yonkers, New York: Hudson River Museum, 2007), pp. 45-6; and see 'Transcript of Interview with Robert Kushner [12 May 2006, New York]'. In Lynn Hershmann Leeson, *!Women Art Revolution: Voices of a Movement*, Stanford University Libraries, https://exhibits.stanford.edu/women-art-revolution/catalog/df572ks9097 (accessed 18 November 2015).
18 Marcia Tucker 'Introduction and Acknowledgements'. In *Bad Girls* [exhibition catalogue] (New York, Cambridge, MA, and London: The Museum of Contemporary Art and The MIT Press, 1994), pp. 5-6.
19 'Meyer Vaisman'. *Arts Magazine* 64(10) (Summer 1990): 96; 'Robert Gober: Interview with Richard Flood'. In Lewis Biggs (ed.), *Robert Gober* [exhibition catalogue] (London and Liverpool: Serpentine Gallery and Tate, 1993), p. 11; and *Joel Otterson: Domestic Partners* [exhibition catalogue] (Los Angeles: Maloney Fine Art, 2012).
20 James Lewis, 'Home Boys'. *Artforum* (October 1991): 105.
21 Ibid.
22 Emily Apter, 'Just Because You're a Man: Maternal Fetishism, Mike Kelley, Mary Kelly and Sally Mann'. *MAKE* 75 (April/May 1997): 8.
23 Nancy Stanton Knox, 'Desperately Seeking Charles: A Portrait of the Artist as an Artisan'. *American Craft* (August/September 2007): 40.
24 Kathy Kubicki, 'Grayson Perry'. *Make* 92 (2002): 39.
25 Cary Levine, 'Manly Crafts: Mike Kelley's (Oxy)Moronic Gender Bending'. *Art Journal* 69, 1-2 (Spring-Summer 2010): 76, and idem, *Pay for Your Pleasures: Mike Kelley, Paul McCarthy and Raymond Pettibon* (Chicago and London: University of Chicago Press, 2013), pp. 107-14.
26 Bob Pease, *Recreating Men: Postmodern Masculinity Politics* (London: Sage, 2000); and David S. Gutterman, 'Postmodernism and the Interrogation of Masculinity'. In Stephen M. Whitehead and Frank J. Barrett (eds), *The Masculinities Reader* (Cambridge: Polity Press, 2001), pp. 56-71
27 Lisa Tickner suggested, for instance, that 'The proper study of womankind is not always or necessarily women; masculinity is a problem for feminism', and Laura Cottingham contented, 'Less attention has been paid to the cultural production of femininity's supposed "opposite": masculinity', see Lisa Tickner, 'Men's Work? Masculinity and Modernism'. *differences* 4(3) (1992): 13; and Laura Cottingham, 'The Masculine Imperative', p. 124.

28   Lynne Segal, 'Introduction to the Third Edition–Men after Feminism: What's Left to Say?' In *Slow Motion: Changing Masculinities, Changing Men* (Houndmills, Basingstoke: Palgrave Macmillan, 2007 [1990]) [third, revised edition], p. xxvi.
29   The play originally opened Off-Broadway in October 1994 but transferred to Broadway in February 1995. Both play and film were directed by Joe Mantello.
30   This image appears in the film version and not in the original stage play. For the original scene [minus James's embroidery hoop] see, Terence McNally, *Love! Valor! Compassion! and A Perfect Ganesh: Two Plays* (London: Plume/Penguin, 1995), pp. 88–92.
31   Cleve Jones (with Jeff Dawson), *Stitching a Revolution: The Making of an Activist* (San Francisco: Harper, 2000), p. 108. The homely and feminine associations of the quilt worked for and against it. Its potential to trivialize, domesticate, and even make palatable, the mass deaths of gay men in an age of insidious homophobia was a central concern of the Quilt's many critics, see, for instance, Douglas Crimp's paper, 'The Spectacle of Mourning', delivered to 'The Names Project: The Transforming Power of the Forbidden Stitch' panel discussion in 1991, published in Douglas Crimp, *Melancholia and Moralism: Essays on AIDS and Queer Politics* (Cambridge: The MIT Press, 2002), pp. 195–220.
32   'Global Health Observatory (GHO) data: HIV/AIDS'. https://www.who.int/gho/hiv/en/ (accessed 1 March 2019).
33   Jen Christensen, 'A Rip in the Quilt'. *The Advocate* (28 February 2006): 28–35; and for an example of an advert for such needlepoint kits, see 'Marketspace [Mail order]'. *The Advocate* (13 December 1994): [n.p.]
34   Marita Sturken, 'Conversations with the Dead: Bearing Witness in the AIDS Memorial Quilt'. *Socialist Review* 92 (April–June 1992): 65–95; Lena Williams, 'Foreign Composition for an American Art: Quilt Making'. *The New York Times* (14 January 1993): C1, C6; and Peter S. Hawkins, 'The Art of Memory and the NAMES Project AIDS Quilt'. *Critical Inquiry* 19(4) (Summer, 1993): 752–79.
35   For the panels stitched by Rod Schelbutt or John Miller see Cindy Ruskin, *The Quilt: Stories from the NAMES Project* (New York: Pocket Books, 1988), pp. 100–1 and 120–1.
36   This version of the story is recorded in David Taffet, 'Highlighting History: UNT special collections displayed in two LGBT exhibits'. *Dallas Voice* (8 June 2018) https://www.dallasvoice.com/highlighting-history/ (accessed 3 March 2019).
37   Parker, *The Subversive Stitch*, pp. 189–215.
38   For Moufarrege's sewing see Debra Wittenberg, 'Portrait of an Artist: Nicolas A. Moufarrege'. *Needlepoint News* (March–April 1986): 34; *DUETS: Nicolas A. Moufarrege: Dean Daderko & Elaine Reichek in Conversation* (Visual Aids: New

York, 2016), p. 28; and Dean Daderko, 'An Ambitious Future, Stitch by Stitch'. In *Nicolas Moufarrege: Recognize My Sign* [exhibition catalogue] (Houston, TX: Contemporary Arts Museum, 2018), pp. 21 and 23.

39   Tim Greathouse, Cynthia Kuebel, Elaine Reichek and Bill Sterling, *Nicolas A. Moufarrege* [exhibition catalogue] (New York: The Clocktower, Institute for Art and Urban Resources, Inc, 1987), p. 15.

40   Dean Daderko in Élizabeth Lebovici, Mounira Al Solh and Dean Daderko. 'Prescient Stitches: The Work of Nicolas Moufarrege'. *Mousse* 63 (April–May 2018): 206.

41   Jean-Honoré Fragonard's *Le Chiffres d'amour* [Love Letters] dates from 1776–8 and Lichtenstein's *Spray* from 1962. The inexpensive needlepoint canvas, which Moufarrege used, was produced by Margot de Paris, one of the longest running 'Tapestry' manufacturers in the world, and is still widely available today. The kit includes, 'Penelope canvas, DMC and Anchor threads, easy to follow instructions, [and] needle'.

42   Douglas Crimp, '*Diss*-Co (A Fragment): From *Before Pictures*, a Memoir of 1970s New York'. *Criticism* 50(1) (Winter 2008): 15.

43   José Esteban Muñoz, *Disidentifications: Queers of Color and the Performance of Politics* (Minneapolis: University of Minnesota Press, 1999), p. 71.

44   Cecilia Brunson, Gabriela Rangel and Susanna V. Temkin, 'Empty Young Man: Autobiography of an Artist as Young Man'. In Karen Marta and Gabriela Rangel (eds), *José Leonilson: Empty Man* (London: Koenig Books for the Americas Society, 2017), p. 50.

45   For affinities in their work see *Oliver Herring, Leonilson* [exhibition brochure] (New York: The Museum of Modern Art, 1996); and Leslie Camhi, 'Sewing circle'. *The Village Voice* 141(6) (6 February 1996): 3–4.

46   Janet Koplos, 'Stitches in Time'. *Art in America* 91(1) (January 2003): 96.

47   D.W. Winnicott, 'Transitional objects and transitional phenomena'. *International Journal of Psychoanalysis* 34(1) (1953): 89–97.

48   'Me Us Them: A Dialogue with Oliver Herring and Ian Berry'. In Ian Berry, *Oliver Herring: Me Us Them* [exhibition catalogue] (Saratoga Springs, New York: The Frances Young Tang Teaching Museum and Art Gallery at Skidmore College, 2009), pp. 5–29.

49   Eve Kosofsky Sedgwick, 'Paranoid Reading and Reparative Reading or, You're So Paranoid, You Probably Think This Essay Is about You'. In *Touching Feeling: Affect, Pedagogy, Performativity* (Durham & London: Duke University Press, 2003), pp. 123–51.

50   Stefano Catalani, 'Codes of Conduct'. *Surface Design Journal* (June 2013): 22.

51  Lisa Duggan, 'The New Homonormativity: The Sexual Politics of Neoliberalism'. In Russ Castronovo and Dana D. Nelson (eds), *Materializing Democracy: Toward a Revitalized Cultural Politics* (Durham and London: Duke University Press, 2002), pp. 175–94.
52  The attraction to working with craft practices and materials that are socially and culturally denigrated perhaps reflects the feelings of worthlessness that many gay men experience. I tentatively explore this in '"Male trouble": Sewing, Amateurism, and Gender'. In Elaine Cheasley Paterson and Susan Surette (eds), *Sloppy Craft: Postdisciplinarity and the Crafts* (London: Bloomsbury, 2015), pp. 27–43.
53  Within the new writing on domestic space as a site for the mediation of modern masculine and homosexual identities John Povtin has contended that, 'The domestic, and not the public domain, I suggest, was the landscape in which the battles over masculine identity and male sexuality were waged', see John Potvin, *Bachelors of a Different Sort: Queer Aesthetics, Material Culture and the Modern Interior in Britain* (Manchester: Manchester University Press, 2014), p. 4.
54  Matt Morris, 'Chicago: Miller & Shellabarger'. *Sculpture* 33(6) (July/August 2014): 72.
55  María Caroline Baulo, 'Leo Chiachio and Danny Giannone: Love Story'. *Fiberarts* 4(1) (Summer 2007): 24–5.
56  Maña Moreno, 'Chiachio & Giannone: Specialists in embroidery'. In *Chiachio & Giannone: Monobordado* [Trans. Jane Brodie] [exhibition catalogue] (Buenos Aires: Pasaje 17 Art Contemporáneo, Galeria de Arte de Apoc y Ospace, 2016), n.p.
57  Ibid.
58  Kosofsky Sedgwick, 'Queer Performativity', p. 5.
59  Peter Hobbs, 'The Sewing Desire Machine'. In Janis Jefferies (ed.), *Reinventing Textiles: Vol. 2: Gender and Identity* (Winchester: Telos, 2001), pp. 49–59.
60  Giulia Lamoni, 'Philomela as Metaphor: Sexuality, Pornography, and Seduction in the Textile Works of Tracey Emin and Ghada Amer'. In Isabelle Loring Wallace and Jennie Hirsh (eds), *Contemporary Art and Classical Myth* (Farnham and Burlington, VT: Ashgate, 2011), pp. 175–97.
61  Michael Bronski, *Culture Clash: The Making of Gay Sensibility* (Boston, MA: South End Press, 1984), p. 165. For a discussion of the object/subject relation and the male-to-male gaze see Kenneth MacKinnon, 'After Mulvey: Male Erotic Objectification'. In Michele Aaron (ed.), *The Body's Perilous Pleasures: Dangerous Desires and Contemporary Culture* (Edinburgh: Edinburgh University Press, 1999), pp. 13–29.
62  Richard Dyer, 'Gay Male Porn: Coming to Terms'. *Jump Cut* 30 (March 1985): 27.

63  Hurlstone's source was James Gardiner, *A Class Apart: The Private Pictures of Montague Glover* (London: The Serpent's Tail, 1992). The quote is from Nigel Hurlstone, 'Stitching Up: Embroidering the Sex Life of a Fetishist Image-Maker'. In Lesley Miller and Alice Kettle (eds), *The Erotic Cloth: Seduction and Fetishism in Textiles* (London and New York: Bloomsbury, 2018), p. 56.

64  Aaron McIntosh, 'An Indecent Obsession'. MFA thesis, Virginia Commonwealth University, 2010, p. 54; and see Gabriel Craig, 'Aaron McIntosh: Queer Country Quilting'. *Surface Design Journal* (Summer 2013): 34–7.

65  Eve Kosofsky Sedgwick, 'Jane Austen and the Masturbating Girl'. In Paula Bennett and Vernon A. Rosario II (eds), *Solitary Pleasures: The Historical, Literary, and Artistic Discourses of Autoeroticism* (New York and London: Routledge, 1995), pp. 133–53.

66  Kenneth Miller, 'These "Kinky Needles" Are Your Queer Fantasies Embroidered', *Hooligan Mag* (23 May 2016), http://www.hooliganmagazine.com/music-reviews/2016/5/23/these-kinky-needles-are-your-queer-fantasies-embroidered (accessed 12 December 2016).

67  'Greg Climer: Pornography Quilts'. http://gregclimer.com/portfolio/pornography-quilts/ (accessed 20 February 2017).

68  'XXX: A Brief History of Gay Porn Films 1971–2016'. https://www.beefcakecraftarcade.com/xxx-a-brief-history-of-gay-porn (accessed 20 February 2017)

69  Zach Nutman, 'Needlepoint'. https://www.nuthouse.studio/needlepoint (accessed 12 August 2018).

70  Like many of the artists under discussion here I am not using needlework to pathologize queerness through the reinscription of shame onto sexual desire. Rather I am trying to understand shame as a 'structure of feeling' as explored by Sedgwick in 'Queer Performativity' (1993); by Douglas Crimp in 'Mario Mortez, For Shame'. In Stephen M. Barber and David L. Clark (eds), *Regarding Sedgwick: Essays on Queer Culture and Critical Theory* (New York and London: Routledge, 2002), pp. 57–70; and by David M. Halperin and Valerie Traub in their edited volume *Gay Shame* (Chicago & London: University of Chicago Press, 2009); or in the discussion of queer shame originating in childhood in Alan Downs's widely read *The Velvet Rage: Overcoming the Pain of Growing Up Gay in a Straight Man's World* (Cambridge, MA: De Capo Press, 2005).

71  For info and statistics see 'The Stitch'n Bitch Niche'. *The Economist* (24 February 2006): 29; and Jenny Wilhide, 'The knitty gritty'. *The Spectator* (23 September 2006): 81.

72 For the presence (and absence) of queer men in the needlecraft books of the new millennium see Alla Myzelev, 'Whip Your Hobby into Shape: Knitting, Feminism and Construction of Gender'. *Textile: The Journal of Cloth and Culture* 7(2) (July 2009): 148–63, and 'Monsieur Tricote: Tricote et masculinité au XXIe siècle/ Here Comes the Knitting Men: Knitting and Masculinity in the early twenty-first century'. *Cahiers des métiers* 5(2) (Printemps/Spring 2012): 101–23.

73 'Men Can Make Kickass Fiber Art Too!' *Feminist Fiber Art* 2 (14 August 2015); and Emily Drury, 'High School Boys Who Knit'. *KnitKnit* 4 (October 2004): 10–11.

74 'Grant Neufeld: community activist for social and environmental justice', http://grantneufeld.ca/media/ (accessed 20 June 2012); and 'Revolutionary Knitting Circle'. In Betty Christiansen, *Knitting for Peace: Make the World a Better Place One Stitch at a Time* (New York: Stewart, Tabori & Chang, 2006), pp. 20–2.

75 Kelly Shindler, 'Lords of the Strings'. *BUST* 36 (December 2005/January 2006): 82–5. In actuality, there are few images of male needleworkers in the best-known overview of the Craftivist movement–*Handmade Nation*. We glimpse a man with an embroidery hoop at a craft fair and we see a quilt by Paul Margolis entitled 'Quilting is for Pussies', a typical homophobic slur directed at any man who takes up a woman's craft (the quilt can be seen in the documentary at 44 mins 52 sec). No needlework by men is included in the associated publication, Faythe Levine and Cortney Heimerl, *Handmade Nation: The Rise of DIY, Art, Craft, and Design* (New York: Princeton Architectural Press, 2008).

76 Christine Kapteijn and Tanya Harrod, *Jonathan Parsons: System + Structure* [exhibition catalogue] (Farnham: James Hockey Gallery, The Surrey Institute of Art & Design, 2000); and Ralph Rugoff et al., *Jeremy Deller: Joy in People* [exhibition catalogue] (London: Hayward Gallery, 2012).

77 For Brennand-Wood's profile as a leading male advocate of embroidery from the 1970s onwards see Moira Kelly, 'This Is Embroidery'. *Crafts* 47 (November/December 1980): 28–31; for Brennand-Wood's flags, see my 'Readymade Redux'. *Selvedge* 45 (March/April 2012): 56–9.

78 *Art Embroidery–Portrait Gallery* [exhibition catalogue] (London: Pfaff, 2005), p. 21. For a discussion of political imagery in Brennand-Wood's work see my essay, 'Pricked by a Needle'. In *Pretty Deadly: New Work by Michael Brennand-Wood* [exhibition catalogue] (Belfast: The Naughton Gallery, Queen's University Belfast, 2009), n.p.

79 Kate Eilertsen, 'Introduction'. In Kate Eilertsen et al., *Nick Cave: Meet Me at the Center of the Earth* [exhibition catalogue] (San Francisco: Yerba Buena Center for the Arts, 2009), p. 18.

80 'Sense of Sound'. *Embroidery* 64(5) (September/October 2013): 22–6.
81 David Revere McFadden, 'The Emergence of an Art Language for the Millennium'. In David Revere McFadden, *Pricked: Extreme Embroidery* [exhibition catalogue] (New York: Museum of Arts and Design, 2007), p. 9.
82 Karen Rosenberg, 'Needling More Than the Feminist Consciousness'. *The New York Times* (28 December 2007): E38; and John Perreault, 'Pricked: Extreme Embroidery'. *Crafts* 210 (January/February 2008): 66.
83 Lisa Graziose Corrin, 'Hanging by a Thread'. In *Loose Threads* [exhibition catalogue] (London: Serpentine Gallery, 1998), p. 12.
84 Richard Dorment, 'Threadbare Display of Knitwit Ideas', *Telegraph* online (5 September 1998) www.telegraph.co.uk/culture/4715547/Threadbare-display-of-knitwit-ideas.html (accessed 20 August 2011).
85 Jean-Christophe Ammann, 'Jochen Flinzer: 53 Weeks of Happiness'. In Jean-Christophe Ammann (ed.), *Jochen Flinzer* [exhibition catalogue] (Frankfurt am Main: Museum für Moderne Kunst, 1996), pp. 38–41; and Janet Koplos, 'Jochen Flinzer at Thomas Rehbein'. *Art in America* 90(3) (March 2002): 138–9.
86 Roland Barthes, 'Préface'. In Renaud Camus, *Tricks: 33 récits* (Paris: Mazarine, 1979), p. viii.
87 Raedecker was nominated for the Turner Prize in 2000, see *Turner Prize 2000* (London: Tate Britain, 2000), n.p.
88 Frank van der Ploeg, 'Penetrations: The "Art Needlework" of Michael Raedecker'. *The Low Countries* 19 (2011): 228–35.
89 Janis Jefferies, 'LETTERS: I can't quite understand all the fuss about Michael Raedecker's work'. *MAKE Magazine* 90 (1 December 2000–February 2001): 2.
90 Janis Jefferies, 'Textiles'. In Fiona Carson and Claire Pajaczkowska (eds), *Feminist Visual Culture* (Edinburgh: Edinburgh University Press, 2000), pp. 200–1.
91 'To Craft To Care: Polly Leonard, interviews exhibition curator, Professor Janis Jefferies, about "Boys Who Sew [December 2003]."' In *Boys Who Sew* [exhibition brochure] (London: Crafts Council, 2004), n.p.
92 Giorgio Verzotti, 'Il racconto del filo: Ricamo e cucito nell-arte contemporanea'. In *Il racconto del filo: Ricamo e cucito nell-arte contemporanea* [exhibition catalogue] (Milan: Skira for Museo di Arte Moderna e Contemporanea di Trento e Rovereto, 2003), pp. 28–36.
93 'Real Boys' Art is Complex'. *Fiberarts* (March/April 1999): 10.
94 Elizabeth A. Brown and Fran Seegull, 'Guys Who Sew'. In *Guys Who Sew* [exhibition catalogue] (Santa Barbara, CA: University Art Museum, University of California, 1994), p. 2.

95 Stephen Beal, *Men of the Cloth: Contemporary Fiber Art* [exhibition catalogue] (Loveland, CO: Loveland Museum/Gallery, 1999), p. 3.

96 William Pollack, *Real Boys: Rescuing Our Sons from the Myths of Boyhood* (New York: Random House, 1998).

97 'Men With Needles And Some Points to Make'. *The New York Times* (7 November 1999): CY16. There were also several broader exhibitions that surveyed men's interest in craft after the millennium. Two notable examples are *Handymen and Girly Boys: Masculinity, Craft, Culture*, Sheery Leedy Contemporary Art, Kansas City, Missouri (2007), curated by Elena Maria Buszek; and *BoysCraft* at the Haifa Museum of Art, Israel (2007–8), curated by Tami Katz-Freiman, and which contained work by forty-one men who used a variety of 'techniques that are culturally associated with "female" or "childlike" forms of expression', see Tami Katz-Freiman, 'Craftsmen in the Factory of Images'. In *BoysCraft* [exhibition catalogue] (Haifa, Israel: Haifa Museum of Art, 2007), pp. 179 and 178.

98 Joe Cunningham, 'Men in Quilts'. In Jean M. Burks and Joe Cunningham, *Man-Made Quilts: Civil War to the Present* [exhibition catalogue] (Shelburne, VT: Shelburne Museum, 2012), pp. 10–26; Joe Cunningham, *Men and the Art of Quiltmaking* (Paducah, KY: American Quilter's Society, 2010), p. 7.

99 Isken, Susan, *Man-Made: Contemporary Male Quilters* [exhibition catalogue] (Los Angeles: Craft & Folk Art Museum, 2015), p. 3.

100 Although there have been some exemplary studies of masculinity in relation textile art (and not just needlework) few, if any, have attempted queer readings; see, for instance, Margo Mensing, 'Close to Home: An Exploration of the Historical Perceptions Concerning Women and Crafts'. *Fiberarts* 20(3) (November–December 1993): 42–6; and Patricia Malarcher, 'Men in Fiber Art'. *Fiberarts* 20(3) (November/December 1993): 47–51.

101 Melissa Boyde and Amanda Lawson, 'Colour Me Lemon'. In HOMO*craft* [exhibition catalogue] (Sydney, NSW: Crafts Council of New South Wales, 1995), p. 6.

102 Peter McNeil, 'Material Boys: Subversion & Celebration'. In *Material Boys–un[Zipped]* [exhibition catalogue] (Sydney: Object Galleries, Australian Centre for Craft and Design, 2000), p. 7.

103 Barbara Morris, '*Nancy Boy* Richmond Art Center'. *Artweek*, 36(4), May 2005, p. 15.

104 Anna-Marie Larsen, 'Boys with Needles'. In *Boys with Needles* [exhibition catalogue] (London, ON: Museum London, 2002), p. 9.

105 John Chaich, 'Queer Threads'. In *Queer Threads: Crafting Identity and Community* [exhibition brochure] (New York: Leslie-Lohman Museum of Gay and Lesbian Art, 2014), p. 5.

106 John Chaich, 'Unraveling Queer Threads'. In John Chaich and Todd Oldham, *Queer Threads: Crafting Identity and Community* (Los Angeles: AMMO Books, 2017), p. viii.

107 Amica De Mouray, 'Gentlemen of the Needle'. *Country Life* CXCI(6) (February 1997): 28–31.

108 Nina Lee Soltwedel, 'Rendering Visible the Formerly Invisible: The Men of the EGA'. *Needle Arts* XXIX(2) (June 1998): 36–44.

109 Ann Cvetkovich, *An Archive of Feelings: Trauma, Sexuality, and Lesbian Cultures* (Durham & London: Duke University Press, 2003), p. 8.

110 For these see Gianfranco Maraniello, 'Detail by Detail: Time Regained'. In *The Needleworks of Francesco Vezzoli* [exhibition catalogue] (Leipzig: Hatje Cantz Verlag für Galerie für Zeitgenössische Kunst Leipzig, 2002), pp. 57–61.

111 Mario Praz, *The House of Life* (Trans. Angus Davidson) (London: Methuen & Co, 1964), pp. 272–3.

112 For the symposium see *The Subversive Stitch Revisited: The Politics of Cloth*, Victoria and Albert Museum, London, 29–30 November 2013, http://www.gold.ac.uk/subversivestitchrevisited/ (accessed 1 July 2014). Some of these papers appeared in a special issue of *Image & Text* (23) (2014); and see Pennina Barnett and Jennifer Harris, 'The Subversive Stitch Revisited'. In Sarah-Joy Floyd (ed.), *Cut Cloth: Contemporary Textiles and Feminism* (Leeds/Manchester: PO Publishing, 2017), pp. 39–52.

113 Matt Smith, 'Unpicking Queer History in the National Trust'. Paper delivered at *The Subversive Stitch Revisited: The Politics of Cloth*, 29 November 2013, Victoria and Albert Museum, London, podcast available at https://soundcloud.com/goldsmithsuol/subversive-stitch-smith?in=goldsmithsuol/sets/the-subversive-stitch (accessed 1 July 2014).

114 Nikki Sullivan, *A Critical Introduction to Queer Theory* (Edinburgh: Edinburgh University Press, 2003), p. 189.

115 Alexander Doty, *Making Things Perfectly Queer: Interpreting Mass Culture* (Minneapolis and London: University of Minnesota Press, 1993), p. 191.

116 For these see Katy Barron, 'Looking In'. In *Looking In: Photographic Portraits of Maud Sulter and Chan-Hyo Bae* [exhibition catalogue] (London: Ben Uri, The London Jewish Museum, 2013), pp. 7–18; James Merry, 'Embroidery Today'.

In *Embroidery: A Maker's Guide* (London: Thames & Hudson/V&A, 2017), p. 6; and Gavin Jantjes, 'Edge, Seam & Space'. In *Nicholas Hlobo: Sculpture, Installation, Performance, Drawing* [exhibition catalogue] (Oslo: Nasjonalmuseet for kunst, arkitektur og design, 2011), pp. 57.

117 Parker, *The Subversive Stitch*, p. 215.

# Chapter 6

1 'Foreword'. In *The Subversive Stitch: Embroidery and the Making of the Feminine* (London: The Women's Press, 1984), p. vi; quote from Oliver Schreiner, *From Man to Man, or Perhaps Only* (London: Virago, 1982 [1926]), p. 187.

2 Olive Schreiner's *The Story of an African Farm* (London: Chapman & Hall, 1890 [1883]), p. 235.

3 This quote is also used to open (as well as a methodological marker) in Maureen Daly Goggin and Beth Fowkes Tobin's edited volume, *Women and the Material Culture of Needlework and Textiles, 1750–1950* (Farnham, Surrey and Burlington, VT: Ashgate, 2009), p. 1.

4 Yaffa Claire Draznin (ed.), *'My Other Self': The Letters of Olive Schreiner and Havelock Ellis, 1884–1920* (New York: Peter Lang, 1992).

5 Thesiger told the reporter that 'they were in a very bad state and so I offered to repair them. The first one I did for love and it was thought so highly of that they commissioned me to do the second,' see 'Men who Embroider', unattributed magazine cutting (early mid-1950s), EFT/000066/13, Ernest Thesiger Archive, Theatre Collection, University of Bristol.

6 The Royal School of Needlework had estimated the cost at £120 but Thesiger took no fee except '30 guineas towards the high cost of the materials and other expenses'. See 'A famous Actor Helps Temple Newsam'. *The Yorkshire Post and Leeds Mercury* (7 June 1955): 4.

7 Gail Carolyn Sirna, *In Praise of Needlewomen: Embroiderers, Knitters, Lacemakers and Weavers in Art* (London: Merrell, 2006), p. 9.

8 Michael Zaki, 'Review of *The Culture of Sewing: Gender, Consumption and Home Dressmaking*. Barbara Burman, ed.' *Business History Review* 74(3) (Autumn 2000): 509.

9 See, in particular, Lacey Jane Roberts, 'Put Your Thing Down, Flip It, and Reverse It: Re-imagining Craft Identities Using the Tactics of Queer Theory'. In Maria Elena Buszek (ed.), *Extra/Ordinary: Craft and Contemporary Art* (Durham and

London: Duke University Press, 2011), pp. 243–59; Ann Cvetkovich, *Depression: A Public Fleeing* (Durham & London: Duke University Press, 2012), pp. 154–202; and Julia Bryan-Wilson, *Fray: Art + Textile Politics* (Chicago & London: Chicago University Press, 2017).

10  Helen Sheumaker's review of Maureen Daly Goggin and Beth Fowkes Tobin's *Women and the Material Culture of Needlework and Textiles*, and its two companion volumes *Women and Things, 1750–1950: Gendered Material Strategies*; and *Material Women, 1750–1950: Consuming Desires and Collecting Practices* (Farnham, Surrey, and Burlington, VT: Ashgate, 2009); in *Winterthur Portfolio* 46(1) (Spring 2012): 93.

11  Clare Hunter, *Threads of Life: A History of the World through the Eye of a Needle* (London: Spectre/Hodder & Stoughton, 2019). Hunter, however, only includes the better-known and most recently discussed examples of men's work (John Craske was the subject of a recent monograph by Julia Blackburn; the embroideries made by Major Alexis Casdagli as a POW were included in the Victoria and Albert Museum's *Power of Making* exhibition; and Fine Cell Work has become well-known through its website).

12  Ariel Shidlo, Michael Schroeder and Jack Drescher (eds), *Sexual Conversion Therapy: Ethical, Clinical and Research Perspectives* (Binghamton, NY: The Haworth Medical Press, 2001), p. 149.

13  Pennina Barnett, 'Afterthoughts on Curating "The Subversive Stitch"'. In Katy Deepwell (ed.), *New Feminist Art Criticism: Critical Strategies* (Manchester and New York: Manchester University Press, 1995), p. 82.

14  Eve Kosofsky Sedgwick, 'A Poem Is Being Written'. *Representations* 17 (Winter 1987): 137.

# Select Bibliography

As I have stated elsewhere the bibliography for men and needlework is not so much elusive as non-existent. There is no single book or article on the subject *per se*. Collated here are key sources that contain reference to needlework in relation to men (largely short articles, book chapters or exhibition catalogues). As there are so few of these I have also included a range of other sources that were critical in shaping my thinking on the subject. Period articles and detailed information on individual artists and designers, exhibitions, or specific works, as well as wider contextual and theoretical material, can be found in the notes to each chapter.

Adams, James Eli, *Dandies and Desert Saints: Styles of Victorian Manhood* (Ithaca and London: Cornell University Press, 1995)

Auther, Elissa, *String, Felt and Thread: The Hierarchy of Art and Craft in American Art* (Minneapolis: University of Minnesota Press, 2010)

Barnett, Pennina, 'Women and Textiles Today'. In *The Subversive Stitch* [exhibition catalogue] (Manchester: Whitworth Art Gallery & Cornerhouse, 1988), pp. 35–60

Barnett, Pennina, 'A Stitch Out of Time'. *Women's Art Magazine* 51 (March/April 1993): 11–13

Barnett, Pennina, 'Afterthoughts on Curating "the Subversive Stitch."' In Katy Deepwell (ed.), *New Feminist Art Criticism: Critical Strategies* (Manchester and New York: Manchester University Press, 1995), pp. 76–86

Barnett, Pennina, and Jennifer Harris, 'The Subversive Stitch Revisited'. In Sarah-Joy Floyd (ed.), *Cut Cloth: Contemporary Textiles and Feminism* (Leeds/Manchester: PO Publishing, 2017), pp. 39–52

Beal, Stephen, *The Very Stuff: Poems on Color, Thread and the Habits of Women* (Loveland, CO: Interweave Press, 1995)

Beal, Stephen, *Men of the Cloth: Contemporary Fiber Art* [exhibition catalogue] (Loveland, CO: Loveland Museum/Gallery, 1999)

Beaudry, Mary C., *Findings: The Material Culture of Needlework and Sewing* (London and New Haven: Yale University Press, 2006)

Beck, Thomasina, *The Embroiderer's Story: Needlework from the Renaissance to the Present Day* (Newton Abbott, Devon: David & Charles, 1995)

Berger, Maurice and Simon Watson, *The Subversive Stitch* [exhibition brochure] (New York: Simon Watson Gallery, 1991)

Berger, Maurice, Brian Wallis and Simon Watson (eds), *Constructing Masculinity* (New York and London: Routledge, 1995)

Breward, Christopher, *The Hidden Consumer: Masculinities, Fashion and City Life 1860–1914* (Manchester and New York: Manchester University Press, 1999)

Breward, Christopher, 'Renouncing Consumption: Men, Fashion and Luxury, 1870–1914'. In Amy de la Haye and Elizabeth Wilson (eds), *Defining Dress: Dress as Object, Meaning and Identity* (Manchester and New York: Manchester University Press, 1999), pp. 48–62

Breward, Christopher, 'Sewing Soldiers'. In Sue Prichard (ed.), *Quilts 1700–2010: Hidden Histories, Untold Stories* (London: V&A Publishing, 2010), pp. 84–7

Brine, Daniel, HOMO*craft* [exhibition catalogue] (Sydney, NSW: Crafts Council of New South Wales, 1995)

Brod, Harry (ed.), *The Making of Masculinities: The New Men's Studies* (Boston, MA, and London: Allen & Unwin, 1987)

Bronski, Michael, *Culture Clash: The Making of Gay Sensibility* (Boston, MA: South End Press, 1984)

Brown, Elizabeth A. and Fran Seegull, *Guys Who Sew* [exhibition catalogue] (Santa Barbara: University of California, 1994)

Burks, Jean M. and Joe Cunningham, *Man-Made Quilts: Civil War to the Present* [exhibition catalogue] (Shelburne, VT: Shelburne Museum, 2012)

Butler, Judith, *Gender Trouble: Feminism and the Subversion of Identity* (New York and London: Routledge, 1990)

Butler, Judith, 'Imitation and Gender Subordination'. In Diana Fuss (ed.), *Inside/Out: Lesbian Theories, Gay Theories* (New York and London: Routledge, 1991), pp. 13–31

Butler, Judith, *Bodies That Matter: On the Discursive Limits of 'Sex'* (New York & London: Routledge, 1993)

Cardinal, Marie, *Le Passé empiété* (Paris: Editions Grasset & Fasquelle, 1983)

Caulfeild, Sophia Frances Anne and Blanche C. Saward, *The Dictionary of Needlework: An Encyclopaedia of Artistic, Plain, and Fancy Needlework* (London: L. Upcott Gill, 1882)

Chaich, John, *Queer Threads: Crafting Identity and Community* [exhibition brochure] (New York: Leslie-Lohman Museum of Gay and Lesbian Art, 2014)

Chaich, John and Todd Oldham, *Queer Threads: Crafting Identity and Community* (Los Angeles: AMMO Books, 2017)

Chodorow, Nancy, *The Reproduction of Mothering: Psychoanalysis and the Sociology of Gender* (Berkeley: University of California Press, 1978)

Christ, Carol, 'Victorian Masculinity and the Angel in the House'. In Martha Vicinus (ed.), *A Widening Sphere: Changing Roles of Victorian Women* (Bloomington & London: Indiana University Press, 1977), pp. 146–62

Christie, A.G.I., *English Medieval Embroidery: A Brief Survey of English Embroidery Dating from the Beginning of the Tenth Century until the End of the Fourteenth* (Oxford: Clarendon Press, 1938)

Claridge, Laura and Elizabeth Langland (eds), *Out of Bounds: Male Writers and Gender(ed.) Criticism* (Amherst: University of Massachusetts, 1990)

Connell, R.W., *Gender and Power: Society, the Person and Sexual Politics* (Cambridge: Polity Press, 1987)

Connell, R.W., 'A Very Straight Gay: Masculinity, Homosexual Experience, and the Dynamics of Gender'. *American Sociological Review* 57(6) (December 1992): 735–51

Connell, R.W., *Masculinities* (Cambridge: Polity Press, 1995)

Corrin, Lisa G., *Loose Threads* [exhibition catalogue] (London: Serpentine Gallery, 1998)

Crowley, Bridget, 'Unlikely Art of Jolly Jack Tar'. *Country Life* CLXXXVI(46) (12 November 1992): 46–7

Cunningham, Joe, *Men and the Art of Quiltmaking* (Puducah, KY: American Quilter's Society, 2010)

Cvetkovich, Ann, *An Archive of Feelings: Trauma, Sexuality, and Lesbian Cultures* (Durham & London: Duke University Press, 2003)

Cvetkovich, Ann, 'Public Feelings'. *South Atlantic Quarterly* 103 (3) (Summer 2007): 459–68

Cvetkovich, Ann, *Depression: A Public Fleeing* (Durham & London: Duke University Press, 2012)

De Mouray, Amica, 'Gentlemen of the Needle'. *Country Life* CXCI(6) (February 1997): 28–31

Doty, Alexander, *Making Things Perfectly Queer: Interpreting Mass Culture* (Minneapolis and London: University of Minnesota Press, 1993)

Doty, Alexander, *Flaming Classics: Queering the Film Canon* (New York and London: Routledge, 2000)

Drury, Emily, 'High School Boys Who Knit'. *KnitKnit* 4 (October 2004): 10–11

Faludi, Susan, *Stiffed: The Betrayal of the Modern Man* (London: Chatto & Windus, 1999)

Felix, Matilda, *Nadelstiche. Sticken in der Kunst der Gegenwart* (Bielefeld: transcript Verlag, 2010)

Flintoff, John-Paul, *Through the Eye of a Needle* (East Meon, Hampshire: Permanent Publications/The Sustainability Centre, 2009) – reissued as *Sew Your Own* (London: Profile, 2010)

Foucault, *The History of Sexuality: Volume 1: The Will to Knowledge* (Trans. Richard Hurley) (London: Penguin, 1998 [1976])

Freeman, June, *Quilting Patchwork and Appliqué, 1700–1982: Sewing as a Woman's Art* [exhibition catalogue] (Colchester and London: The Minories and Crafts Council, 1983)

Freeman, June, *Knitting: A Common Art* [exhibition catalogue] (Colchester and Aberystwyth: The Minories and Aberystwyth Arts Centre, 1986)

Frye, Susan, *Pens and Needles: Women's Textiles in Early Modern England* (Philadelphia: University of Pennsylvania Press, 2010)

Furneaux, Holly, *Military Men of Feeling: Emotion, Touch and Masculinity in the Crimean War* (Oxford: Oxford University Press, 2016)

Furneaux, Holly, *Created in Conflict: British Soldier Art from the Crimean War to Today* [exhibition catalogue] (Compton Verney, Warwickshire: Compton Verney Art Gallery & Park, 2018)

Furneaux, Holly and Sue Prichard, 'Contested Objects: Curating Soldier Art'. *Museum & Society* 13(4) (2015): 447–61

Gay Left Collective, *Homosexuality: Power and Politics* (London: Verso, 1980)

Goggin, Maureen Daly, 'An "Essamplaire Essai" on the Rhetoricity of Needlework Sampler-Making: A Contribution to Theorizing and Historicizing Rhetorical Praxis'. *Rhetoric Review* 21(4) (2002): 309–38

Goggin, Maureen Daly and Beth Fowkes Tobin (eds), *Women and the Material Culture of Needlework and Textiles, 1750–1950* (Farnham, Surrey and Burlington, VT: Ashgate, 2009)

Gschwandtner, Sabrina, *KnitKnit: Profiles + Projects from Knitting's New Wave* (New York: Stewart, Tabori & Chang, 2007)

Hall, Donald E., *Fixing Patriarchy: Feminism and Mid-Victorian Male Novelists* (New York: New York University Press, 1996)

Hall, Donald E., *Queer Theories* (Basingstoke: Palgrave Macmillan, 2003)

Halperin, David M., *Saint Foucault: Towards a Gay Hagiography* (Oxford and New York: Oxford University Press, 1995)

Halperin, David M., 'How to Do the History of Homosexuality'. *GLQ: A Journal of Lesbian and Gay Studies* 6(1) (2000): 87–123

Halperin, David M., *How to be Gay* (Cambridge, MA: The Belknap Press of Harvard University Press, 2012)

Halperin, David M. and Valerie Traub (eds), *Gay Shame* (Chicago & London: University of Chicago Press, 2009)

Harris, Jennifer, 'Embroidery in Women's Lives 1300–1900'. In *The Subversive Stitch* [exhibition catalogue] (Manchester: Whitworth Art Gallery & Cornerhouse, 1988), pp. 7–33

Hartley, Paddy, 'The Forgotten Fighters'. *Embroidery* 69(1) (January/February 2018): 36–7

Hearn, Jeff and David Morgan (eds), *Men, Masculinities & Social Theory* (London: Unwin Hyman, 1990)

Hesketh, Sally, 'Needlework in the Lives and Novels of the Brontë Sisters'. *Brontë Studies* 1 (June 1997): 72–85

Hobbs, Peter, 'The Sewing Desire Machine'. In Janis Jefferies (ed.), *Reinventing Textiles: Vol. 2: Gender and Identity* (Winchester: Telos, 2001), pp. 49–59

Huish, Marcus B., *Samplers & Tapestry Embroideries* (London: Longmans, Green & Co., 1913)

Hunter, Clare, *Threads of Life: A History of the World through the Eye of a Needle* (London: Spectre/Hodder & Stoughton, 2019)

Isken, Susan, *Man-Made: Contemporary Male Quilters* [exhibition catalogue] (Los Angeles: Craft & Folk Art Museum, 2015)

Jagose, Annamarie, *Queer Theory: An Introduction* (New York: New York University Press, 1996)

Jardine, Alice and Paul Smith (eds), *Men in Feminism* (New York and London: Routledge, 1987)

Jefferies, Janis, 'Textiles: What Can She Know?' In Fiona Carson and Claire Pajaczkowska (eds), *Feminist Visual Culture* (Edinburgh: Edinburgh University Press, 2000), pp. 189–205

Jefferies, Janis, *Boys Who Sew* [exhibition brochure] (London: Crafts Council, 2004)

Johnson, Pamela, 'Art and Women's Work? News from the "Knitting Circle."' *Oral History* (*The Crafts* Special Issue) 18 (2) (Autumn 1990): 50–3

Jones, Cleve (with Jeff Dawson), *Stitching a Revolution: The Making of an Activist* (San Francisco: Harper, 2000)

Katz-Freiman, Tami, *BoysCraft* [exhibition catalogue] (Haifa, Israel: Haifa Museum of Art, 2007)

Kimmel, Michael S., 'The Contemporary "Crisis" of Masculinity in Historical Perspective'. In Harry Brod (ed.), *The Making of Masculinities: The New Men's Studies* (Boston, MA, and London: Allen & Unwin, 1987), pp. 121–53

Kimmel, Michael S., *Manhood in America: A Cultural History* (Oxford University Press US, 2006 [1996])

Kimmel, Michael S. and Amy Aronson (eds), *Men & Masculinities: A Social, Cultural, and Historical Encyclopedia*, 2 vols (Santa Barbara, CA: ABC-CLIO, 2004)

King, Natalie, *The Subversive Stitch* [exhibition catalogue] (Melbourne: Monash University Gallery, 1991)

Langland, Elizabeth, *Nobody's Angels: Middle-Class Women and Domestic Ideology in Victorian Culture* (Ithaca and London: Cornell University Press, 1995)

Larsen, Anna-Marie, *Boys with Needles* [exhibition catalogue] (London, ON: Museum London, 2002)

Lauretis, Teresa de, 'Queer Theory: Lesbian and Gay Sexualities. An Introduction'. *differences: A Journal of Feminist Cultural Studies* 3(2) (Summer 1991): iii–xviii

Lewis, James, 'Home Boys'. *Artforum* (October 1991): 101–5

Lloyd, Christopher, *The Burdens of Intimacy: Psychoanalysis and Victorian Masculinity* (Chicago & London: Chicago University Press, 1999)

Lynes, Russell, 'Confessions of a Needlepointer'. *House Beautiful* 108(11) (November 1966): 252–3, 294–5

Lynes, Russell, 'The Mesh Canvas'. *Art in America* 56(3) (May/June 1968): 29–49

Lynes, Russell, 'The Pleasure of Making It'. *House & Garden* 142(1) (July 1972): 50–1, 82

Lynes, Russell, 'The Needlepoint Boom'. *New York Times Magazine* (11 July 1972): 56–8

Macdonald, Anne L., *No Idle Hands: The Social History of American Knitting* (New York: Ballantine Books, 1988)

MacInnes, John, *The End of Masculinity: The Confusion of Sexual Genesis and Sexual Difference in Modern Society* (Buckingham: Open University Press, 1998)

McBrinn, Joseph, *Pretty Deadly: New Work by Michael Brennand-Wood* [exhibition catalogue] (Belfast: The Naughton Gallery, Queen's University Belfast, 2009)

McBrinn, Joseph, 'Readymade Redux'. *Selvedge* 45 (March/April 2012): 56–9

McBrinn, Joseph, 'Yarns and Tails'. *Embroidery* 63(3) (September/October 2012): 36–41

McBrinn, Joseph, 'Happy Ever After'. *Embroidery* 63(4) (November/December 2012): 26–31

McBrinn, Joseph, '"Male Trouble": Sewing, Amateurism, Gender'. In Elaine Cheasley Patterson and Susan Surette (eds): *Sloppy Craft: Postdisciplinarity and the Crafts* (London: Bloomsbury, 2015), pp. 27–43

McBrinn, Joseph, 'Needlepoint for Men: Craft and Masculinity in Postwar America'. *The Journal of Modern Craft* 8(3) (November 2015): 301–31

McBrinn, Joseph, '"Nothing is more terrifying to me than to see Ernest Thesiger sitting under the lamplight doing this embroidery": Ernest Thesiger (1879–1961),

"Expert Embroider."' *Text: Journal for the Study of Textile Art, Design and History* 43 (2015–16): 20–6.

McBrinn, Joseph, 'The Clever Needlemen: The Disabled Soldiers' Embroidery Industry and the Embroiderers' Guild'. *Embroidery* 68(1) (January/February 2017): 50–5

McBrinn, Joseph, 'Queer Hobbies: Ernest Thesiger and Interwar Embroidery'. *Textile: Cloth and Culture* 15(3) (September 2017): 292–322

McBrinn, Joseph, '"The work of masculine fingers": The Disabled Soldiers' Embroidery Industry, 1918–1955'. *Journal of Design History* 31(1) (February 2018): 1–23 (advance access, epw043, https://doi.org/10.1093/jdh/epw043 [21 October 2016])

McBrinn, Joseph, 'The Spectacle of Masculinity: Men and the Visual Culture of the Suffrage Campaign'. In Miranda Garrett and Zoë Thomas (eds), *Suffrage and the Arts: Visual Culture, Politics and Enterprise* (London: Bloomsbury, 2018), pp. 205–31

McBrinn, Joseph, '"Knitting is the saving of life: Adrian has taken to it too": Needlework, Gender and the Bloomsbury Group'. In Lisa Binkley and Joanna Amos (eds), *Stitching the Self: Identity and the Needle Arts* (London: Bloomsbury, 2020), pp. 67–79, 187–93

McFadden, David Revere, *Radical Lace and Subversive Knitting* [exhibition catalogue] (New York: Museum of Arts and Design, 2006)

McFadden, David Revere, *Pricked: Extreme Embroidery* [exhibition catalogue] (New York: Museum of Arts and Design, 2007)

Maines, Rachel, *Hedonizing Technologies: Paths to Pleasure in Hobbies and Leisure* (Baltimore, MD: Johns Hopkins University Press, 2009)

Malarcher, Patricia, 'Men in Fiber Art'. *Fiberarts* 20(3) (November/December 1993): 47–51

Mangan, J.A. and James Walvin (eds), *Manliness and Morality: Middle-Class Masculinity in Britain and America, 1800–1940* (Manchester: Manchester University Press, 1987)

*Material Boys – un[Zipped]* [exhibition catalogue] (Sydney: Object Galleries, Australian Centre for Craft and Design, 2000)

Mavor, Carol, *Reading Boyishly: Roland Barthes, J.M. Barrie, Jacques Henri Lartigue, Marcel Proust and D.W. Winnicott* (Durham and London: Duke University Press, 2007)

Mensing, Margo, 'Close to Home: An Exploration of Historical Perceptions Concerning Women and Crafts'. *Fiberarts* 20(3) (November/December 1993): 42–6

Mosse, George L., *The Image of Man: The Creation of Modern Masculinity* (New York and Oxford: Oxford University Press, 1996)

Muñoz, José Esteban, *Disidentifications: Queers of Color and the Performance of Politics* (Minneapolis: University of Minnesota Press, 1999)

Myzelev, Alla, 'Whip Your Hobby into Shape: Knitting, Feminism and Construction of Gender'. *Textile: The Journal of Cloth and Culture* 7(2) (July 2009):148–63

Myzelev, Alla, 'Monsieur Tricote: Tricote et masculinité au XXIe siècle/Here Comes the Knitting Men: Knitting and Masculinity in the Early Twenty-First Century'. *Cahiers des métiers* 5(2) (Printemps/Spring 2012): 101–23

Nectar, Iris, 'Men Can Make Kickass Fiber Art Too!' *Feminist Fiber Art* 2 (August 2016) (http://feministfiberart.com/post/127075600687/here-is-the-digital-version-of-the-second-zine (accessed 14 September 2017)

Neuland-Kitzerow, Dagmar, Salwa Joram and Erika Karasek (eds), *Inlaid Patchwork in Europe from 1500 to the Present/Tuchinstarsien in Europa von 1500 bid heute* (Regensburg and Berlin: Schnell & Steiner GMBH/Museum Europäischer Kulturen, Staatliche Mussen zu Berlin, 2009)

Newport, Mark, 'The Masculine in Fiber Art'. *Surface Design Journal* 22(3) (Spring 1998): 28–33

Obler, Bibiana, 'Taeuber, Arp, and the Politics of Cross-Stitch'. *The Art Bulletin* 91(2) (June 2009): 207–29

Obler, Bibiana, *Intimate Collaborations: Kandinsky & Münter, Arp & Taeuber* (New Haven and London: Yale University Press, 2014)

Olliver, Clyde, 'Forget-Me-Not: British Servicemen's Embroidery'. *Embroidery* 54(1) (January 2003): 38–9

Pascoe, C.J. and Tristan Bridges (eds), *Exploring Masculinities: Identity, Inequality, Continuity, and Change* (New York and Oxford: Oxford University Press, 2015)

Parker, Rozsika, 'Old Mistresses'. *Spare Rib* 10 (April 1973): 11–13.

Parker, Rozsika, 'Art of Course Has No Sex. But Artists Do'. *Spare Rib* 25 (July 1974): 34–5

Parker, Rozsika, 'The Word for Embroidery Was Work'. *Spare Rib* 37 (July 1975): 41–5

Parker, Rozsika (and Amanda Sebestyen) 'A Literature of Our Own [an interview with Elaine Showalter]'. *Spare Rib* 78 (January 1979): 27–30

Parker, Rozsika, 'Images of Men'. *Spare Rib* 99 (October 1980): 5–8

Parker, Rozsika, *The Subversive Stitch: Embroidery and the Making of the Feminine* (London: The Women's Press, 1984) [Reissued by The Women's Press in 1989, and then with revisions, in 1996]

Parker, Rozsika, 'Foreword'. In *The Subversive Stitch* [exhibition catalogue] (Manchester: Whitworth Art Gallery & Cornerhouse, 1988), pp. 5–6

Parker, Rozsika, *Torn in Two: The Experience of Maternal Ambivalence* (London: Virago, 1995)
Parker, Rozsika, '"Killing the Angel in the House": Creativity, Femininity and Aggression'. *International Journal of Psychoanalysis* 79(4) (1998): 757–74
Parker, Rozsika, 'Introduction'. In *The Subversive Stitch: Embroidery and the Making of the Feminine* (London: I.B. Tauris, 2010 [new edition]), pp. xi–xxii
Parker, Rozsika and Griselda Pollock, *Old Mistresses: Women, Art and Ideology* (London: Pandora Press, 1981)
Parker, Rozsika and Griselda Pollock (eds), *Framing Feminism: Art and the Women's Movement 1970–85* (London: Pandora, 1987)
Perchuk, Andrew and Helaine Posner (eds), *The Masculine Masquerade: Masculinity and Representation* (Cambridge, MA: MIT Press, 1995)
Prain, Leanne, *Hoopla: The Art of Unexpected Embroidery* (Vancouver: Arsenal Pulp Press, 2011)
Prichard, Sue, 'Precision Patchwork: Nineteenth Century Military Quilts'. *Textile History* 41(1) (2010): 214–26
Prichard, Sue (ed.), *Quilts 1700–2010: Hidden Histories, Untold Stories* (London: V&A Publishing, 2010)
Richmond, Vivienne, 'Men's Needlework'. In *Clothing the Poor in Nineteenth-Century England* (Cambridge: Cambridge University Press, 2013), pp. 117–20
Rock, Daniel, *Textile Fabrics: A Descriptive Catalogue of the Collection of Church-Vestments, Dresses, Silk Stuffs, Needlework and Tapestries, Forming that Section of the South Kensington Museum* (London: Chapman and Hall, 1870)
Roper, Michael, 'Mothering Men'. In *The Secret Battle: Emotional Survival in the Great War* (Manchester and New York: Manchester University Press, 2009), pp. 119–203
Roper, Michael and John Tosh (eds), *Manful Assertions: Masculinities in Britain since 1800* (London and New York: Routledge, 1991)
Rutt, Richard, *A History of Hand Knitting* (London: B.T. Batsford, 1987)
Sedgwick, Eve Kosofsky, *Between Men: English Literature and Male Homosocial Desire* (New York: Columbia University Press, 1985)
Sedgwick, Eve Kosofsky, 'The Beast in the Closet: James and the Writing of Homosexual Panic'. In Ruth Bernard Yeazell (ed.), *Sex, Politics, and Science in the Nineteenth-Century Novel* (Baltimore and London: Johns Hopkins University Press, 1986), pp. 148–86
Sedgwick, Eve Kosofsky, 'A Poem Is Being Written'. *Representations* 17 (Winter 1987): 110–43
Sedgwick, Eve Kosofsky, *Epistemology of the Closet* (Berkeley: University of California Press, 1990)
Sedgwick, Eve Kosofsky, 'Queer Performativity: Henry James's *The Art of the Novel*'. *GLQ: A Journal of Lesbian and Gay Studies* 1(1) (1993): 1–16

Sedgwick, Eve Kosofsky, *Tendencies* (Durham: Duke University Press, 1993)
Sedgwick, Eve Kosofsky, 'Inside Henry James: Toward a Lexicon for *The Art of the Novel*'. In Monica Dorenkamp and Richard Henke (eds), *Negotiating Lesbian and Gay Subjects* (New York and London: Routledge, 1995), pp. 131–48
Sedgwick, Eve Kosofsky, 'Shame and Performativity: Henry James's New York Edition Prefaces'. In David McWhirter (ed.), *Henry James's New York Edition: The Construction of Authorship* (Stanford: Stanford University Press, 1995), pp. 206–39
Sedgwick, Eve Kosofsky, *Touching Feeling: Affect, Pedagogy, Performativity* (Durham & London: Duke University Press, 2003)
Segal, Lynne, *Slow Motion: Changing Masculinities, Changing Men* (London: Virago, 1990)
Segal, Lynne, *Slow Motion: Changing Masculinities, Changing Men* (Houndmills, Basingstoke: Palgrave Macmillan, 2007 [Third, Revised Edition])
Sestay, Catherine J., *Needlework: A Selected Bibliography with Special Reference to Embroidery and Needlepoint* (Metuchen, NJ: Scarecrow Press, 1982)
Shindler, Kelly, 'Lords of the Strings'. *BUST* 36 (December 2005/January 2006): 82–5
Silverman, Kaja, *Male Subjectivity at the Margins* (New York and London: Routledge, 1992)
Smith, Claire, 'Doing Time: Patchwork as a Tool of Social Rehabilitation in British Prisons'. *V&A Journal Online* 1 (Autumn 2008), http://www.vam.ac.uk/content/journals/research-journal/issue-01/doing-time-patchwork-as-a-tool-of-social-rehabilitiation-in-british-prisons/ (accessed 1 December 2011)
Soltwedel, Nina Lee, 'Rendering Visible the Formerly Invisible: The Men of the EGA'. *Needle Arts* XXIX(2) (June 1998): 36–44
Stoller, Debbie, *Son of Stitch'n Bitch: 45 Projects to Knit & Crochet for Men* (New York: Workman Publishing, 2007)
*The Subversive Stitch* [exhibition catalogue] (Manchester: Whitworth Art Gallery & Cornerhouse, 1988)
*The Subversive Stitch Revisited: The Politics of Cloth*, Victoria and Albert Museum, London, 29–30 November 2013, http://www.gold.ac.uk/subversivestitchrevisited/ (accessed 1 July 2014). Some of these papers appeared in a special issue of *Image & Text* (23) (2014)
Sullivan, Nikki, *A Critical Introduction to Queer Theory* (Edinburgh: Edinburgh University Press, 2003)
Tamboukou, Maria, *Sewing, Fighting and Writing: Radical Practices in Work, Politics and Culture* (London and New York: Rowan & Littlefield, 2016)
Thesiger, Ernest, 'Needlework as a Hobby'. *The Home Magazine* XXXIV(119) (March 1926): 27–8, 90
Thesiger, Ernest, *Practically True* (London: William Heinemann, 1927)
Thesiger, Ernest, *Adventures in Embroidery* (London and New York: The Studio, 1941)

Tickner, Lisa, *The Spectacle of Women: Imagery and the Suffrage Campaign, 1907–14* (London: Chatto & Windus, 1987)
Troy, Virginia Gardner, *The Modernist Textile: Europe and America, 1890–1940* (London: Lund Humphries, 2006)
Tucker, Marcia, *A Labor of Love* [exhibition catalogue] (New York: The New Museum of Contemporary Art, 1996)
Turner, William B., *A Genealogy of Queer Theory* (Philadelphia: Temple University Press, 2000)
Turney, Joanne, *The Culture of Knitting* (Oxford and New York: Berg, 2009)
Verzotti, Giorgio et al., *Il racconto del filo: Ricamo e cucito nell–arte contemporanea/ The Tale of Thread: Embroidery and Sewing in Contemporary Art* [exhibition catalogue] (Milan: Skira for Museo di Arte Moderna e Contemporanea di Trento e Rovereto, 2003)
Warner, Michael (ed.), *Fear of a Queer Planet: Queer Politics and Social Theory* (Minneapolis and London: University of Minnesota Press, 1993)
West, Janet, 'Nautical Woolwork Pictures'. *Antique Collecting* 22 (1988): 31–5
West, Janet, 'Sailor Wool Pictures'. *The Mariner's Mirror* 85(1) (1999): 90–1
Whitehead, Stephen M., *Men and Masculinities: Key Themes and New Directions* (Cambridge: Polity Press, 2002)
Whitehead, Stephen M. and Frank J. Barrett (eds), *The Masculinities Reader* (Cambridge: Polity Press, 2001)
Williams, Raymond, 'Structures of Feeling'. In *Marxism and Literature* (Oxford and New York: Oxford University Press, 1977), pp. 128–35
Williams, Raymond, 'The Significance of 'Bloomsbury' as a Social and Cultural Group'. In Derek Crabtree and A.P. Thirlwall (eds), *Keynes and the Bloomsbury Group* (London and Basingstoke: Macmillan, 1980), pp. 40–67
Winnicott, D.W., 'Transitional Objects and Transitional Phenomena'. *International Journal of Psychoanalysis* 34(1) (1953): 89–97
Winnicott, D.W., 'String'. *Child Psychology and Psychiatry* 1 (January 1960): 52 and 51
Winnicott, D.W., 'Mirror-Role of Mother in Family Life and Child Development'. [1967] In *Playing and Reality* (London: Tavistock Publications, 1971), pp. 111–18
Woolf, Virginia, *Orlando: A Biography* (London: The Hogarth Press, 1928)
Woolf, Virginia, *A Room of One's Own* (London: The Hogarth Press, 1929)
Woolf, Virginia, *Killing the Angel in the House: Seven Essays* (London: Penguin, 1995 [1931])
Yee, Lydia and Anastasia Aukeman (eds), *Division of Labor: 'Women's Work' in Contemporary Art* [exhibition catalogue] (New York: The Bronx Museum of the Arts, 1995)

# Index

Abstract Expressionism 105, 106
activism 8, 44, 139, 150
affection 8, 69, 129, 187
AIDS
    AIDS epidemic 39, 45, 125, 126
    AIDS Quilt 126–8, 152–3, 204
Alexander, Brett 146
Alford, Lady Marian 80, 189
amateur 3, 7, 20, 36, 40, 65, 89, 104, 111, 115–16, 121, 123, 126, 129, 137–8, 150, 164, 184
Amer, Ghada 135, 206
American Needlepoint Guild 106
'Angel in the House' 40, 54, 55, 56, 58, 86, 181
Aoyama, Satoru 154, *155*
appliqué 9, 24, 64, 72, 116, 121, 141
appropriation 31, 42, 55, 122, 147
archive 22, 80, 119, 133, 134
Arey, Capt. Garrison Burdett 6, 7, 166
*Art in America* (magazine) 105, 106
art needlework 54, 66, 95
Arts and Crafts Exhibition Society 64, 72
Arts and Crafts movement 13, 23, 54
Atelier François Lesage 21
Auden, W.H. 35, 175

Bae, Chan-Hyo 155
Ballets Russes 66, 97
bargello 92
Barney, Matthew 21
Beal, Stephen 22, 147, 172, 210
Beauchamp, 7th Earl (William Lygon) 81, 189, 190
'Beefcake Craft Arcade' (Matthew Monthei) 138, 207
Bell, Vanessa 67, 71, 72, *73*, 95
Benson, E.F. 'Fred' 55, 59, 64, 68, 78, 135, 183, 186, *186*
    and Disabled Soldiers' Embroidery Industry 78–9
    and needlework 59
    novels,
        *The Countess of Lowndes Square and Other Stories* 59, 183
        *David Blaize* 60
        *Dodo* 59
        *Dodo the Second* 59, 60, 183
        *The Freaks of Mayfair* 60, *61*, 135, 183
        *Mapp and Lucia* 62, 183
        *Paul* 59, 68, 183, 184
    fictional male needleworkers,
        Aunt Georgie 60, 61, 62, 135, 183
        Georgie Pillson 62
        Oliver Bowman 59, 62
        Seymour Sturgis 59, 60, 62
        Thomas Beckwith 62.
        *Also see* A.C. 'Arthur' Benson and R.H. 'Hugh' Benson 62–5
Berlin woolwork 6, 50, 54, 58, 66, 67, 72, 74, 94, 99, 104, 148
Berwick, Mary 88
Björk 155
Blampied. Edmund 60
Bloomsbury group 66, 79, 89, 148, 185, 187
Boetti, Alighiero 21, 143, 154, 172
boys
    'bad boys' 121, 140, 146
    'boys that sew club' 145–6
    'effeminophobia' 85, 190
    needlework and boyhood 4, 12, 47, 50–5, 137, 139, 160
Box, Richard 18
Brennand-Wood, Michael 141–2, 208
*British Workman, The* (magazine) 4, *5*
Broderers Company 13
Brown, Wendell 19, 171
Bulley, Margaret H. 72, 187
*BUST* (magazine) *140*, 208
Butler, Judith 43, 177

Cadmus, Paul 93, 94, 97, 102, 193, 196
camp 7, 17, 27, 32, 62, 77, 83, 98, 127
capitalism 3, 13, 138

Cardinal, Marie 15, 171
Casdagli, Major Alexis 161, 213
castration 14, 16
Cave, Nick 141–2, 208
Celtic Revival 41–2
Chalmers, Jamie ('Mr. X-Stitch') 25, 26
Chaplin, Charlie 29, *30*
Charleston 69
Chiachio, Leo and Daniel Giannone 133, *134*, 206
Chicago, Judy 2, 109, 110, 126
childbirth 14, 85, 159
children's literature 179
Christie, Grace 81
cis-gender 8, 44
cissy (*see* sissy)
class 4, 5, 19, 20, 44, 50, 123, 141, 160
Climer, Greg 138, 207
Colby, Max 138
compulsory heterosexuality 43, 117, 137
convalescence 52, 77
conversion therapy 161
Cold War 45, 97
Cole, Jack 94
Connell, R.W. 8, 43, 166, 168, 178
*Country Life* (magazine) 150
craft
    as a construct like masculinity 131, 164–5
    craft book phenomenon 109–10, 113, 140
    as modern concept 13, 46
*Craft Horizons* (magazine) 192, 200
Craftivism 11, 45, 208
Craske, John 75, *76*, 77, 79, 161, 188, 213
crewel 109
crochet, crocheting 8, 9, 21, 27, 33, 49, 58, 59, 72, 92, 104, 111, 121, 131–2, 133, 141, 143
cross-stitch 9, 20, 25, 37, 66, 67, 74, 78, 89, 99, 160
*Cross Stitcher* (magazine) 20
Crumpler, John Glazbey 52, *53*
Cuevas, Ben 131–2
Cunningham, Joe ('Joe the Quilter') 148, 210
Curry, John 27, 173
Cvetkovich, Ann 44, 160
    'archives of feeling' 151

DaCosta, Morton 110
Davidson, Angus 69, 186, 211 123, 203

Deller, Jeremy 141, 208
Delvoye, Wim 21
Disabled Soldiers' Embroidery Industry 74, 77–9, 83, 95, 188–9, 194
DIY 11, 50, 137
Documenta 21, 37
drag 43, 125, 130
dressmaking 9, 11, 72, 113, 116
Duke of Gloucester 49–50, 180
Duke of Windsor 1, 49–50, 55, 104, 115, 150, 180, 182
    as celebrated male needleworker 1, 49–50, 55, 104, 115, 150
    and Disabled Soldiers' Embroidery Industry 79, 194
    HRH Prince of Wales 1, 49, 79, 92, 182, 194
    King Edward VIII 1, 49
Dutton, William Rush 89–90, 192

effeminacy 1, 27, 31, 34, 58–60, 64, 69, 70, 81, 89, 90, 96, 97, 103, 126, 131
Eidson, Wendy 140
Ellis, Havelock 34, 81–2, 157–8, 190, 195, 212
Embroiderers' Guild 70, 83, 94, 150
Embroiderers' Guild of American (EGA), 106, 151
embroidery. *See* needlework
Emin, Tracey 135
Everett, Kenny 27, 174
exhibitions
    *Boy Oh Boy* 147
    *Boys Who Sew* 146
    *Boys with Needles* 149
    *BoysCraft* 210
    *Created in Conflict: British Soldier Art from the Crimean War to Today* 168
    *Embroiderers' Guild Exhibition* 70–1, 94
    *Exhibition of 20th Century Needlework* 72
    *Exhibition of Modern British Embroidery* 71
    *Exhibition of Modern Embroideries and Decorative Art* 80
    *Fibremen International* 147
    *Grafton Group* 67
    *Guys Who Sew* 147
    *HOMOcraft* 149

*Il racconto del filo: Ricamo e cucito nell–arte contemporanea/The tale of thread: Embroidery and sewing in contemporary art* 147
*Inlaid Patchwork in Europe from 1500 to the Present/Tuchinstarsien in Europa von 1500 bid heute* 167
*A Labor of Love* 121
*Loose Threads* 143–4
*Man-Made: Contemporary Male Quilters* 148
*Man-Made Quilts: Civil War to the Present* 148
*Material Boys–un[Zipped]* 149
*Men of Cloth* 148
*Men of the Cloth: Contemporary Fiber Art* 147
*Men Who Sew* 147
*The Mesh Canvas* 106
*Modern Designs in Needlework* 71, 95
*Nancy Boy* 149
*National Exhibition of Amateur Needlework Exhibition of English Needlework (Past and Present)* 55, 71, 79
*Needlework of Today* 96, 103
*Pricked: Extreme Embroidery* 142
*Queer Threads: Crafting Identity & Community* 149
*Radical Lace and Subversive Knitting* 142
*The Subversive Stitch* (Manchester) 119
*The Subversive Stitch* (Melbourne) 120
*The Subversive Stitch* (New York) 120

Fassett, Kaffe *18*, 119
Faught, Josh 152, *153*
feeling/feelings 14, 28, 33, 44, 65, 70, 77, 105, 108, 124, 125, 129, 131, 133, 135, 137, 146, 151, 154, 158, 160, 161
femininity
    definition of 7
    feminine as social category 3
    male femininity 9, 60, 82, 158, 168–9
    needlework and construction of the feminine 3–4
feminism
    and 'l'écriture féminine' 14
fiber art 22, 116, 139

film
    *Breakfast on Pluto* 31
    *Demolition Man* 30
    *Die Hard 2*
    *Harry Potter and the Half Blood Prince* 31
    *Homicidal* 31
    *Jamaica Inn*
    *Love! Valour! Compassion!* 135, 128
    *Mr. Lucky* 29
    *Modern Times* 29, *30*
    *Monsieur Beaucaire* 29
    *Psycho* 30
    *Silence of the Lambs* 31
    *Talk to Her/Hable con ella* 31
Fine Cell Work 24, 161
First World War 22, 45, 49, 52, 55, 60, 66, 68, 89, 90, 96, 147
Flinzer, Jochen 143, *144*
Fonda, Henry 27, 110, 200
Forster, E.M. 59, 65, 93–4
French, Jared 93, 97, 98
Fry, Gavin 22, 148, 172
Fry, Roger 66–71
FullMano (José Teixeira) 138

gaming 47
Gartner Jr., Louis J. 100–3, *102*
gay (*see* homosexual/homosexuality, queer)
Gay Liberation Front (GLF) 35
Gay Liberation movement 35, 108
gender
    and binary identity 8, 40, 42, 105, 128
    as biological destiny 42
    mutability, relationality 8, 40, 125
Gilliam, Sam 19
Gimson, Ernest *23*
Gober, Robert 121, 123, *124*
Goggin, Maureen Daly 52, 161
'Golden Thimble'
    competition 106
    prize 80, 95
González-Torres, Félix 38, 106
*Good Housekeeping* (magazine) 192, 200
Grant, Duncan 67–72, *73*, 77, 86, 89, 94, 182
Grant, Ethel ('Mrs. Bartle Grant') 69–72, *73*, 186

*Graphic, The* (magazine) 28
Greenberg, Clement 87–9, 92, 105, 115
'great masculine renunciation' 42
Grier, Rosey
    as celebrated male needleworker 7–8, 110–11, 113, *114*, 147
    *Needlepoint for Men* 7, 113, *114*, 140
gros point 74, 91, 106
Gustaf V of Sweden, King 91, *92*

Hackleton, John Nichols 50
Hall, Ed 141
Hall, Radclyffe 82, 158
Hand & Lock 21
Harrison, Edmund 14, *15*
Hartley, Paddy 22, 172
Hercules 7, 16
Herring, Oliver 120, 130–1, 145
Hlobo, Nicholas 155
HMP Wandsworth 24
hobby/hobbies 1, 11, 49, 50, 66, 67, 89–95, 109–10, 151, 158
    hobbycrafts 11, 105
Hodges, Jim 38–9
Hogarth, Mary 70–3
Holland, Ton of 138
Hollinghurst, Alan 34–5, 169, 175, 185
Holstein, Jonathan 110–11, 113
*Home Magazine, The* (magazine) 83–4
homosexual/homosexuality
    'birth of the homosexual' 33
    homoeroticism 36, 111, 134
    'homosexual panic' 45, 65, 69, 96
Honeyman, Raymond 18
Hopkins, Arthur *28*
*House Beautiful* (magazine) 98
*House & Garden* (magazine) 78, 100, 108
Hudson, Rock 1, 26, 110
Hunting, James 138
Hurlstone, Nigel 135, *136*

Illes, Robert E. 111–13, *112*
*Illustrated London News, The* (magazine) 54
Inman, John 27
invalid/invalidism 16, 52, 57, 75

inversion 33–4, 78, 81, 96, 157–8
    invert 34, 68, 81, 96
Isermann, Jim 120, 121

James, Henry 56, 58–9, 62–5, 78, 80, 85–6
    'The Beast in the Jungle' 65
Jefferies, Janis 144–6

Kains-Jackson, Charles 64
Kelley, Mike 121, *122*, 124, 143
Kimmel, Michael 116
Kipling, John Lockwood *29*
'Kinky Needles' (Juan Diego) 137
Kinsey, Alfred 98
Kirstein, Lincoln 93, 97
kitsch 105, 115, 116, 128
knitting 9, 11, 12, 17, 18, 27, 29, 30–7, 41, 43, 57, 59, 60, 69, 72, 89, 92, 95, 109, 111, 115, 120, 139–40, 142
Kushner, Robert 120, 123
Kyle, Scott Ramsay 138

labour 2, 4, 44, 53, 55, 78, 108, 110, 125, 132, 145, 154, 160
lace-making 9, 21, 29, 32, 116–17, 142, 153, 160
Lawrence, D.H. 75, *76*, 77
Lawrence, Frieda 75, *76*
Leclerq, Jules 21
LeDray, Charles 120, 124–5
Lee, Kang Seung 135, *136*, 137
Leonilson, José 135, *136*, 137
*Life* (magazine) 96, 113–15
Lion, Ralph 74
Lippard, Lucy 2, 111
Lomas, Isaac 51
Lovibond, Phyllis *23*
Loving, Al 19
Lynes, George Platt 93–4, 97–8, *99*, 100, *101*, 103, 117
Lynes, Russell
    as celebrated male needleworker *101*, 103–8, 111
    and Clement Greenberg 105

McIntosh, Aaron 135, *136*, 137
McPhee, Angus 20–1
McQueen, Alexander 21

Maines, Rachel 2, 110
manbroidery 24–6
    manbroiderer 26
masculinity/masculinities
    definition of 3, 7, 13
    as feeling 77
    hegemonic masculinity 43, 160
    hypermasculinity 4, 18
    manliness 55, 60, 62
    masculine ideal 3, 18, 43
    'masculinity crisis' 45, 60, 116, 122, 160
    masculine as social category 9
    toxic masculinity 9
masturbation
    autoeroticism 137
    'plain sewing' 35, 157–8, 175
Materson, Ray 21
Medalla, David 37, *38*, 143
men (*see* masculinity)
Merry, James 155
Metropolitan District Schools (London) 53
Miller, Dutes and Stan Shellabarger *132*, 132–3
Mitford, Nancy 81, 183, 190
modernism 46, 66–7, 87–9, 92, 97, 109, 117, 120, 121
monks 14, 63
Morrell, Lady Ottoline 71, 75
Morris, Jane (née Burden) 22, 172
Morris, May 22
Morris, William 22–3, 56, 64
Morstad, Julie *140*
Mortellito, Nina 109
mothers/mothering 14, 16, 22–3, 24, 32, 38–9, 51, 56–7, 62, 64, 68, 69, 70–1, 77, 80, 83–6, 95, 96, 103, 104, 115, 116, 124, 128, 137, 151, 160, 173, 176, 180, 183, 190
    men and mothering 83–6
    needlework as maternal 15, 17, 22, 24, 44, 51, 55, 70, 85, 116, 128, 137
Moufarrege, Nicolas 120, 128–30
Murder, Johnny 25
Museum of Modern Art (MoMA) 93

NAMES Project Memorial AIDS Quilt 126–8, 152

*Needle Arts* (magazine) *151*
needlemen/needleman 7, 27, 83, 159
needlework
    amateur 3, 7, 20, 36, 40, 65, 89, 104, 111, 115–16, 121, 123, 126, 129, 137–8, 150, 164, 184
    aristocratic 7, 58, 74, 91–2, 150
    and decadence 60
    decorative v. plain 169
    definition of 9
    and domesticity 17, 109
    and education of boys 52–4
    and 'flight from masculinity' 55, 60, 96
    as impersonation, parody and mimicry, passing, cross-dressing and drag 42–3
    as male parturition 85, 191
    men's absence in its history xvii, 2, 40, 43, 44, 160–1
    needlecrafts 9, 18
    needlepoint 9, 94, 101
    and nerves, trauma and hysteria, xvii, 44, 52, 68
    professional 7, 13, 18, 21, 139
    as reparative 55, 83, 89, 110, 131
    representations of the male needleworker 4–5, 30
Neufeld, Grant *139*
neurasthenia (war neurosis) 52
Newport, Mark 18, *19*, 22
Nicholson, Ben 87–8
Norbury, James *17*
Nutman, Zach 138

occupational therapy 7, 52, 83, 89–91
Oedipal crisis 31
Oedipus 16
Oldenburg, Claes 110, 120
Olliver, Clyde 22
Omega workshop 67–72
Opus Anglicanum 2, 13, 14, 72, 113
Otterson, Joel 123
Overstreet, Joe 20
Overton, Paul 25

Paradiso, John Thomas 138
Parker, Rozsika ('Rosie')
    'Killing the Angel in the House' 55

*Old Mistresses* 3
*Spare Rib* 35, 120
*The Subversive Stitch* xvii, 1, 3, 9, 11, 15, 26, 35, 44, 50, 81, 120, 128, 138, 155, 157, 161–2
Parsons, Jonathan 141
patchwork 9, 14, 24, 68, 126, 129, 137
Patmore, Coventry 181
patriarchy 9, 12, 40, 42, 43, 166
Pattern and Decoration movement 123
Penn & Fletcher 21
*People* (magazine) 111
Perlin, Bernard 94, 97, 100
Perry, Grayson 18, 124
petit point 9, 62, 69, 74, 78–80, 95, 102
photography 64, 98–101, 117–18, 134, 135, 141, 154
Pippet, Gabriel 63
pleasure 4–8, 17, 20, 43, 44, 51, 52, 77, 103, 108, 135, 137, 138, 151, 157, 158, 160, 162
pornography/porn/porno
    gay pornography 36, 94, 117, 134–8
    *Also see*
    Maria E. Piñeres 135
    Michael Bronski 125
    Richard Dyer 125
Porter, Allen 99, *100*, 103
postmodernism 120, 125
prison 9, 21, 24, 29, 32, 52, 55
Puryear, Duane Kearns *127*, 128

*Queen, The* (magazine) *79*
queer
    'queer domesticity' 134, 206
    'queer moments' 154
    'queer performativity' 86
    'queer voice' 34
    *queering* 31, 43, 47, 149, 154, 155, 161
    *Also see*
    Annamarie Jagose 165
    David Halperin 34, 165
    Donald E. Hall 177
    Eve Kosofsky Sedgwick 16, 44, 65, 69, 85, 103, 131, 133, 137, 160, 162
    Michael Warner 165
    Nikki Sullivan 154, 211

Teresa de Lauretis 165
William B. Turner 165
quilts, quilting 4, 8, 9, 15, 18, 19, 20, 24, 27, 39, 68, 80, 89–90, 91, 110–11, 121, 126–8, 129, 131, 137, 138, 140, 148, 149, 150, 152

Raedecker, Michael 38, 144, *145*
rag rugs 9, 88
Ranken, William B. 80–1
Rauschenberg, Robert 116, 120
Read, Herbert 87–9
Reichek, Elaine 7, 120
Revolutionary Knitting Circle (RKC) 139
Roberts, Winifred 88
Rock, Daniel 80
Rosário, Arthur Bisop 21, 129
Rossbach, Ed 116, *117*
Royal School of Needlework 21, 83, *85*, 91, 109, 150, 158, 197
Ruskin, John 181
Rutt, Richard 119

sailors 2, 4–7, 22, 29, 49, 52, 91, 104, 133–4, 147
Saja, Richard 39
samplers 2, 7, 22, 23, 27, 31, 50–3, 68, 82, 129, 144
Schreiner, Olive 157–8
Second World War 17, 24, 45, 83, 88, 90, 96, 103, 117, 151
Sedgwick, Eve Kosofsky
    reparative v. paranoid reading 131
Segal, Lynne 125
sewing (*see* needlework)
sexology 33, 81, 82, 87, 96, 98, 157
Shairp, Mordaunt 81
shame 44, 51, 85, 108, 133, 137–8, 146, 160
Shenton, David 37
Shonibare MBE, Yinka 143, *144*, 145
Showalter, Elaine 14, 16, 41
silence 44, 70, 103, 126–8, 159
sissy/sissiness 2, 12, 27, 51, 63–5, 108, 113, 179
*Sketch, The* (magazine) 60, *61*
Smith, Ernie 21

Smith, Matt 152, *153*, 154
Smith-Dorrien, Lady *85*
soldiers 12, 49, 52, 72, 77–9, 83, 85, 91, 95, 167–8, 188
*Spare Rib* (magazine) 35, 119
*Sports Illustrated* (magazine) 172, 200
Stella, Frank 105–6, *107*
Stone-blossom 93–4
Strachey, Lytton 69–70
Sturgis, Howard
    *Belchamber* 58–9, 65
    and needlework 56–9, 62, 64
Style-Art Needlepoint Inc *36*
subculture 34, 46, 70, 97–8, 128–9, 138
*Subversive Stitch, The* 1, 3, 9, 11, 15, 26, 35, 44, 50, 81, 120, 128, 138, 155, 157, 161–2
'subversive stitch' 14, 46, 154
suffrage movement 45, 55, 75, 80
superheroes 18
    *Also see*
    Marvel Comics 'X-Men' 26
surveillance 34, 45, 97, 134, 162

tapestry 22, 32, 56, 63–4, 68, 72, 74–5, 78, 80, 94, 123, 145
tatting 9
Tcheltichew, Pavel 99
tenderness 44, 135
Tennyson, Alfred (Lord) 44, 181
Thesiger, Ernest
    *Adventures in Embroidery* 7, 190
    as celebrated male needleworker 7–8, 72–86, *82*, *84*, 150
    and Disabled Soldiers' Embroidery Industry 77–80
Tom of Finland 37, *38*
Tooker, George 97
Tree, Lady Angela 24
Tryon, Wyndham 71
Tutill, George 141
TV series
    *30 Rock* 32
    *Are You Being Served?* 27, 32
    *The Big Bang Theory* 32
    *Curb Your Enthusiasm* 32
    *Family Guy* 32
    *Friends* 32
    *Great British Sewing Bee* 12
    *Home Improvement* 32
    *Keeping Up Appearances* 32
    *Porridge* 32
    *Will & Grace* 32–3
Turner Prize 21, 124
Tuymans, Luc 21

Vaisman, Meyer 121, 123, 145
Venice Biennale 21
vernacular 19, 88, 128
Vezzoli, Francesco *152*
Victoria and Albert Museum 71, 78, 91, 152
video games 47, 179
Vincent, Nathan 131
*Vogue* (magazine) 60, 70, *71*, 72, 78, 91, 95, 98, 115

Warhol, Andy 106, 117–18
*Weldon's Antique Tapestry* 72–5
White, Edmund 34, 175, 182
Whitney Biennial 21
Wilde, Oscar 74, 80–1
Williams, Raymond 44, 160, 178, 187
    'structures of feeling' 44, 129, 154, 160, 207
Willis, Norman *20*
Wilson, Erica 109, 111
Wilson, Fred 120
Wilson, James 50, *51*
Winnicott, D.W.
    mirroring 24, 85
    string 70
    transitional objects 70
Wojnarowicz, David 128
women (*see* femininity)
Woolf, Virginia
    'Killing the Angel in the House' 55
    *Orlando* 70
    *A Room of One's Own* xvii, 163
World Health Organization 126

Yore, Paul 138